T0222266

Practical MongoDB

Architecting, Developing, and
Administering MongoDB

Shakuntala Gupta Edward

Navin Sabharwal

Apress®

Practical MongoDB: Architecting, Developing, and Administering MongoDB

Shakuntala Gupta Edward
Ghaziabad, Uttar Pradesh, India

Navin Sabharwal
New Delhi, Delhi, India

ISBN-13 (pbk): 978-1-4842-0648-5
DOI 10.1007/978-1-4842-0647-8

ISBN-13 (electronic): 978-1-4842-0647-8

Library of Congress Control Number: 2015959699

Managing Director: Welmoed Spahr
Acquisitions Editor: Celestin Suresh John
Developmental Editor: Douglas Pundick
Technical Reviewer: Gopala Manchukunda
Editorial Board: Steve Anglin, Mark Beckner, Ewan Buckingham, Gary Cornell, Louise Corrigan,
  James DeWolf, Jonathan Gennick, Robert Hutchinson, Celestin Suresh John, Michelle Lowman,
  James Markham, Susan McDermott, Matthew Moodie, Jeffrey Pepper, Douglas Pundick,
  Ben Renow-Clarke, Gwenan Spearing, Matt Wade, Steve Weiss
Coordinating Editor: Rita Fernando
Copy Editor: Mary Behr
Compositor: SPi Global
Indexer: SPi Global

Distributed to the book trade worldwide by Springer Science+Business Media New York, 233 Spring Street, 6th Floor, New York, NY 10013. Phone 1-800-SPRINGER, fax (201) 348-4505, e-mail orders-ny@springer-sbm.com, or visit www.springeronline.com. Apress Media, LLC is a California LLC and the sole member (owner) is Springer Science + Business Media Finance Inc (SSBM Finance Inc). SSBM Finance Inc is a Delaware corporation.

For information on translations, please e-mail rights@apress.com, or visit www.apress.com.

Apress and friends of ED books may be purchased in bulk for academic, corporate, or promotional use. eBook versions and licenses are also available for most titles. For more information, reference our Special Bulk Sales–eBook Licensing web page at www.apress.com/bulk-sales.

Any source code or other supplementary materials referenced by the author in this text is available to readers at www.apress.com. For detailed information about how to locate your book's source code, go to www.apress.com/source-code/.

Printed on acid-free paper

Dedicated to people who made my life worth living and carved me into an individual I am today and to God who shades every step of my life.

—Shakuntala Gupta Edward

Dedicated to the people I love and the God I trust.

—Navin Sabharwal

Contents at a Glance

Contents

About the Authors

Shakuntala Gupta Edward has been working with database technologies since 10 years. Her experience ranges from SQL Server, Oracle Databases, Analytics platforms and Big Data technologies like MongoDB, Cassandra and SAP HANA.

Shakuntala is an accomplished architect with experience in leveraging diverse database technologies to create products and solutions in various business domains.

Shakuntala has been involved in developing products and solutions leveraging big data technologies MongoDB and Cassandra. Shakuntala holds a Master's Degree in Computer Applications.

Navin Sabharwal is an innovator, thought leader, author, and consultant in the areas Reporting and Analytics, RDBMS Technologies including SQL Server, Oracle, MySQL Big Data Technologies, Hadoop, MongoDB and SAP HANA. Navin has been using big data technologies in creating products and services in the areas of IT service management, product development, cloud computing, cloud lifecycle management, and social network product development.

Navin has created niche award-winning products and solutions and has filed numerous patents in diverse fields such as IT services, assessment engines, ranking algorithms, capacity planning engines, and knowledge management.

Navin has authored the following books: *Cloud Computing First Steps* (CreateSpace, ISBN#: 978-1478130086), *Apache Cloudstack Cloud Computing* (Packt Publishing, ISBN#: 978-1782160106), *Cloud Capacity Management* (Apress, ISBN #: 978-1430249238). Navin holds a Masters in Information Technology and is a Certified Project Management Professional.

The authors can be reached at architectbigdata@gmail.com.

About the Technical Reviewers

Prasoon Kumar is a seasoned technology professional and trainer with more than 18 years of strong experience in building world-class software products. He topped IIT-JEE in 1993, among 100 thousand applicants, arguably the most challenging and competitive exam in the world.

He is based out of Bangalore now having worked with companies like MongoDB, Justdial, Avaya etc both in India and Silicon Valley, USA. He has used mysql, MongoDB, HBase, Apache Solr, Elasticsearch, PHP, Node.JS to build scalable backends for complex applications.

He takes up the role of evangelising polyglot persistence and NoSQL solutions for scale-out datastore. He has worked with large eCommerce, FSI, healthcare and publishing companies of India for their scalability needs of document management, high-traffic portal. He has done tuning, optimisation, backup, recovery, migration and upgrades for datastores of TB's of sizes. He blogs on technology, business, hackathons and entrepreneurship at http://prasoonk.wordpress.comText.

Sundar Rajan Raman is a Big Data Architect currently working in Bank Of America. He holds Bachelor Of Technology degree from National Institute of Technology, Silcha, India. Being a seasoned Java and J2EE programmer from the base he has worked companies such as AT&T, Singtel, Deutsche Bank. He is a Messaging platform specialist with vast experience on Sonic MQ, Websphere MQ, TIBCO with respective certifications. His current focus is on Big Data technologies. He is currently working with Hadoop and its echo systems such as Pig, HIVE, Oozie and Storm, Spark etc. He has Architected an analytical engine based on Mongo DB for AT&T. More information is available on https://in.linkedin.com/pub/sundar-rajan-raman/7/905/488.

Acknowledgments

Special thanks go out to the people who have helped in creation of this book Rajeev Pratap Singh and Amit Agrawal for helping with the code snippets and Dheeraj Raghav for the creative inputs in the design of this book.

A ton of thanks go out to Stuti Awasthi for being the initiator and inspiration for this book.

The authors will like to acknowledge the creators of big data technologies and the open source community for providing such powerful tools and technologies to code with and enable products and solutions which solve real business problems easily and quickly.

Preface

Data warehousing as an industry has been around for quite a number of years now. Relational databases have been used to store data for decades while SQL has been the de-facto language to interact with RDBMS. With the emergence of Social Networking, Internet of Things and huge volumes of unstructured data on the internet the needs of data storage, processing and analytics just exploded. Traditional RDBMS systems and storage technologies were not designed to handle such vast variety and volumes of data.

Thus was born the Big Data technologies which now power various internet scale companies and their huge amounts of data. Companies like Facebook, Twitter, Google and yahoo are leveraging the big data technologies to provide products and services at internet scale which support millions of users.

This book will help our readers to appreciate the big data technologies, their emergence, need and then we will provide a deep dive technical perspective on architecting solutions using MongoDB. The book will enable our readers to understand the key use cases where big data technologies fit in and also provide them pointers on where Big Data technologies should be used carefully or combined with traditional RDBMS technologies to provide a feasible solution.

Along with the architecture the book aims to provide a step by step guide on learning MongoDB and creating applications and solutions using MongoDB.

We sincerely hope our readers will enjoy reading the book as much as we have enjoyed writing it.

About this Book

This book:

- Acts as a guide that helps the reader in grasping the various buzz words in Big Data technologies and getting a grip over various aspects of Big Data.

- Acts as a guide for people in order to understand about NoSQL and Document based database and how they are different from the traditional relational database.

- Provides insight into architecting solutions using MongoDB, it also provides information on the limitations of MongoDB as a tool.

- Methodically covers architecture, development, administration and data model of MongoDB.

- Cites examples in order to make the users comfortable in getting started with the technology.

What you need for this book

MongoDB supports the most popular platforms.

Download the latest stable production release of MongoDB from the MongoDB downloads page (`http://www.mongodb.org/downloads/`).

In this book we have focused on using MongoDB on a 64-bit Windows platform and at places have cited references on how to work with MongoDB running on Linux.

We will be using 64-bit Windows 2008 R2 and LINUX for examples of the installation process.

Who this book is for

This book would be of interest to Programmers, Big Data Architects, Application Architects, Technology Enthusiasts, Students, Solution Experts and those wishing to choose the right big data products for their needs.

The book covers aspects on Big Data, NOSQL and details on architecture and development on MongoDB. Thus it serves the use cases of developers, architects and operations teams who work on MongoDB.

CHAPTER 1

Big Data

"Big data is a term used to describe data that has massive volume, comes in a variety of structures, and is generated at high velocity. This kind of data poses challenges to the traditional RDBMS systems used for storing and processing data. Bid data is paving way for newer approaches of processing and storing data."

In this chapter, we will talk about big data basics, sources, and challenges. We will introduce you to the three Vs (volume, velocity, and variety) of big data and the limitations that traditional technologies face when it comes to handling big data.

Getting Started

Big data, along with *cloud*, *social*, *analytics*, and *mobility*, are buzz words today in the information technology world. The availability of the Internet and electronic devices for the masses is increasing every day. Specifically, smartphones, social networking sites, and other data-generating devices such as tablets and sensors are creating an explosion of data. Data is generated from various sources in various formats such as video, text, speech, log files, and images. A single second of a high-definition (HD) video generates 2,000 times more bytes than that of a single page of text.

Consider the following statistics about Facebook, as reported on the company's web site:

1. There were 968 million daily active users on average for June of 2015. There were 844 million mobile daily active users on average for June of 2015.

2. There were 1.49 billion monthly active users as of June 30, 2015. There were 1.31 billion mobile monthly active users as of June 30, 2015.

3. There were 4.5 billion likes generated daily as of May 2013, which is a 67 percent increase from August 2012.

Figure 1-1 depicts the statistics of Twitter.

© Shakuntala Gupta Edward, Navin Sabharwal 2015
S.G. Edward and N. Sabharwal, *Practical MongoDB*, DOI 10.1007/978-1-4842-0647-8_1

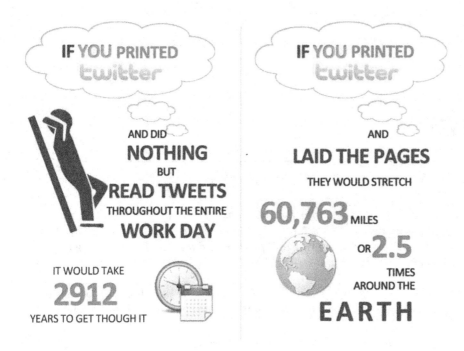

IF YOU PRINTED
twitter

AND DID
NOTHING
BUT
READ TWEETS
THROUGHOUT THE ENTIRE
WORK DAY

IT WOULD TAKE
2912
YEARS TO GET THOUGH IT

IF YOU PRINTED
twitter

AND
LAID THE PAGES
THEY WOULD STRETCH
60,763 MILES
OR **2.5**
TIMES
AROUND THE
EARTH

Figure 1-1. *If you printed Twitter…*

Here's another example: consider the amount of data that a simple event like going to a movie can generate. You start by searching for a movie on movie review sites, reading reviews about that movie, and posting queries. You may tweet about the movie or post photographs of going to the movie on Facebook. While travelling to the theater, your GPS system tracks your course and generates data.

You get the picture: smartphones, social networking sites, and other media are creating flood of data for companies to process and store. When the size of data poses challenges to the ability of typical software tools to capture, process, store, and manage data, then we have big data in hand. Figure 1-2 graphically defines big data.

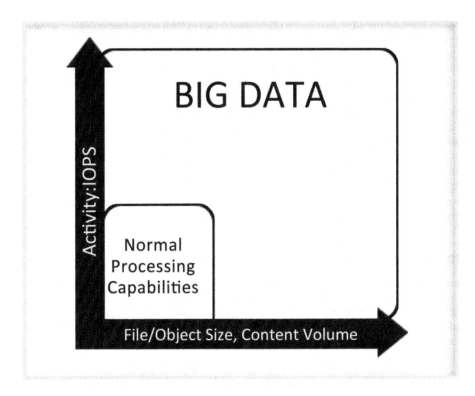

Figure 1-2. *Definition of Big Data*

Big Data

Big data is data that has high volume, is generated at high velocity, and has multiple varieties. Let's look at few facts and figures of big data.

Facts About Big Data

Various research teams around the world have done analysis on the amount of data being generated. For example, IDC's analysis revealed that the amount of digital data generated in a single year (2007) is larger than the world's total capacity to store it, which means there is no way in which to store all of the data that is being generated. Also, the rate at which data is getting generated will soon outgrow the rate at which data storage capacity is expanding.

The following sections cover insights from the MGI (McKinsey Global Institute) report (www.mckinsey.com/insights/business_technology/big_data_the_next_frontier_for_innovation) that was published in May 2011. The study makes the case that the business and economic possibilities of big data and its wider implications are important issues that business leaders and policy makers must tackle.

The Size of Big Data Varies Across Sectors

The growth of big data is a phenomenon that is observed in every sector.MGI estimates that enterprises around the world used more than 7 exabytes of incremental disk drive data storage capacity in 2010; what's interesting is that nearly 80 percent of that total seemed to duplicate data that was stored elsewhere.

MGI also estimated that, by 2009, nearly all sectors in the US economy had at least an average of 200 terabytes of stored data per company and that many sectors had more than 1 petabyte in mean stored data per company.

Some sectors exhibited far higher levels of data intensity than others; in this case, data intensity refers to the average amount of data getting accumulated across companies/firms of that sector, implying that they have more potential to capture value from big data.

Financial services sectors, including banking, investment, and securities services, are highly transaction-oriented; they are also required by regulations to store data. The analysis shows that they have the most digital data stored per firm on average.

Communications and media firms, utilities, and government also have significant digital data stored per enterprise or organization, which appears to reflect the fact that such entities have a high volume of operations and multimedia data.

Discrete and process manufacturing have the highest aggregate data stored in bytes. However, these sectors rank much lower in intensity terms, since they are fragmented into a large number of firms.

The Big Data Type Varies Across Sectors

The MGI research also shows that the type of data stored also varies by sector. For instance, retail and wholesale, administrative parts of government, and financial services all generate significant amounts of text and numerical data including customer data, transaction information, and mathematical modeling and simulations. Sectors such as manufacturing, health care, media and communications are responsible for higher percentages of multimedia data. And image data in the form of X-rays, CT, and other scans dominate data storage volumes in health care.

In terms of geographic spread of big data, North America and Europe have 70% of the global total currently. Thanks to cloud computing, data generated in one region can be stored in another country's datacenter. As a result, countries with significant cloud and hosting provider offerings tend to have high storage of data.

Big Data Sources

In this section, we will cover the major factors that are contributing to the ever increasing size of data. Figure 1-3 depicts the major contributing sources.

WHAT ARE THE MOST IMPORTANT FACTORS DRIVING
THE GROWTH OF DATA GLOBALLY?

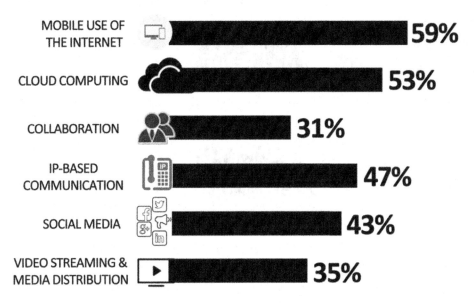

Figure 1-3. Sources of data

As highlighted in the MGI report, the major sources of this data are

- Enterprises, which are collecting data with more granularities now, attaching more details with every transaction in order to understand consumer behavior.

- Increase in multimedia usage across industries such as health care, product companies, etc.

- Increased popularity of social media sites such as Facebook, Twitter, etc.

- Rapid adoption of smartphones, which enable users to actively use social media sites and other Internet applications.

- Increased usage of sensors and devices in the day-to-day world, which are connected by networks to computing resources.

The MGI report also projects that the number of machine-to-machine devices such as sensors (which are also referred as the Internet of Things, or IoT) will grow at a rate exceeding 30 percent annually over the next five years.

Thus, the rate of growth of data is increasing and so is the diversity. Also, the model of data generation has changed from few companies generating data and others consuming it to everyone generating data and everyone consuming it. This is due to the penetration of consumer IT and internet technologies along with trends like social media. Figure 1-4 depicts the change in the data generation model.

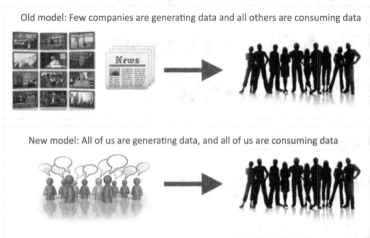

The Model Has Changed

The model of generating and consuming data has changed

Old model: Few companies are generating data and all others are consuming data

New model: All of us are generating data, and all of us are consuming data

Figure 1-4. *Data model*

Three Vs of Big Data

We have defined big data as data with three Vs:volume, velocity, and variety, as shown in Figure 1-5. Let's look at the three Vs. It is imperative that organizations and IT leaders focus on these aspects.

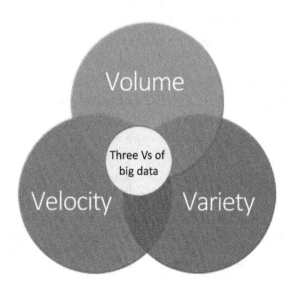

Figure 1-5. *The three Vs of big data. The "big" isn't just the volume*

Volume

Volume in big data means the size of the data. As discussed in the previous sections, various factors contribute to the size of big data: as businesses are becoming more transaction-oriented, we see ever increasing numbers of transactions; more devices are getting connected to the Internet, which is adding to the volume; there is an increased usage of the Internet; and there is an increase in the digitization of content. Figure 1-6 depicts the growth in digital universe since 2009.

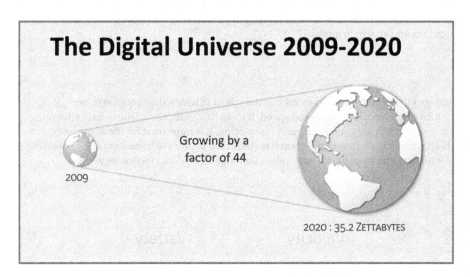

Figure 1-6. *Digital universe size*

In today's scenario, data is not just generated from within the enterprise; it's also generated based on transactions with the extended enterprise and customers. This requires extensive maintenance of customer data by the enterprises. A petabyte scale is becoming commonplace these days. Figure 1-7 depicts the data growth rate.

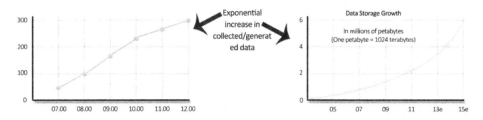

Figure 1-7. *Growth rate*

This huge volume of data is the biggest challenge for big data technologies. The storage and processing power needed to store, process, and make accessible the data in a timely and cost effective manner is massive.

Variety

The data generated from various devices and sources follows no fixed format or structure. Compared to text, CSV or RDBMS data varies from text files, log files, streaming videos, photos, meter readings, stock ticker data, PDFs, audio, and various other unstructured formats.

There is no control over the structure of the data these days. New sources and structures of data are being created at a rapid pace. So the onus is on technology to find a solution to analyze and visualize the huge variety of data that is out there. As an example, to provide alternate routes for commuters, a traffic analysis application needs data feeds from millions of smartphones and sensors to provide accurate analytics on traffic conditions and alternate routes.

Velocity

Velocity in big data is the speed at which data is created and the speed at which it is required to be processed. If data cannot be processed at the required speed, it loses its significance. Due to data streaming in from social media sites, sensors, tickers, metering, and monitoring, it is important for the organizations to speedily process data both when it is on move and when it is static (see Figure 1-8). Reacting and processing quickly enough to deal with the velocity of data is one more challenge for big data technology.

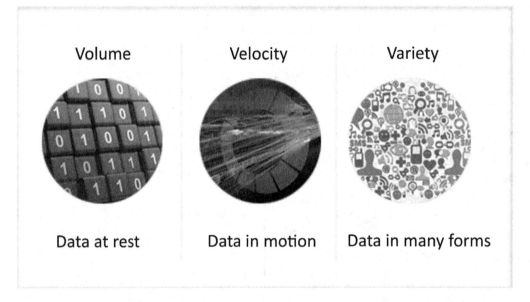

Figure 1-8. The three aspects of data

Real-time insight is essential in many big data use cases. For example, an algorithmic trading system takes real-time feeds from the market and social media sites like Twitter to make decisions on stock trading. Any delay in processing this data can mean millions of dollars in lost opportunities on a stock trade.

There is a fourth V that is talked about whenever big data is discussed. The fourth V is veracity, which means not all the data out there is important, so it's essential to identify what will provide meaningful insight, and what should be ignored.

Usage of Big Data

This section will focus on ways of using big data for creating value for organizations. Before we delve into how big data can be made usable to the organizations, let's first look at why big data is important.

Big data is a completely new source of data; it's data that is generated when you post on a blog, like a product, or travel. Previously, such minutely available information was not captured. Now it is and organizations that embrace such data can pursue innovations, improve their agility, and increase their profitability.

Big data can create value for any organization in a variety of ways. As listed in the MGI report, this can be broadly categorized into five ways of usage of big data.

Visibility

Accessibility to data in a timely fashion to relevant stakeholders generates a tremendous amount of value. Let's understand this with an example. Consider a manufacturing company that has R&D, engineering, and manufacturing departments dispersed geographically. If the data is accessible across all these departments and can be readily integrated, it can not only reduce the search and processing time but will also help in improving the product quality according to the present needs.

Discover and Analyze Information

Most of the value of big data comes from when the data collected from outside sources can be merged with the organization's internal data. Organizations are capturing detailed data on inventories, employees, and customers. Using all of this data, they can discover and analyze new information and patterns; as a result, this information and knowledge can be used to improve processes and performance.

Segmentation and Customizations

Big data enables organizations to create tailor-made products and services to meet specific segment needs. This can also be used in the social sector to accurately segment populations and target benefit schemes for specific needs. Segmentation of customers based on various parameters can aid in targeted marketing campaigns and tailoring of products to suit the needs of customers.

Aiding Decision Making

Big data can substantially minimize risks, improve decision making, and uncover valuable insights. Automated fraud alert systems in credit card processing and automatic fine-tuning of inventory are examples of systems that aid or automate decision-making based on big data analytics.

Innovation

Big data enables innovation of new ideas in the form of products and services. It enables innovation in the existing ones in order to reach out to large segments of people. Using data gathered for actual products, the manufacturers can not only innovate to create the next generation product but they can also innovate sales offerings.

As an example, real-time data from machines and vehicles can be analyzed to provide insight into maintenance schedules; wear and tear on machines can be monitored to make more resilient machines; fuel consumption monitoring can lead to higher efficiency engines. Real-time traffic information is already making life easier for commuters by providing them options to take alternate routes.

Thus, big data is not just the volume of data. It's the opportunities in finding meaningful insights from the ever-increasing pool of data. It's helping organizations make more informed decisions, which makes them more agile. It not only provides the opportunity for organizations to strengthen existing business by making informed decisions, it also helps in identifying new opportunities.

Big Data Challenges

Big data also poses some challenges. In this section, we will highlight a few of them.

Policies and Procedures

As more and more data is gathered, digitized, and moved around the globe, the policy and compliance issues become increasingly important. Data privacy, security, intellectual property, and protection are of immense importance to organizations.

Compliance with various statutory and legal requirements poses a challenge in data handling. Issues around ownership and liabilities around data are important legal aspects that need to be dealt with in cases of big data.

Moreover, many big data projects leverage the scalability features of public cloud computing providers. This poses a challenge for compliance.

Policy questions on who owns the data, what is defined as fair use of data, and who is responsible for accuracy and confidentiality of data also need to be answered.

Access to Data

Accessing data for consumption is a challenge for big data projects. Some of the data may be available to third parties, and gaining access can be a legal, contractual challenge.

Data about a product or service is available on Facebook, Twitter feeds, reviews, and blogs, so how does the product owner access this data from various sources owned by various providers?

Likewise, contractual clauses and economic incentives for accessing big data need to be tied in to enable the availability of data by the consumer.

Technology and Techniques

New tools and technologies built specifically to address the needs of big data must be leveraged, rather than trying to address the aforementioned issues through legacy systems. The inadequacy of legacy systems to deal with big data on one hand and the lack of experienced resources in newer technologies is a challenge that any big data project has to manage.

Legacy Systems and Big Data

In this section, we will discuss the challenges that organizations are facing when managing big data using legacy systems.

Structure of Big Data

Legacy systems are designed to work with structured data where tables with columns are defined. The format of the data held in the columns is also known.

However, big data is data with many structures. It's basically unstructured data such as images, videos, logs, etc.

Since big data can be unstructured, legacy systems created to perform fast queries and analysis through techniques like indexing based on particular data types held in various columns cannot be used to hold or process big data.

Data Storage

Legacy systems use big servers and NAS and SAN systems to store the data. As the data increases, the server size and the backend storage size has to be increased. Traditional legacy systems typically work in a scale-up model where more and more compute, memory, and storage needs to be added to a server to meet the increased data needs. Hence the processing time increases exponentially, which defeats the other important requirement of big data, which is velocity.

Data Processing

The algorithms in legacy system are designed to work with structured data such as strings and integers. They are also limited by the size of data. Thus, legacy systems are not capable of handling the processing of unstructured data, huge volumes of such data, and the speed at which the processing needs to be performed.

As a result, to capture value from big data, we need to deploy newer technologies in the field of storing, computing, and retrieving, and we need new techniques for analyzing the data.

Big Data Technologies

You have seen what big data is. In this section we will briefly look at what technologies can handle this humongous source of data. The technologies in discussion need to efficiently accept and process different types of data.

The recent technology advancements that enable organizations to make the most of its big data are the following:

1. New storage and processing technologies designed specifically for large unstructured data

2. Parallel processing

3. Clustering

4. Large grid environments

5. High connectivity and high throughput

6. Cloud computing and scale-out architectures

There are a growing number of technologies that are making use of these technological advancements. In this book, we will be discussing MongoDB, one of the technologies that can be used to store and process big data.

Summary

In this chapter you learned about big data. You looked into the various sources that are generating big data, and the usage and challenges posed by big data. You also looked why newer technologies are needed to store and process big data.

In the following chapters, you will look into a few of the technologies that help organizations manage big data and enable them to get meaningful insights from big data.

CHAPTER 2

NoSQL

"NoSQL is a new way of designing Internet-scale database solutions. It is not a product or technology but a term that defines a set of database technologies that are not based on the traditional RDBMS principles."

In this chapter, we will cover the definition and basics of NoSQL. We will introduce you to the CAP theorem and will talk about the NRW notations. We will compare the ACID and BASE approaches and finally conclude the chapter by comparing NoSQL and SQL database technologies.

SQL

The idea of RDBMS was borne from E.F. Codd's 1970 whitepaper titled "A relational model of data for large shared data banks." The language used to query RDBMS systems is SQL (Sequel Query Language).

RDBMS systems are well suited for structured data held in columns and rows, which can be queried using SQL. The RDBMS systems are based on the concept of ACID transactions. ACID stands for Atomic, Consistent, Isolated, and Durable, where

- **Atomic** implies either all changes of a transaction are applied completely or not applied at all.

- **Consistent** means the data is in a consistent state after the transaction is applied. This means after a transaction is committed, the queries fetching a particular data will see the same result.

- **Isolated** means the transactions that are applied to the same set of data are independent of each other. Thus, one transaction will not interfere with another transaction.

- **Durable** means the changes are permanent in the system and will not be lost in case of any failures.

NoSQL

NoSQL is a term used to refer to non-relational databases. Thus, it encompasses majority of the data stores that are not based on the conventional RDBMS principles and are used for handling large data sets on an Internet scale.

Big data, as discussed in the previous chapter, is posing challenges to the traditional ways of storing and processing data, such as the RDBMS systems. As a result, we see the rise of NoSQL databases, which are designed to process this huge amount and variety of data within time and cost constraints.

© Shakuntala Gupta Edward, Navin Sabharwal 2015
S.G. Edward and N. Sabharwal, *Practical MongoDB*, DOI 10.1007/978-1-4842-0647-8_2

Thus NoSQL databases evolved from the need to handle big data; traditional RDBMS technologies could not provide adequate solutions. Figure 2-1 shows the rise of un/semi-structured data over the years as compared to structured data.

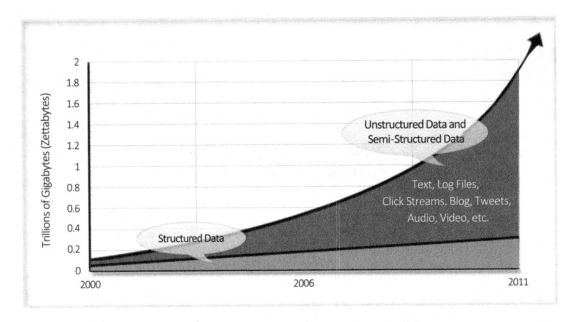

Figure 2-1. *Structured vs. un/Semi-Structured data*

Some examples of big data use cases that are a good fit for NoSQL databases are the following:

- **Social Network Graph**: Who is connected to whom? Whose post should be visible on the user's wall or homepage on a social network site?

- **Search and Retrieve**: Search all relevant pages with a particular keyword ranked by the number of times a keyword appears on a page.

Definition

NoSQL doesn't have a formal definition. It represents a form of persistence/data storage mechanism that is fundamentally different from RDBMS. But if pushed to define NoSQL, here it is: NoSQL is an umbrella term for data stores that don't follow the RDBMS principles.

■ **Note**   The term was used initially to mean "do not use SQL if you want to scale." Later this was redefined to "not only SQL," which means that in addition to SQL other complimentary database solutions exist.

A Brief History of NoSQL

In 1998, Carlo Strozzi coined the term *NoSQL*. He used this term to identify his database because the database didn't have a SQL interface. The term resurfaced in early 2009 when Eric Evans (a Rackspace employee) used this term in an event on open source distributed databases to refer to distributed databases that were non-relational and did not follow the ACID features of relational databases.

ACID vs. BASE

In the introduction, we mentioned that the traditional RDBMS applications have focused on ACID transactions. Howsoever essential these qualities may seem, they are quite incompatible with availability and performance requirements for applications of a Web scale.

Let's say, for example, that you have a company like OLX, which sells products such as unused household goods (old furniture, vehicles, etc.) and uses RDBMS as its database. Let's consider two scenarios.

First scenario: Let's look at an e-commerce shopping site where a user is buying a product. During the transaction, the user locks a part of database, the inventory, and every other user must wait until the user who has put the lock completes the transaction.

Second scenario: The application might end up using cached data or even unlocked records, resulting in inconsistency. In this case, two users might end up buying the product when the inventory actually was zero.

The system may become slow, impacting scalability and user experience.

In contrary to the ACID approach of traditional RDBMS systems, NoSQL solves the problem using an approach popularly called as BASE. Before explaining BASE, let's explore the concept of the CAP theorem.

CAP Theorem (Brewer's Theorem)

Eric Brewer outlined the CAP theorem in 2000. This is an important concept that needs to be well understood by developers and architects dealing with distributed databases. The theorem states that when designing an application in a distributed environment there are three basic requirements that exist, namely consistency, availability, and partition tolerance.

- **Consistency** means that the data remains consistent after any operation is performed that changes the data, and that all users or clients accessing the application see the same updated data.

- **Availability** means that the system is always available.

- **Partition Tolerance** means that the system will continue to function even if it is partitioned into groups of servers that are not able to communicate with one another.

The CAP theorem states that at any point in time a distributed system can fulfil only two of the above three guarantees (Figure 2-2).

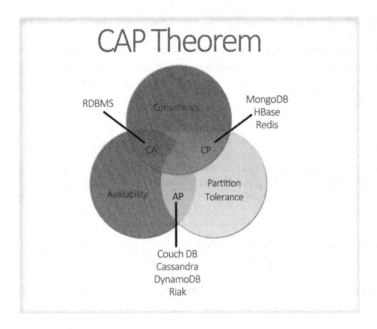

Figure 2-2. *CAP Theorem*

The BASE

Eric Brewer coined the BASE acronym. BASE can be explained as

- **Basically Available** means the system will be available in terms of the CAP theorem.

- **Soft state** indicates that even if no input is provided to the system, the state will change over time. This is in accordance to eventual consistency.

- **Eventual consistency** means the system will attain consistency in the long run, provided no input is sent to the system during that time.

Hence BASE is in contrast with the RDBMS ACID transactions.

You have seen that NoSQL databases are eventually consistent but the eventual consistency implementation may vary across different NoSQL databases.

NRW is the notation used to describe how the eventual consistency model is implemented across NoSQL databases where

- **N** is the number of data copies that the database has maintained.

- **R** is the number of copies that an application needs to refer to before returning a read request's output.

- **W** is the number of data copies that need to be written to before a write operation is marked as completed successfully.

Using these notation configurations, the databases implement the model of eventual consistency.

Consistency can be implemented at both read and write operation levels.

Write Operations

N=W implies that the write operation will update all data copies before returning the control to the client and marking the write operation as successful. This is similar to how the traditional RDBMS databases work when implementing synchronous replication. This setting will slow down the write performance.

If write performance is a concern, which means you want the writes to be happening fast, you can set W=1, R=N. This implies that the write will just update any one copy and mark the write as successful, but whenever the user issues a read request, it will read all the copies to return the result. If either of the copies is not updated, it will ensure the same is updated, and then only the read will be successful. This implementation will slow down the read performance.

Hence most NoSQL implementations use N>W>1. This implies that greater than one node needs to be updated successfully; however, not all nodes need to be updated at the same time.

Read Operations

If R is set to 1, the read operation will read any data copy, which can be outdated. If R>1, more than one copy is read, and it will read most recent value. However, this can slow down the read operation.

Using N<W+R always ensures that a read operation retrieves the latest value. This is because the number of written copies and read copies are always greater than the actual number of copies, ensuring that at least one read copy has the latest version. This is **quorum assembly**.

Table 2-1 compares ACID vs. BASE.

Table 2-1. *ACID vs. BASE*

ACID	BASE
Atomicity	Basically Available
Consistency	Eventually Consistency
Isolation	Soft State
Durable	

NoSQL Advantages and Disadvantages

In this section, you will look at the advantages and disadvantages of NoSQL databases.

Advantages of NoSQL

Let's talk about the advantages of NoSQL databases.

- **High scalability:** This scaling up approach fails when the transaction rates and fast response requirements increase. In contrast to this, the new generation of NoSQL databases is designed to scale out (i.e. to expand horizontally using low-end commodity servers).

- **Manageability and administration**: NoSQL databases are designed to mostly work with automated repairs, distributed data, and simpler data models, leading to low manageability and administration.

- **Low cost**: NoSQL databases are typically designed to work with a cluster of cheap commodity servers, enabling the users to store and process more data at a low cost.

- **Flexible data models**: NoSQL databases have a very flexible data model, enabling them to work with any type of data; they don't comply with the rigid RDBMS data models. As a result, any application changes that involve updating the database schema can be easily implemented.

Disadvantages of NoSQL

In addition to the above mentioned advantages, there are many impediments that you need to be aware of before you start developing applications using these platforms.

- **Maturity**: Most NoSQL databases are pre-production versions with key features that are still to be implemented. Thus, when deciding on a NoSQL database, you should analyze the product properly to ensure the features are fully implemented and not still on the To-do list.

- **Support**: Support is one limitation that you need to consider. Most NoSQL databases are from start-ups which were open sourced. As a result, support is very minimal as compared to the enterprise software companies and may not have global reach or support resources.

- **Limited Query Capabilities**: Since NoSQL databases are generally developed to meet the scaling requirement of the web-scale applications, they provide limited querying capabilities. A simple querying requirement may involve significant programming expertise.

- **Administration**: Although NoSQL is designed to provide a no-admin solution, it still requires skill and effort for installing and maintaining the solution.

- **Expertise**: Since NoSQL is an evolving area, expertise on the technology is limited in the developer and administrator community.

Although NoSQL is becoming an important part of the database landscape, you need to be aware of the limitations and advantages of the products to make the correct choice of the NoSQL database platform.

SQL vs. NoSQL Databases

Now you know the details regarding NoSQL databases. Although NoSQL is increasingly getting adopted as a database solution, it's not here to replace SQL or RDBMS databases. In this section, you will look at the differences between SQL and NoSQL databases.

Let's do a quick recap of the RDBMS system. RDBMS systems have prevailed for about 30 years, and even now they are the default choice of the solution architect for data storage for an application. If we will list a few of the good points of RDBMS system, first and the foremost is the use of SQL, which is a rich declarative query language used for data processing. It is well understood by users. In addition, the RDBMS system offers ACID support for transactions, which is a must in many sectors, such as banking applications.

However, the biggest drawbacks of the RDBMS system are its difficulty in handling schema changes and scaling issues as data increases. As data increases, the read read/write performance degrades. You face scaling issues with RDBMS systems because they are mostly designed to scale up and not scale out.

In contrast to the SQL RDBMS databases, NoSQL promotes the data stores, which break away from the RDBMS paradigm.

Let's talk about technical scenarios and how they compare in RDBMS vs. NoSQL:

- **Schema flexibility:** This is a must for easy future enhancements and integration with external applications (outbound or inbound).

  RDBMS are quite inflexible in their design. Adding a column is an absolute no-no, especially if the table has some data. The reasons range from default value, indexes, and performance implications. More often than not, you end up creating new tables, and increasing the complexity by introducing relationships across tables.

- **Complex queries:** The traditional designing of the tables leads to developers writing complex JOIN queries, which are not only difficult to implement and maintain but also take substantial database resources to execute.

- **Data update:** Updating data across tables is probably one of the more complex scenarios, especially if they are a part of the transaction. Note that keeping the transaction open for a long duration hampers the performance. You also have to plan for propagating the updates to multiple nodes across the system. And if the system does not support multiple masters or writing to multiple nodes simultaneously, there is a risk of node failure and the entire application moving to read-only mode.

- **Scalability:** Often the only scalability that may be required is for read operations. However, several factors impact this speed as operations grow. Some of the key questions to ask are:

  - What is the time taken to synchronize the data across physical database instances?

  - What is the time taken to synchronize the data across datacenters?

  - What is the bandwidth requirement to synchronize data?

  - Is the data exchanged optimized?

  - What is the latency when any update is synchronized across servers? Typically, the records will be locked during an update.

  NoSQL-based solutions provide answers to most of the challenges listed above.

  Let's now see what NoSQL has to offer against each technical question mentioned above.

- **Schema flexibility:** Column-oriented databases store data as columns as opposed to rows in RDBMS. This allows the flexibility of adding one or more columns as required, on the fly. Similarly, document stores that allow storing semi-structured data are also good options.

- **Complex queries:** NoSQL databases do not have support for relationships or foreign keys. There are no complex queries. There are no JOIN statements.

  Is that a drawback? How does one query across tables?

  It is a functional drawback, definitely. To query across tables, multiple queries must be executed. A database is a shared resource, used across application servers and must not be released from use as quickly as possible. The options involve a combination of simplifying the queries to be executed, caching data, and performing complex operations in the application tier. A lot of databases provide in-built entity-level caching. This means that when a record is accessed, it may be automatically cached transparently by the database. The cache may be in-memory distributed cache for performance and scale.

- **Data update:** Data updating and synchronization across physical instances are difficult engineering problems to solve. Synchronization across nodes within a datacenter has a different set of requirements compared to synchronizing across multiple datacenters. One would want the latency within a couple of milliseconds or tens of milliseconds at the best. NoSQL solutions offer great synchronization options.

  MongoDB, for example, allows concurrent updates across nodes, synchronization with conflict resolution, and eventually, consistency across the datacenters within an acceptable time that would run in few milliseconds. As such, MongoDB has no concept of isolation. Note that now because the complexity of managing the transaction may be moved out of the database, the application will have to do some hard work.

  An example of this is a two-phase commit while implementing transactions (`http://docs.mongodb.org/manual/tutorial/perform-two-phase-commits/`).

  A plethora of databases offer multiversion concurrency control (MCC) to achieve transactional consistency.

  Well, as Dan Pritchett (`www.addsimplicity.com/`), Technical Fellow at eBay puts it, eBay.com does not use transactions. Note that PayPal does use transactions.

- **Scalability:** NoSQL solutions provider greater scalability for obvious reasons. A lot of the complexity that is required for transaction-oriented RDBMS does not exist in ACID non-compliant NoSQL databases. Interestingly, since NoSQL does not provide cross-table references and there are no JOIN queries possible, and because you can't write a single query to collate data across multiple tables, one simple and logical solution is to—at times—duplicate the data across tables. In some scenarios, embedding the information within the primary entity—especially in one-to-one mapping cases—may be a great idea.

Table 2-2 compares SQL and NoSQL technologies.

Table 2-2. *SQL vs. NoSQL*

	SQL Databases	NoSQL Databases
Types	All types support SQL standard.	Multiple types exists, such as document stores, key value stores, column databases, etc.
Development History	Developed in 1970.	Developed in 2000s.
Examples	SQL Server, Oracle, MySQL.	MongoDB, HBase, Cassandra.
Data Storage Model	Data is stored in rows and columns in a table, where each column is of a specific type. The tables generally are created on principles of normalization. Joins are used to retrieve data from multiple tables.	The data model depends on the database type. Say data is stored as a key-value pair for key-value stores. In document-based databases, the data is stored as documents. The data model is flexible, in contrast to the rigid table model of the RDBMS.
Schemas	Fixed structure and schema, so any change to schema involves altering the database.	Dynamic schema, new data types, or structures can be accommodated by expanding or altering the current schema. New fields can be added dynamically.
Scalability	Scale up approach is used; this means as the load increases, bigger, expensive servers are bought to accommodate the data.	Scale out approach is used; this means distributing the data load across inexpensive commodity servers.
Supports Transactions	Supports ACID and transactions.	Supports partitioning and availability, and compromises on transactions. Transactions exist at certain level, such as the database level or document level.
Consistency	Strong consistency.	Dependent on the product. Few chose to provide strong consistency whereas few provide eventual consistency.
Support	High level of enterprise support is provided.	Open source model. Support through third parties or companies building the open source products.
Maturity	Have been around for a long time.	Some of them are mature; others are evolving.
Querying Capabilities	Available through easy-to-use GUI interfaces.	Querying may require programming expertise and knowledge. Rather than an UI, focus is on functionality and programming interfaces.
Expertise	Large community of developers who have been leveraging the SQL language and RDBMS concepts to architect and develop applications.	Small community of developers working on these open source tools.

Categories of NoSQL Databases

In this section, you will quickly explore the NoSQL landscape. You will look at the emerging categories of NoSQL databases. Table 2-3 shows a few of the projects in the NoSQL landscape, with the types and the players in each category.

Table 2-3. *NoSQL Categories*

Category	Brief Description	For E.g.
Document-based	Data is stored in form of documents. For instance, {Name="Test User", Address="Address1", Age:8}	MongoDB
XML database	XML is used for storing data.	MarkLogic
Graph databases	Data is stored as node collections. The nodes are connected via edges. A node is comparable to an object in a programming language.	GraphDB
Key-value store	Stores data as key-value pairs.	Cassandra, Redis, memcached

The NoSQL databases are categorized on the basis of how the data is stored. NoSQL mostly follows a horizontal structure because of the need to provide curated information from large volumes, generally in near real-time. They are optimized for insert and retrieve operations on a large scale with built-in capabilities for replication and clustering.

Table 2-4 briefly provides a feature comparison between the various categories of NoSQL databases.

Table 2-4. *Feature Comparison*

Feature	Column-Oriented	Document Store	Key-Value Store	Graph
Table-like schema support (columns)	Yes	No	No	Yes
Complete update/fetch	Yes	Yes	Yes	Yes
Partial update/fetch	Yes	Yes	Yes	No
Query/filter on value	Yes	Yes	No	Yes
Aggregate across rows	Yes	No	No	No
Relationship between entities	No	No	No	Yes
Cross-entity view support	No	Yes	No	No
Batch fetch	Yes	Yes	Yes	Yes
Batch update	Yes	Yes	Yes	No

The important thing when considering a NoSQL project is the feature set you are interested in. When deciding on a NoSQL product, first you need to understand the problem requirements very carefully, and then you should look at other people who have already used the NoSQL product to solve similar problems. Remember that NoSQL is still maturing, so this will enable you to learn from peers and previous deployments, and make better choices.

In addition, you also need to consider the following questions.

- How big is the data that needs to be handled?

- What throughput is acceptable for read and write?

- How is consistency is achieved in the system?

- Does the system need to support high write performance or high read performance?

- How easy is the maintainability and administration?

- What needs to be queried?

- What is the benefit of using NoSQL?

We recommend that you start small but significant, and consider a hybrid approach wherever possible.

Summary

In this chapter, you learned about NoSQL. You should now understand what NoSQL is and how it is different from SQL. You also looked into the various categories of NoSQL.

In the following chapters, you will look into MongoDB, which is a document-based NoSQL database.

CHAPTER 3

■ ■ ■

Introducing MongoDB

"MongoDB is one of the leading NoSQL document store databases. Itenables organizations to handle and gain meaningful insights from Big Data."

Some leading enterprises and consumer IT companies have leveraged the capabilities of MongoDB in their products and solutions. The MongoDB 3.0 release introduced a pluggable storage engine and the Ops Manager, which has extended the set of applications that are best suited for MongoDB.

MongoDB derives its name from the word "humungous."Like other NoSQL databases, MongoDB also doesn't comply with the RDBMS principles. It doesn't have the concepts of tables, rows, and columns. Also, it doesn't provide features of ACID compliance, JOINS, foreign keys, etc.

MongoDB stores data as Binary JSON documents (also known as BSON). The documents can have different schemas, which means that the schema can change as the application evolves. MongoDB is built for scalability, performance, and high availability.

In this chapter, we will talk a bit about MongoDB's creation and the design decisions. We will look at the key features, components, and architecture of MongoDB in the following chapters.

History

In the later part of 2007, Dwight Merriman, Eliot Horowitz, and their team decided to develop an online service. The intent of the service was to provide a platform for developing, hosting, and auto-scaling web applications, much in line with products such as the Google App Engine or Microsoft Azure. Soon they realized that no open source database platform suited the requirements of the service.

"We felt like a lot of existing databases didn't really have the 'cloud computing' principles you want them to have: elasticity, scalability, and … easy administration, but also ease of use for developers and operators," Merriman said. "[MySQL] doesn't have all those properties."[1] So they decided to build a database that would not comply with the RDBMS model.

A year later, the database for the service was ready to use. The service itself was never released but the team decided in 2009 to open source the database as MongoDB. In March of 2010,the release of MongoDB 1.4.0 was considered production-ready. The latest production release is 3.0and it was released in March 2015.MongoDB was built under the sponsorship of 10gen, a New York–based startup.

---

[1]The Register, Cade Metz, "MongoDB daddy: My baby beats Google BigTable",
www.theregister.co.uk/2011/05/25/the_once_and_future_mongodb/), May 25, 2011.

S.G. Edward and N. Sabharwal, *Practical MongoDB*, DOI 10.1007/978-1-4842-0647-8_3

MongoDB Design Philosophy

In one of his talks, Eliot Horowitz mentioned that MongoDB wasn't designed in a lab and is instead built from the experiences of building large scale, high availability, and robust systems. In this section, we will briefly look at some of the design decisions that led to what MongoDB is today.

Speed, Scalability, and Agility

The design team's goal when designing MongoDB was to create a database that was fast, massively scalable, and easy to use. To achieve speed and horizontal scalability in a partitioned database, as explained in the CAP theorem, the consistency and transactional support have to be compromised. Thus, per this theorem, MongoDB provides high availability, scalability, and partitioning at the cost of consistency and transactional support. In practical terms, this means that instead of tables and rows, MongoDB uses documents to make it flexible, scalable, and fast.

Non-Relational Approach

Traditional RDBMS platforms provide scalability using a scale-up approach, which requires a faster server to increase performance. The following issues in RDBMS systems led to why MongoDB and other NoSQL databases were designed the way they are designed:

- In order to scale out, the RDBMS database needs to link the data available in two or more systems in order to report back the result. This is difficult to achieve in RDBMS systems since they are designed to work when all the data is available for computation together. Thus the data has to be available for processing at a single location.

- In case of multiple Active-Active servers, when both are getting updated from multiple sources there is a challenge in determining which update is correct.

- When an application tries to read data from the second server, and the information has been updated on the first server but has yet to be synchronized with the second server, the information returned may be stale.

The MongoDB team decided to take a non-relational approach to solving these problems. As mentioned, MongoDB stores its data in BSON documents where all the related data is placed together, which means everything is in one place. The queries in MongoDB are based on keys in the document, so the documents can be spread across multiple servers. Querying each server means it will check its own set of documents and return the result. This enables linear scalability and improved performance.

MongoDB has a primary-secondary replication where the primary accepts the write requests. If the write performance needs to be improved, then sharding can be used; this splits the data across multiple machines and enables these multiple machines to update different parts of the datasets. Sharding is automatic in MongoDB; as more machines are added, data is distributed automatically.

JSON-Based Document Store

MongoDB uses a JSON-based (JavaScript Object Notation) document store for the data. JSON/BSON offers a schema-less model, which provides flexibility in terms of database design. Unlike in RDBMSs, changes can be done to the schema seamlessly.

This design also makes for high performance by providing for grouping of relevant data together internally and making it easily searchable.

A JSON document contains the actual data and is comparable to a row in SQL. However, in contrast to RDBMS rows, documents can have dynamic schema. This means documents within a collection can have different fields or structure, or common fields can have different type of data.

A document contains data in form of key-value pairs. Let's understand this with an example:

```
{
"Name": "ABC",
"Phone": ["1111111",
........"222222"
........],
"Fax":..
}
```

As mentioned, keys and values come in pairs. The value of a key in a document can be left blank. In the above example, the document has three keys, namely "Name," "Phone," and "Fax." The "Fax" key has no value.

Performance vs. Features

In order to make MongoDB high performance and fast, certain features commonly available in RDBMS systems are not available in MongoDB. MongoDB is a document-oriented DBMS where data is stored as documents. It does not support JOINs, and it does not have fully generalized transactions. However, it does provide support for secondary indexes, it enables users to query using query documents, and it provides support for atomic updates at a per document level. It provides a replica set, which is a form of master-slave replication with automated failover, and it has built-in horizontal scaling.

Running the Database Anywhere

One of the main design decisions was the ability to run the database from anywhere, which means it should be able to run on servers, VMs, or even on the cloud using the pay-for-what-you-use service. The language used for implementing MongoDB is C++, which enables MongoDB to achieve this goal. The 10gen site provides binaries for different OS platforms, enabling MongoDB to run on almost any type of machine.

SQL Comparison

The following are the ways in which MongoDB is different from SQL.

1. MongoDB uses documents for storing its data, which offer a flexible schema (documents in same collection can have different fields). This enables the users to store nested or multi-value fields such as arrays, hashes, etc. In contrast, RDBMS systems offer a fixed schema where a column's value should have a similar data type. Also, it's not possible to store arrays or nested values in a cell.

2. MongoDB doesn't provide support for JOIN operations, like in SQL. However, it enables the user to store all relevant data together in a single document, avoiding at the periphery the usage of JOINs. It has a workaround to overcome this issue. We will be discussing this in more detail in a later chapter.

3. MongoDB doesn't provide support for transactions in the same way as SQL. However, it guarantees atomicity at the document level. Also, it uses an isolation operator to isolate write operations that affect multiple documents, but it does not provide "all-or-nothing" atomicity for multi-document write operations.

Summary

In this chapter, you got to know MongoDB, its history, and brief details on design of the MongoDB system. In the next chapters, you will learn more about MongoDB's data model.

■ ■ ■

CHAPTER 4

The MongoDB Data Model

"MongoDB is designed to work with documents without any need of predefined columns or data types (unlike relational databases), making the data model extremely flexible."

In this chapter, you will learn about the MongoDB data model. You will also learn what flexible schema (polymorphic schema) means and why it's a significant contemplation of MongoDB data model.

The Data Model

In the previous chapter, you saw that MongoDB is a document-based database system where the documents can have a flexible schema. This means that documents within a collection can have different (or same) sets of fields. This affords you more flexibility when dealing with data.

In this chapter, you will explore MongoDB's flexible data model. Wherever required, we will demonstrate the difference in the approach compared to RDBMS systems.

A MongoDB deployment can have many databases. Each database is a set of collections. Collections are similar to the concept of tables in SQL; however, they are schemaless. Each collection can have multiple documents. Think of a document as a row in SQL. Figure 4-1 depicts the MongoDB database model.

© Shakuntala Gupta Edward, Navin Sabharwal 2015
S.G. Edward and N. Sabharwal, *Practical MongoDB*, DOI 10.1007/978-1-4842-0647-8_4

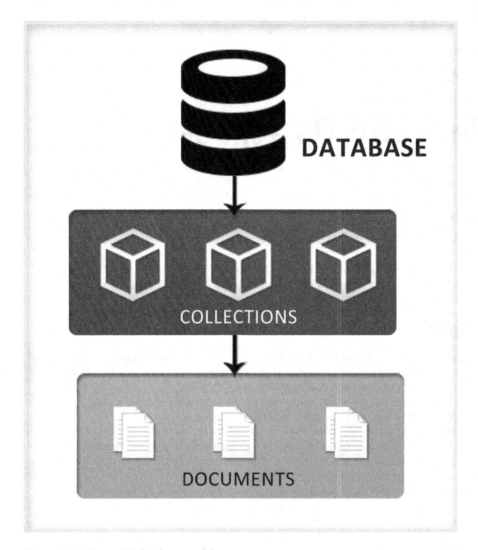

Figure 4-1. *MongoDB database model*

In an RDBMS system, since the table structures and the data types for each column are fixed, you can only add data of a particular data type in a column. In MongoDB, a collection is a collection of documents where data is stored as key-value pairs.

Let's understand with an example how data is stored in a document. The following document holds the name and phone numbers of the users:

```
{"Name": "ABC", "Phone": ["1111111",      "222222" ] }
```

Dynamic schema means that documents within the same collection can have the same or different sets of fields or structure, and even common fields can store different types of values across documents. There's no rigidness in the way data is stored in the documents of a collection.

Let's see an example of a Region collection:

```
{ "R_ID" : "REG001",  "Name" : "United States" }
{ "R_ID" :1234,  "Name" : "New York" , "Country" : "United States" }
```

In this code, you have two documents in the Region collection. Although both documents are part of a single collection, they have different structures: the second collection has an additional field of information, which is country. In fact, if you look at the "R_ID" field, it stores a STRING value in the first document whereas it's a number in the second document.

Thus a collection's documents can have entirely different schemas. It falls to the application to store the documents in a particular collection together or to have multiple collections.

JSON and BSON

MongoDB is a document-based database. It uses Binary JSON for storing its data.

In this section, you will learn about JSON and Binary-JSON (BSON). JSON stands for JavaScript Object Notation. It's a standard used for data interchange in today's modern Web (along with XML). The format is human and machine readable. It is not only a great way to exchange data but also a nice way to store data.

All the basic data types (such as strings, numbers, Boolean values, and arrays) are supported by JSON. The following code shows what a JSON document looks like:

```
{
"_id" : 1,
"name" : { "first" : "John", "last" : "Doe" },
"publications" : [
        {
          "title" : "First Book",
          "year" : 1989,
          "publisher" : "publisher1"
        },
        { "title" : "Second Book",
          "year" : 1999,
          "publisher" : "publisher2"
        }
]
}
```

JSON lets you keep all the related pieces of information together in one place, which provides excellent performance. It also enables the updating of a document to be independent. It is schemaless.

Binary JSON (BSON)

MongoDB stores the JSON document in a binary-encoded format. This is termed as BSON. The BSON data model is an extended form of the JSON data model.

MongoDB's implementation of a BSON document is fast, highly traversable, and lightweight. It supports embedding of arrays and objects within other arrays, and also enables MongoDB to reach inside the objects to build indexes and match objects against queried expressions, both on top-level and nested BSON keys.

The Identifier (_id)

You have seen that MongoDB stores data in documents. Documents are made up of key-value pairs. Although a document can be compared to a row in RDBMS, unlike a row, documents have flexible schema. A key, which is nothing but a label, can be roughly compared to the column name in RDBMS. A key is used for querying data from the documents. Hence, like a RDBMS primary key (used to uniquely identify each row), you need to have a key that uniquely identifies each document within a collection. This is referred to as _id in MongoDB.

If you have not explicitly specified any value for a key, a unique value will be automatically generated and assigned to it by MongoDB. This key value is immutable and can be of any data type except arrays.

Capped Collection

You are now well versed with collections and documents. Let's talk about a special type of collection called a capped collection.

MongoDB has a concept of capping the collection. This means it stores the documents in the collection in the inserted order. As the collection reaches its limit, the documents will be removed from the collection in FIFO (first in, first out) order. This means that the least recently inserted documents will be removed first.

This is good for use cases where the order of insertion is required to be maintained automatically, and deletion of records after a fixed size is required. One such use cases is log files that get automatically truncated after a certain size.

■ **Note** MongoDB itself uses capped collections for maintaining its replication logs. Capped collection guarantees preservation of the data in insertion order, so queries retrieving data in the insertion order return results quickly and don't need an index. Updates that change the document size are not allowed.

Polymorphic Schemas

As you are already conversant with the schemaless nature of MongoDB data structure, let's now explore polymorphic schemas and use cases.

A polymorphic schema is a schema where a collection has documents of different types or schemas. A good example of this schema is a collection named Users. Some user documents might have an extra fax number or email address, while others might have only phone numbers, yet all these documents coexist within the same Users collection. This schema is generally referred to as a polymorphic schema.

In this part of the chapter, you'll explore the various reasons for using a polymorphic schema.

Object-Oriented Programming

Object-oriented programming enables you to have classes share data and behaviors using inheritance. It also lets you define functions in the parent class that can be overridden in the child class and thus will function differently in a different context. In other words, you can use the same function name to manipulate the child as well as the parent class, although under the hood the implementations might be different. This feature is referred to as polymorphism.

The requirement in this case is the ability to have a schema wherein all of the related sets of objects or objects within a hierarchy can fit in together and can also be retrieved identically.

Let's consider an example. Suppose you have an application that lets the user upload and share different content types such as HTML pages, documents, images, videos, etc. Although many of the fields are common across all of the above-mentioned content types (such as Name, ID, Author, Upload Date, and Time), not all fields are identical. For example, in the case of images, you have a binary field that holds the image content, whereas an HTML page has a large text field to hold the HTML content.

In this scenario, the MongoDB polymorphic schema can be used wherein all of the content node types are stored in the same collection, such as LoadContent, and each document has relevant fields only.

```
// "Document collections" - "HTMLPage" document
{
_id: 1,
title: "Hello",
type: "HTMLpage",
text: "<html>Hi..Welcome to my world</html>"
}
...
// Document collection also has a "Picture" document
{
_id: 3,
title: "Family Photo",
type: "JPEG",
sizeInMB: 10,........
}
```

This schema not only enables you to store related data with different structures together in a same collection, it also simplifies the querying. The same collection can be used to perform queries on common fields such as fetching all content uploaded on a particular date and time as well as queries on specific fields such as finding images with a size greater than X MB.

Thus object-oriented programming is one of the use cases where having a polymorphic schema makes sense.

Schema Evolution

When you are working with databases, one of the most important considerations that you need to account for is the schema evolution (i.e. the change in the schema's impact on the running application). The design should be done in a way as to have minimal or no impact on the application, meaning no or minimal downtime, no or very minimal code changes, etc.

Typically, schema evolution happens by executing a migration script that upgrades the database schema from the old version to the new one. If the database is not in production, the script can be simple drop and recreation of the database. However, if the database is in a production environment and contains live data, the migration script will be complex because the data will need to be preserved. The script should take this into consideration. Although MongoDB offers an Update option that can be used to update all the documents' structure within a collection if there's a new addition of a field, imagine the impact of doing this if you have thousands of documents in the collection. It would be very slow and would have a negative impact on the underlying application's performance. One of the ways of doing this is to include the new structure to the new documents being added to the collection and then gradually migrating the collection in the background while the application is still running. This is one of the many use cases where having a polymorphic schema will be advantageous.

For example, say you are working with a Tickets collection where you have documents with ticket details, like so:

```
// "Ticket1" document (stored in "Tickets" collection")
{
_id: 1,
Priority: "High",
type: "Incident",
text: "Printer not working"
}..........
```

At some point, the application team decides to introduce a "short description" field in the ticket document structure, so the best alternative is to introduce this new field in the new ticket documents. Within the application, you embed a piece of code that will handle retrieving both "old style" documents (without a short description field) and "new style" documents (with a short description field). Gradually the old style documents can be migrated to the new style documents. Once the migration is completed, if required the code can be updated to remove the piece of code that was embedded to handle the missing field.

Summary

In this chapter, you learned about the MongoDB data model. You also looked at identifiers and capped collections. You concluded the chapter with an understanding of how the flexible schema helps.

In the following chapter, you will get started with MongoDB. You will perform the installation and configuration of MongoDB.

CHAPTER 5

■ ■ ■

MongoDB - Installation and Configuration

"MongoDB is a cross-platform database."

In this chapter, you will go over the process of installing MongoDB on Windows and Linux.

Select Your Version

MongoDB runs on most platforms. A list of all the available packages is available on the MongoDB downloads page at www.mongodb.org/downloads.

The correct version for your environment will depend on your server's operating system and the kind of processor. MongoDB supports both 32-bit and 64-bit architecture but it's recommended to use 64-bit in your production environment.

■ **32-bit limitation** This is due to the usage of memory mapped files in MongoDB. This limits the 32-bit builds to around 2GB of data. It's recommended to use a 64-bit build for a production environment for performance reasons.

The latest MongoDB production release is 3.0.4 at the time of writing this book. Downloads for MongoDB are available for Linux, Windows, Solaris, and Mac OS X.

The MongoDB download page is divided in the following sections:

- Current Stable Release (3.0.4) – 6/16/2015

- Previous Releases (stable)

- Development Releases (unstable)

The current release is the most stable recent version available, which at time of writing of the book is 3.0.4. When a new version is released, the prior stable release is moved to the Previous Releases section.

The development releases, as the name suggests, are the versions that are still under development and hence are tagged as unstable. These versions can have additional features but they may not be stable since they are still in the development phase. You can use the development versions to try out new features and provide feedback to 10gen regarding the features and issues faced.

© Shakuntala Gupta Edward, Navin Sabharwal 2015
S.G. Edward and N. Sabharwal, *Practical MongoDB*, DOI 10.1007/978-1-4842-0647-8_5

Installing MongoDB on Linux

This section covers installing MongoDB on a LINUX system. For the following demonstration, we will be using an Ubuntu Linux distribution. You can install MongoDB either manually or via repositories. We will walk you through both options.

Installing Using Repositories

In LINUX, repositories are the online directories that contain software. Aptitude is the program used to install software on Ubuntu. Although MongoDB might be present in the default repositories, there is the possibility of an out-of-date version, so the first step is to configure Aptitude to look at the custom repository.

1. Issue the following to import the `public.GPG` key for MongoDB:

    ```
    sudo apt-key adv --keyserver hkp://keyserver.ubuntu.com:80 --recv 7F0CEB10
    ```

2. Next, use the following command to create the `/etc/apt/sources.list.d/mongodb-org-3.0.list` file:

    ```
    echo "deb http://repo.mongodb.org/apt/ubuntu "$(lsb_release -sc)"/
    mongodb-org/3.0 multiverse" | sudo tee /etc/apt/sources.list.d/
    mongodb-org-3.0.list
    ```

3. Finally, use the following command to reload the repository:

    ```
    sudo apt-get update
    ```

    Now Aptitude is aware of the manually added repository.

4. Next, you need to install the software. The following command should be issued in the shell to install MongoDB's current stable version:

    ```
    sudo apt-get install -y mongodb-org
    ```

You've successfully installed MongoDB, and that's all there is to it.

Installing Manually

In this section, you will see how MongoDB can be installed manually. This knowledge is important in the following cases:

- When the Linux distribution doesn't use Aptitude.

- When the version you require is not available through repositories or is not part of the repository.

- When you need to run multiple MongoDB versions simultaneously.

The first step in a manual installation is to decide on the version of MongoDB to use and then download from the site. Next, the package needs to be extracted using the following command:

```
$ tar -xvf mongodb-linux-x86_64-3.0.4.tgz
mongodb-linux-i686-3.0.4/THIRD-PARTY-NOTICES
mongodb-linux-i686-3.0.4/GNU-AGPL-3.0
mongodb-linux-i686-3.0.4/bin/mongodump
. . . . . . . . . . . .
mongodb-linux-i686-3.0.4/bin/mongosniff
mongodb-linux-i686-3.0.4/bin/mongod
mongodb-linux-i686-3.0.4/bin/mongos
mongodb-linux-i686-3.0.4/bin/mongo
```

This extracts the package content to a new directory, namely mongodb-linux-x86_64-3.0.4 (which is located under your current directory). The directory contains many subdirectories and files. The main executable files are under the subdirectory bin.

This completes the MongoDB installation successfully.

Installing MongoDB on Windows

Installing MongoDB on Windows is a simple matter of downloading the msi file for the selected build of Windows and running the installer.

The installer will guide you through installation of MongoDB.

Following the wizard, you will reach the Choose Setup Type screen. There are two setup types available wherein you can customize your installation. In this example, select the setup type as Custom.

An installation directory needs to be specified when selecting Custom, so specify the directory to C:\PracticalMongoDB.

Note that MongoDB can be run from any folder selected by the user because it is self-contained and has no dependency on the system. If the setup type of Complete is selected, the default folder selected is C:\Program Files\MongoDB.

Clicking Next will take you to the Ready to installation screen. Click Install.

This will start the installation and will show the progress on a screen. Once the installation is complete, the wizard will take you to the completion screen.

Clicking Finish completes the setup. After successful completion of the above steps, you have a directory called C:\PracticalMongoDB with all the relevant applications in the bin folder. That's all there is to it.

Running MongoDB

Let's see how to start running and using MongoDB.

Preconditions

A data folder is required for storing the files. This by default is C:\data\db in Windows and /data/db in LINUX systems.

These data directories are not created by MongoDB, so before starting MongoDB the data directory needs to be manually created and you need to ensure that proper permissions are set (such as that MongoDB has read, write, and directory creation permissions).

If the MongoDB is started before you create the folder, it will throw an error message and will fail to run.

Starting the Service

Once the directories are created and permissions are in place, execute the mongod application (placed under the bin directory) to start the MongoDB core database service.

In continuation of the above installation, the same can be started by opening the command prompt in Windows (which needs to be run as administrator) and executing the following:

```
c:\>c:\practicalmongodb\bin\mongod.exe
```

In case of Linux, the mongod process is started in the shell.

This will start the MongoDB database on the localhost interface. It will listen for connections from the mongo shell on port 27017.

As mentioned, the folder path needs to be created before starting the database, which by default is c:\data\db. An alternative path can also be provided when starting the database service by using the **–dbpath** parameter.

```
C:\>C:\practicalmongodb\bin\mongod.exe --dbpath
C:\NewDBPath\DBContents
```

Verifying the Installation

The relevant executable will be present under the subdirectory bin. The following can be checked under the bin directory in order to vet the success of the installation step:

- Mongod: the core database server

- Mongo: The database shell

- Mongos: The auto-sharding process

- Mongoexport: The export utility

- Mongoimport: The import utility

Apart from the above, there are other applications available in the bin folder.

The mongo application launches the mongo shell, which supplies access to the database contents and lets you fire selective queries or execute aggregation against the data in MongoDB.

The mongod application, as you saw above, is used to start the database service, or daemon.

Multiple flags can be set when launching the applications. For example, –dbpath can be used to specify an alternative path for where the database files should be stored. To get the list of all available options, include the --help flag when launching the service.

MongoDB Shell

The mongo shell comes as part of the standard distribution of MongoDB. The shell provides a full database interface for MongoDB, enabling you play around with the data stored in MongoDB using a JavaScript environment, which has complete access to the language and all the standard functions.

Once database services have started, you can fire up the mongo shell and start using MongoDB. This can be done using Shell in Linux or the command prompt in Windows (run as administrator).

You must refer to the exact location of the executable, such as in the C:\practicalmongodb\bin\ folder in a Windows environment.

Open the command prompt (run as administrator) and type `mongo.exe`. Press the Enter key. This will start the mongo shell.

```
C:\>C:\practicalmongodb\bin\mongo.exe
MongoDB shell version: 3.0.4
connecting to: test
>
```

If no parameters are specified when starting the service, it connects to the default database named `test` on the localhost instance.

The database will be created automatically when connected to it. MongoDB offers this feature of automatically creating a database if an attempt is made to access a one that is not there.

The next chapter offers more information on working with the mongo shell.

Securing the Deployment

You know how to install and start using MongoDB via the default configurations. Next, you need to ensure that the data that is stored within the database is secure in all aspects.

In this section, you will look at how to secure your data. You will change the configuration of the default installation to ensure that your database is more secure.

Using Authentication and Authorization

Authentication verifies the user's identity, and authorization determines the level of actions that the user can perform on the authenticated database.

This means the users will be able to access the database only if they log in using the credentials that have access on the database. This disables anonymous access to the database. After the user is authenticated, authorization can be used to ensure that the user has only the required amount of access needed to accomplish the tasks at hand.

Both authentication and authorization exist at a per-database level. The users exist in the context of a single logical database.

The information on the users is maintained in a collection named `system.users`, which exists in the admin database. This collection maintains the credentials needed for authenticating the user wherein it stores the user id, password, and the database against which it is created, plus privileges needed for authorizing the user.

MongoDB uses a role-based approach for authorization (the roles of read, readWrite, readAnyDatabase, etc.). If needed, the user administrator can create custom roles.

A privilege document within the `system.users` collection is used for storing each user roles. The same document maintains the credentials for authenticated users.

An example of a document in the `system.users` collection is as follows:

```
{
_id : "practicaldb.Shaks",
user : "Shaks",
db : "practicaldb",
credentials : {.......},
roles : [
{ role: "read", db: "practicaldb" },
{ role: "readWrite", db: "MyDB" }
],
......
}
```

This document tells us that the user Shaks is associated with database `practicaldb` and it has read roles in the `practicaldb` database and a readWrite role in the `MyDB` database. Note that a user name and the associated database uniquely identifies a user within MongoDB, so if you have two users with the same name, but they are associated with different databases, then they are considered as two unique users. Thus a user can have multiple roles with different authorization levels on different databases.

The available roles are

- read: This provides a read-only access of all the collections for the specified database.

- readWrite: This provides a read-write access to any collection within the specified database.

- dbAdmin: This enables the user to perform administrative actions within the specified database such as index management using ensureIndex, dropIndexes, reIndex, indexStats, renaming collections, creating collections, etc.

- userAdmin: This enables the user to perform readWrite operations on the system.users collection of the specified database. It also enables altering permissions of existing users or creating new users. This is effectively the SuperUser role for the specified database.

- clusterAdmin: This role enables the user to grant access to administrative operations that alter or display information about the complete system. clusterAdmin is applicable only on the admin database.

- readAnyDatabase: This role enables user to read from any database in the MongoDB environment.

- readWriteAnyDatabase: This role is similar to readWrite except it is for all databases.

- userAdminAnyDatabase: This role is similar to the userAdmin role except it applies to all databases.

- dbAdminAnyDatabase: This role is the same as dbAdmin, except it applies to all databases.

- Starting from version 2.6, a user admin can also create user-defined roles to adhere to the policy of least privilege by providing access at collection level and command level. A user-defined role is scoped to the database in which it's created and is uniquely identified by the combination of the database and the role name. All the user defined roles are stored in the system.roles collection.

Enabling Authentication

Authentication is disabled by default, so use --auth to enable authentication. While starting mongod, use mongod --auth. Before enabling authentication, you need to have at least one admin user. As you saw above, an admin user is a user who is responsible for creating and managing other users.

It is recommended that in production deployments such users are created solely for managing users and should not be used for any other roles. In a MongoDB deployment, this user is the first user that needs to be created; other users of the system can be created by this user.

The admin user can be created either way: before enabling the authentication or after enabling the authentication.

In this example, you will first create the admin user and then enable the auth settings. The below steps should be executed on the Windows platform.

Start the mongod with default settings:

```
C:\>C:\practicalmongodb\bin\mongod.exe
C:\practicalmongodb\bin\mongod.exe --help for help and startup options

2015-07-03T23:11:10.716-0700 I CONTROL  Hotfix KB2731284 or later update is installed, no
need to zero out data files
2015-07-03T23:11:10.716-0700 I JOURNAL  [initandlisten] journal dir=C:\data\db\journal

......................................................

2015-07-03T23:11:10.763-0700 I CONTROL  [initandlisten] MongoDB starting : pid=2776
port=27017 dbpath=C:\data\db\ 64-bit host=ANOC9
2015-07-03T23:11:10.763-0700 I CONTROL  [initandlisten] targetMinOS: Windows 7/W
indows Server 2008 R2
2015-07-03T23:11:10.763-0700 I CONTROL  [initandlisten] db version v3.0.4
2015-07-03T23:11:10.764-0700 I CONTROL  [initandlisten] OpenSSL version: OpenSSL
1.0.1j-fips 19 Mar 2015
2015-07-03T23:11:10.764-0700 I CONTROL  [initandlisten] build info: windows sys.
getwindowsversion(major=6, minor=1, build=7601, platform=2, service_pack='Service Pack 1')
BOOST_LIB_VERSION=1_49
2015-07-03T23:11:10.771-0700 I NETWORK  [initandlisten] waiting for connections
on port 27017
```

Creating the Admin User

Run another instance of command prompt by running it as an administrator and execute the mongo application:

```
C:\>C:\practicalmongodb\bin\mongo.exe
MongoDB shell version: 3.0.4
connecting to: test
>
```

Switching to the Admin Database

Note that admin db is a privileged database that the user needs access to in order to execute certain administrative commands such as creating an admin user.

```
>db = db.getSiblingDB('admin')
```

Admin

The user needs to be created with either of the roles: userAdminAnyDatabase or userAdmin:

```
>db.createUser({user: "AdminUser", pwd: "password", roles:["userAdminAnyDatabase"]})
Successfully added user: { "user" : "AdminUser", "roles" : [ "userAdminAnyDatabase" ] }
```

Next, authenticate using this user. Restart the mongod with auth settings:

```
C:\>C:\practicalmongodb\bin\mongod.exe -auth
C:\practicalmongodb\bin\mongod.exe --help for help and startup options
2015-07-03T23:11:10.716-0700 I CONTROL  Hotfix KB2731284 or later update is installed, no
need to zero out data files
2015-07-03T23:11:10.716-0700 I JOURNAL  [initandlisten] journal dir=C:\data\db\journal
.................................................
2015-07-03T23:11:10.763-0700 I CONTROL  [initandlisten] MongoDB starting : pid=2776
port=27017 dbpath=C:\data\db\ 64-bit host=ANOC9
2015-07-03T23:11:10.763-0700 I CONTROL  [initandlisten] targetMinOS: Windows 7/W
indows Server 2008 R2
2015-07-03T23:11:10.763-0700 I CONTROL  [initandlisten] db version v3.0.4
2015-07-03T23:11:10.764-0700 I CONTROL  [initandlisten] OpenSSL version: OpenSSL
1.0.1j-fips 19 Mar 2015
2015-07-03T23:11:10.764-0700 I CONTROL  [initandlisten] build info: windows sys.
getwindowsversion(major=6, minor=1, build=7601, platform=2, service_pack='Service Pack 1')
BOOST_LIB_VERSION=1_49
2015-07-03T23:11:10.771-0700 I NETWORK  [initandlisten] waiting for connections
on port 27017
```

Start the mongo console and authenticate against the admin database using the AdminUser user created above:

```
C:\>c:\practicalmongodb\bin\mongo.exe
MongoDB shell version: 3.0.4
connecting to: test
>use admin
switched to db admin
>db.auth("AdminUser", "password")
1
>
```

Creating a User and Enabling Authorization

In this section, you will create a user and assign a role to the newly created user. You have already authenticated using the admin user, as shown:

```
C:\>c:\practicalmongodb\bin\mongo.exe
MongoDB shell version: 3.0.4
connecting to: test
>use admin
switched to db admin
>db.auth("AdminUser", "password")
1
>
```

Switch to the Product database and create user Alice and assign read access on the product database, like so:

```
>use product
switched to db product
>db.createUser({user: "Alice"
... , pwd:"Moon1234"
... , roles: ["read"]
... }
... )
Successfully added user: { "user" : "Alice", "roles" : [ "read" ] }
```

Next, validate that the user has read-only access on the database:

```
>db
product
>show users
{
        "_id" : "product.Alice",
        "user" : "Alice",
        "db" : "product",
        "roles" : [
                {
                        "role" : "read",
                        "db" : "product"
                }
        ]
}
```

Next, connect to a new mongo console and log in as Alice to the Products database to issue read-only commands:

```
C:\>c:\practicalmongodb\bin\mongo.exe -u Alice -p Moon1234 product
2015-07-03T23:11:10.716-0700 I CONTROL  Hotfix KB2731284 or later update is installed, no
need to zero-out data files
MongoDB shell version: 3.0.4
connecting to: products
```

Post successful authentication the following entry will be seen on the mongod console.

```
2015-07-03T23:11:26.742-0700 I ACCESS   [conn2] Successfully authenticated as principal
Alice on product
```

Controlling Access to a Network

By default, mongod and mongos bind to all the available IP addresses on a system. In this section, you will look at configuration options for restricting network exposure. The code below is executed on the Windows platform:

```
C:\>c:\practicalmongodb\bin\mongod.exe --bind_ip 127.0.0.1 --port 27017 --rest
2015-07-03T00:33:49.929-0700 I CONTROL  Hotfix KB2731284 or later update is installed, no
need to zero out data files
2015-07-03T00:33:49.946-0700 I JOURNAL  [initandlisten] journal dir=C:\data\db\journal
2015-07-03T00:33:49.980-0700 I CONTROL  [initandlisten] MongoDB starting : pid=1144
port=27017 dbpath=C:\data\db\ 64-bit host=ANOC9
2015-07-03T00:33:49.980-0700 I CONTROL  [initandlisten] targetMinOS: Windows 7/Windows
Server 2008 R2
2015-07-03T00:33:49.980-0700 I CONTROL  [initandlisten] db version v3.0.4
2015-07-03T00:33:49.980-0700 I CONTROL  [initandlisten] OpenSSL version: OpenSSL1.0.1j-fips
19 Mar 2015
2015-07-03T00:33:49.980-0700 I CONTROL  [initandlisten] build info: windows
sys.getwindowsversion(major=6, minor=1, build=7601, platform=2, service_pack='Service Pack 1')
BOOST_LIB_VERSION=1_49
2015-07-03T00:33:49.981-0700 I CONTROL  [initandlisten] allocator: system
2015-07-03T00:33:49.981-0700 I CONTROL  [initandlisten] options: { net: { bindIp:
"127.0.0.1", http: { RESTInterfaceEnabled: true, enabled: true }, port: 27017} }
2015-07-03T00:33:49.990-0700 I NETWORK  [initandlisten] waiting for connections on port
27017
2015-07-03T00:33:49.990-0700 I NETWORK  [websvr] admin web console waiting for connections
on port 28017
2015-07-03T00:34:22.277-0700 I NETWORK  [initandlisten] connection accepted from
127.0.0.1:49164 #1 (1 connection now open)
```

You have started the server with bind_ip, which has one value set as 127.0.0.1, which is the localhost interface.

The bind_ip limits the network interfaces of the incoming connections for which the program will listen. Comma-separated IP addresses can be specified. In your case, you have restricted the mongod to listen to only the localhost interface.

When the mongod instance is started, by default it waits for any incoming connection on port 27017. You can change this using -port.

Just changing the port does not reduce the risk much. In order to completely secure the environment, you need to allow only trusted clients to connect to the port using firewall settings.

Changing this port also changes the HTTP status interface port, which by default is 28017. This port is available on a port that is X+1000, where X represents the connection port.

This web page exposes diagnostic and monitoring information, which includes operational data, a variety of logs, and status reports regarding the database instances. It provides management-level statistics that can be used for administration purpose. This page is by default read-only; to make it fully interactive, you will use the REST settings. This configuration makes the page fully interactive, helping the administrators troubleshoot any performance issues. Only trusted client access should be allowed on this port using firewalls.

It is recommended to disable the HTTP Status page as well as the REST configuration in the production environment.

Use Firewalls

Firewalls are used to control access within a network. They can be used to allow access from a specific IP address to specific IP ports, or to stop any access from any untrusted hosts. They can be used to create a trusted environment for your mongod instance where you can specify what IP addresses or hosts can connect to which ports or interfaces of the mongod.

On the Windows platform, use netsh to configure the incoming traffic for port 27017:

```
C:\>netsh advfirewall firewall add rule name="Open mongod port 27017" dir=in action=allow
protocol=TCP localport=27017
Ok.
C:\>
```

This code says that all of the incoming traffic is allowed on port 27017, so any application servers can connect to the mongod.

Encrypting Data

You have seen that MongoDB stores all its data in a data directory that in Windows defaults to C:\data\db and /data/db in Linux. The files are stored unencrypted in the directory because there's no provisioning of methods for automatically encrypting the files in Mongo. Any attacker with file system access can read the data stored in the files. It's the application's responsibility to ensure that sensitive information is encrypted before it's written to the database.

Additionally, operating system-level mechanisms such as file system-level encryption and permissions should be implemented in order to prevent unauthorized access to the files.

Encrypting Communication

It's often a requirement that communication between the mongod and the client (mongo shell, for instance) is encrypted. In this setup, you will see how to add one more level of security to the above installation by configuring SSL, so that the communication between the mongod and mongo shell (client) happens using a SSL certificate and key.

It is recommended to use SSL for communication between the server and the client.

Starting from Version 3.0, most of the MongoDB distributions now have support included for SSL. The below commands are executed on a Windows platform.

The first step is to generate the .pem file that will contain the public key certificate and the private key. MongoDB can use either a self-signed certificate or any valid certificate issued by a certificate authority.

In this book, you will use the following commands to generate a self-signed certificate and private key.

1. Install OpenSSL and Microsoft Visual C++ 2008 redistributable as per the MongoDB distribution and the Windows platform. In this book, you have installed the 64-bit version.

2. Run the following command to create a public key certificate and a private key:

```
C:\> cd c:\OpenSSL-Win64\bin
C:\OpenSSL-Win64\bin\>openssl
```

This opens the OpenSSL shell where you need to enter the following command:

```
OpenSSL>req -new -x509 -days 365 -nodes -out C:\practicalmongodb\
mongodb-cert.crt -keyout C:\practicalmongodb\mongodb-cert.key
```

The above step generates a certificate key named mongodb-cert.key and places it in the C:\practicalmongodb folder.

3. Next, you need to concatenate the certificate and the private key to the .pem file. In order to achieve this, run the following commands at the command prompt:

```
C:\> more C:\practicalmongodb\mongodb-cert.key > temp
C:\> copy \b temp C:\practicalmongodb\mongodb-cert.crt > C:\practicalmongodb\
mongodb.pem
```

Now you have a .pem file. Use the following runtime options when starting the mongod:

```
C:\> C:\practicalmongodb\bin\mongod –sslMode requireSSL --sslPEMKeyFile C:\practicalmongodb\
mongodb.pem

2015-07-03T03:45:33.248-0700 I CONTROL  Hotfix KB2731284 or later update is installed, no
need to zero-out data files
2015-07-03T02:54:30.630-0700 I JOURNAL  [initandlisten] journal dir=C:\data\db\journal
2015-07-03T02:54:30.670-0700 I CONTROL  [initandlisten] MongoDB starting : pid=2
816 port=27017 dbpath=C:\data\db\ 64-bit host=ANOC9
2015-07-03T02:54:30.670-0700 I CONTROL  [initandlisten] targetMinOS: Windows 7/Windows
Server 2008 R2
2015-07-03T02:54:30.670-0700 I CONTROL  [initandlisten] db version v3.0.4
2015-07-03T02:54:30.670-0700 I CONTROL  [initandlisten] OpenSSL version: OpenSSL1.0.1j-fips
19 Mar 2015
2015-07-03T02:54:30.670-0700 I CONTROL  [initandlisten] build info: windows sys.
getwindowsversion(major=6, minor=1, build=7601, platform=2, service_pack='Service Pack 1')
BOOST_LIB_VERSION=1_49
2015-07-03T02:54:30.671-0700 I CONTROL  [initandlisten] allocator: system
2015-07-03T02:54:30.671-0700 I CONTROL  [initandlisten] options: { net: { ssl: {
 PEMKeyFile: "c:\practicalmongodb\mongodb.pem", mode: "requireSSL" } } }
2015-07-03T02:54:30.680-0700 I NETWORK  [initandlisten] waiting for connections
on port 27017 ssl
2015-07-03T03:33:43.708-0700 I NETWORK  [initandlisten] connection accepted from
 127.0.0.1:49194 #2 (1 connection now open)
```

■ **Note**   Using a self-signed certificate is not recommended in a production environment unless it's a trusted network because it will leave you vulnerable to man-in-the-middle attacks.

You will next connect to the above mongod using the mongo shell. When you run mongo with a -ssl option, you need to either specify -sslAllowInvalidCertificates or -sslCAFile. Let's use -sslAllowInvalidCertificates.

Open a terminal window and enter the following:

```
C:\>C:\practicalmongodb\bin>mongo --ssl --sslAllowInvalidCertificates
2015-07-03T02:30:10.774-0700 I CONTROL  Hotfix KB2731284 or later update is installed, no
need to zero-out data files
MongoDB shell version: 3.0.4
connecting to: test
```

Provisioning Using MongoDB Cloud Manager

In the starting of the chapter, you learned how to install and configure MongoDB using Windows and Linux. In this part of the chapter, you will look at how to use MongoDB Cloud Manager.

Mongo DBCloud Manager is a monitoring solution built in by the developer of the database. Prior to version 2.6, MongoDB Cloud Manager (formerly known as MongoDB Monitoring Service or MMS) was used for monitoring and administering MongoDB only. Starting from version 2.6, major enhancements have been introduced to MongoDB Cloud Manager including backup, point-in-time recovery, and an automation feature, making the task of operating MongoDB simpler than before. The automation feature provides power capabilities to administrators to quickly create, upgrade, scale, or shut down MongoDB instances in few clicks.

In this part of the book, you will see how to get started with MongoDB Cloud Manager. You will deploy a standalone MongoDB instance on AWS using MongoDB Cloud Manager.

When you start with MongoDB Cloud Manager, it asks to install an automation agent on each server, which is then used by the MongoDB Cloud Manager for communicating with the server.

In order to start provisioning, you first need to create your profile on MongoDB Cloud Manager.

Enter the following URL: https://cloud.mongodb.com. Click the Login or Sign up for Free button, based on whether you have an account or not.

Since you are starting for the first time, clicked the Sign up for Free button. This sends you to the page depicted in Figure 5-1.

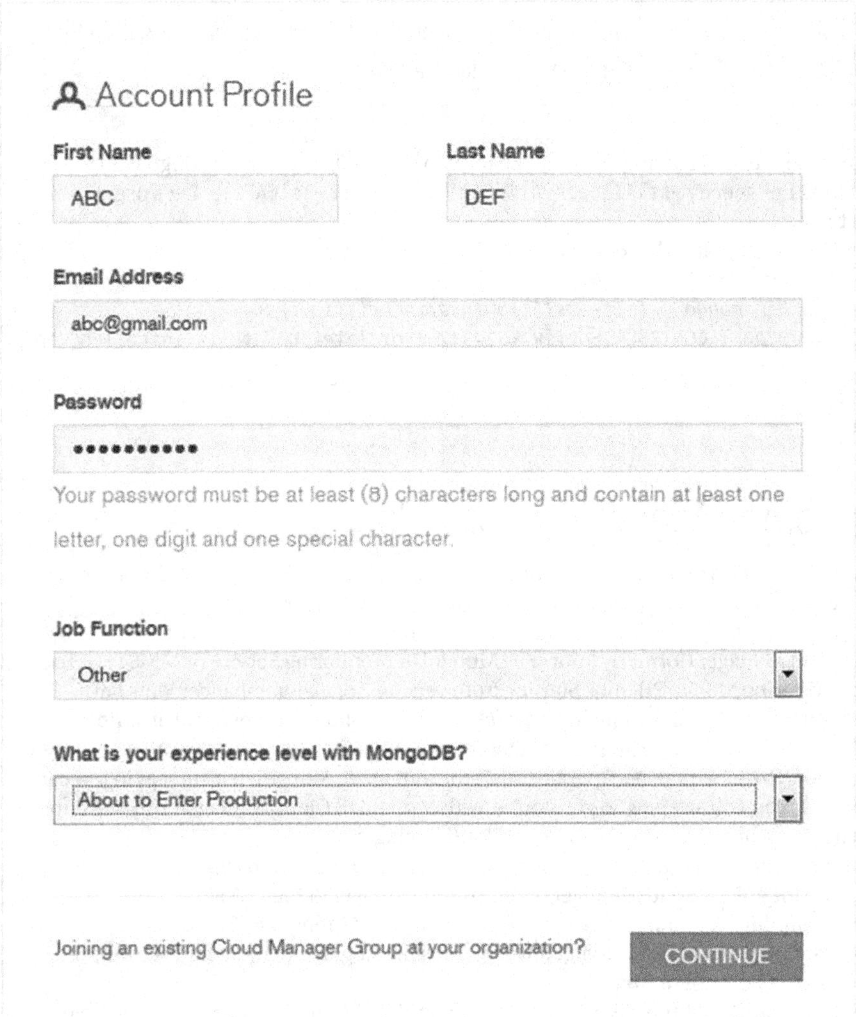

Figure 5-1. *Account Profile*

You will be creating a new profile. However, MongoDB provides an option for joining as existing Cloud Manager group.

Enter all the relevant details, as shown in Figure 5-1, and click Continue. This sends you to the page for providing company information. Once you complete the profile and company information, accept the terms and click the Create Account button. This completes the profile creation. The next step is to create a group (Figure 5-2).

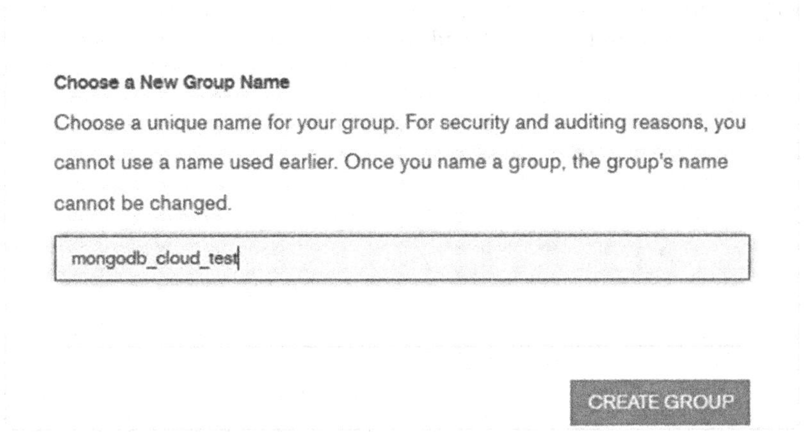

Choose a New Group Name

Choose a unique name for your group. For security and auditing reasons, you
cannot use a name used earlier. Once you name a group, the group's name
cannot be changed.

mongodb_cloud_test

CREATE GROUP

Figure 5-2. *Create Group*

Provide a unique name for the group, and click Create Group. Next is the deployment selection
page shown in Figure 5-3, where you have the option to build a new deployment or manage an existing
deployment.

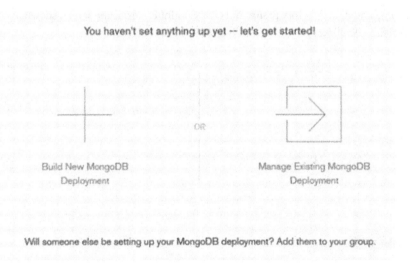

You haven't set anything up yet -- let's get started!

OR

Build New MongoDB
Deployment

Manage Existing MongoDB
Deployment

Will someone else be setting up your MongoDB deployment? Add them to your group.

Figure 5-3. *Deployment*

Select to build a new deployment. Next, you'll be prompted for the location of where to build the
deployment (i.e. Local, AWS, or other remote environment). In this example, select AWS. Clicking the Deploy
in AWS option leads you to choose between provision on your own and using Cloud Manager to provision.

Select the "I will Provision" option, which means you will be using a machine that is already provisioned
to you on AWS.

The next screen provides options for the deployment type (i.e. standalone, replica set, or sharded cluster). You are doing a standalone deployment, so click the Create Standalone box. This sends you to the screen shown in Figure 5-4.

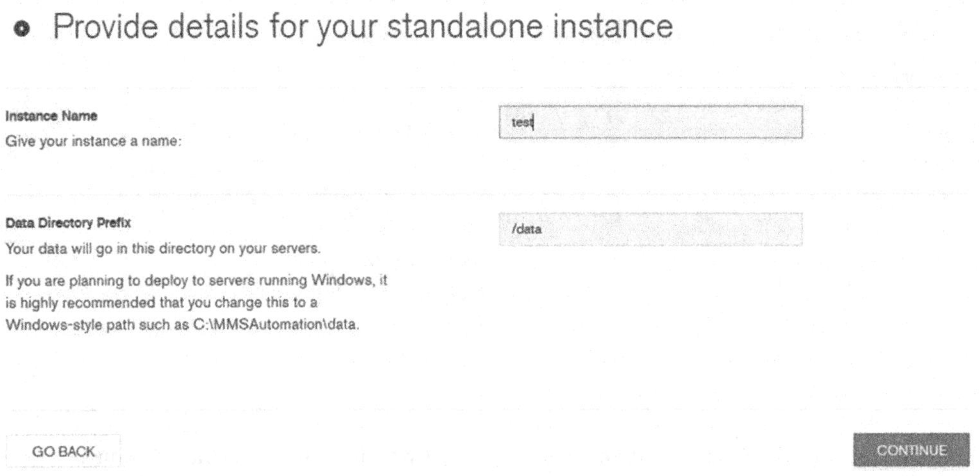

● Provide details for your standalone instance

Instance Name
Give your instance a name:

test

Data Directory Prefix
Your data will go in this directory on your servers.

/data

If you are planning to deploy to servers running Windows, it
is highly recommended that you change this to a
Windows-style path such as C:\MMSAutomation\data.

GO BACK   CONTINUE

Figure 5-4. Details for a standalone instance

Provide the instance name and data directory prefix, and click Continue. Next is the screen shown in Figure 5-5, which prompts you to install an automation agent on each server

Install an Automation Agent on each server.

Before we can create your MongoDB deployment, you'll need to download and follow the instructions for installing an Automation Agent on each server.

Please ensure that ports 27000 through 27020 are not currently in use by other processes on these servers, and that your firewall allows traffic on these ports between the servers.

I have 1   ▲▼ servers:

One Server

⌂ INSTALL AGENT   ▾

Select your server's OS:
♨ RHEL/CentOS 7.X - RPM
♨ RHEL/CentOS (5.X, 6.X)/SUSE/Amazon Linux - RPM
♨ Ubuntu (12.04+) - DEB
♨ RHEL/CentOS 7.X - TAR
♨ Other Linux - TAR
🍎 Mac OS X - TAR
⊞ Windows - MSI

CONTINUE

⚠ Install 1 more agent(s)

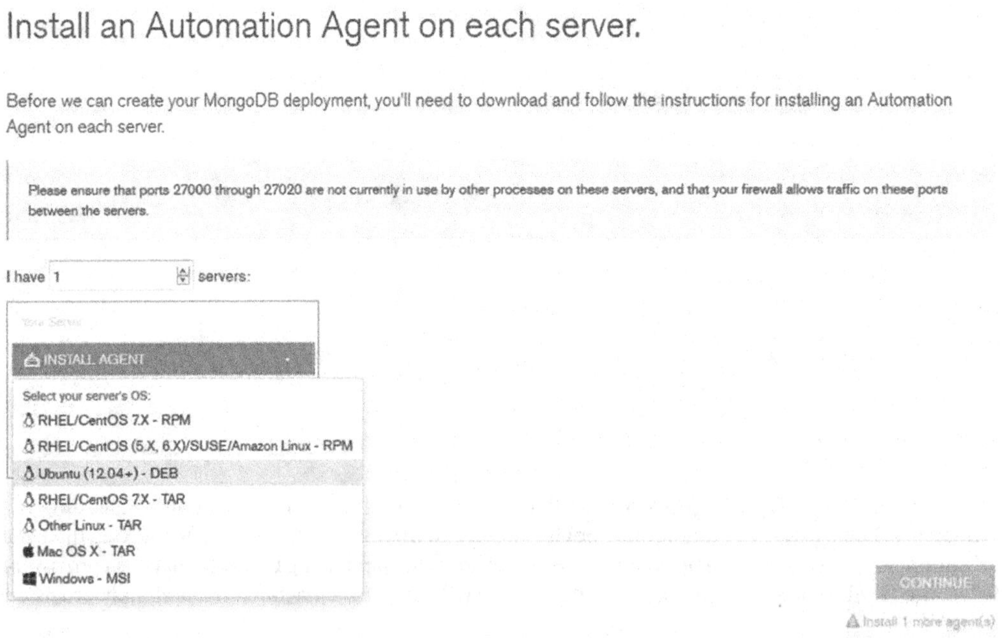

Figure 5-5. Installing an automation agent

This screen has an option for specifying the number of servers. In this example, you specify 1. Next, you need to specify the platform. Choose Ubuntu. Then the screen in Figure 5-6 appears.

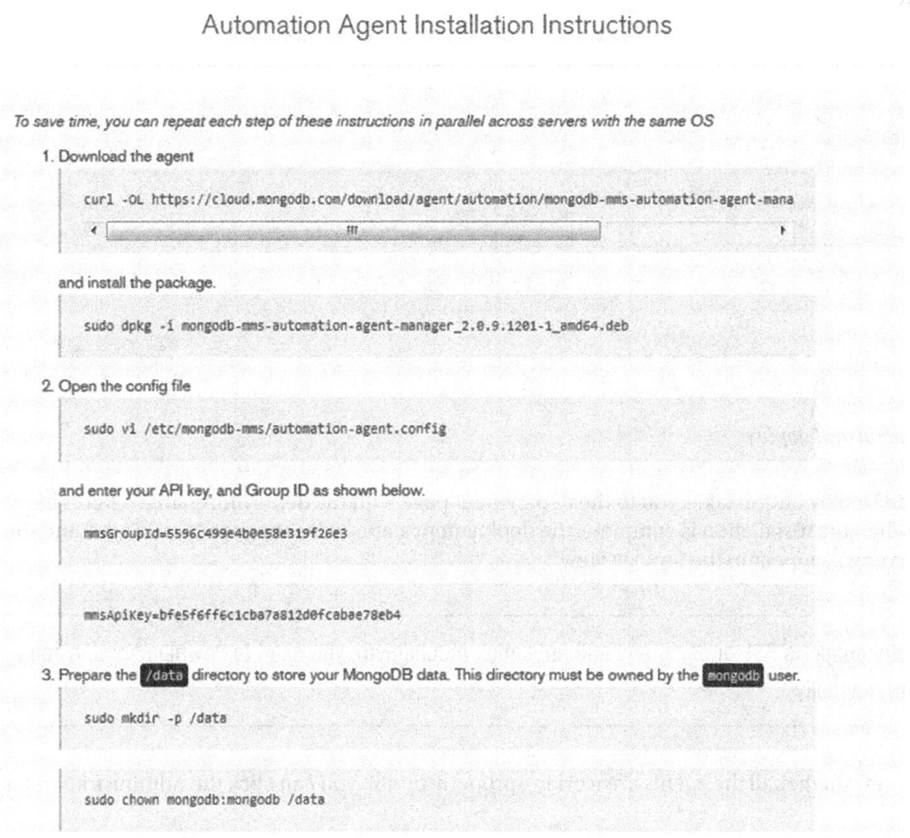

Automation Agent Installation Instructions

To save time, you can repeat each step of these instructions in parallel across servers with the same OS

1. Download the agent

```
curl -OL https://cloud.mongodb.com/download/agent/automation/mongodb-mms-automation-agent-mana
```

and install the package.

```
sudo dpkg -i mongodb-mms-automation-agent-manager_2.0.9.1201-1_amd64.deb
```

2. Open the config file

```
sudo vi /etc/mongodb-mms/automation-agent.config
```

and enter your API key, and Group ID as shown below.

```
mmsGroupId=5596c499e4b0e58e319f26e3
```

```
mmsApiKey=bfe5f6ff6c1cba7a812d0fcabae78eb4
```

3. Prepare the `/data` directory to store your MongoDB data. This directory must be owned by the `mongodb` user.

```
sudo mkdir -p /data
```

```
sudo chown mongodb:mongodb /data
```

Figure 5-6. *Automation agent installation instructions*

Follow the steps.

Before you implement the step where you start the agent, you need to ensure that all the relevant ports are open (443, 4949, 27000 to 27018).

Once all the steps are completed, click the Verify Agent button. Post verification, if everything is working as needed, you'll see a Continue button.

When you click Continue, you will go to the Review and Deploy page shown in Figure 5-7 where you can see all of the processes that are going to get deployed. Here an automation agent downloads and installs the monitoring and backup agent.

Review & Deploy

You are about to deploy the following MongoDB processes on your servers. The Automation Agent will also install the other agents needed for monitoring and (optionally) backing up your deployment.

Figure 5-7. *Review and deploy*

Clicking the Deploy button takes you to the deployment page with the deploying changes status as "In progress." When the installation is complete, the deployment status will change to "Goal State" and the provisioned server will appear in the toplogy view.

If your deployment supports SSL or using any authentication mechanism, you need to download and install a monitoring agent manually.

In order to vet whether all the agents are working properly or not, you can click the Administration tab on the console.

The Cloud Manager can deploy MongoDB replica sets, sharded clusters, and standalones on any Internet-connected server. The servers need only be able to make outbound TCP connections to the Cloud Manager.

Summary

In this chapter, you learned how to install MongoDB on the Windows and Linux platforms. You also looked at some important configurations that are necessary to ensure secure and safe usage of the database. You concluded the chapter by provisioning using MongoDB Cloud Manager.

In the following chapter, you will get started with MongoDB Shell.

CHAPTER 6

■ ■ ■

Using MongoDB Shell

"mongo shell comes with the standard distribution of MongoDB. It offers a JavaScript environment with complete access to the language and the standard functions. It provides a full interface for the MongoDB database."

In this chapter, you learn the basics of the mongo shell and how to use it to manage MongoDB documents. Before you delve into creating applications that interact with the database, it is important to understand how the MongoDB shell works.

There's no better way to get a feel for a MongoDB database than to get started with the MongoDB shell. The MongoDB shell introduction has been divided into three parts in order to make it easier for the readers to grasp and practice the concepts.

The first section covers the basic features of the database, including the basic CRUD operators. The next section covers advanced querying. The last section of the chapter explains the two ways of storing and retrieving data: embedding and referencing.

Basic Querying

This section will briefly discuss the CRUD operations (Create, Read, Update, and Delete). Using basic examples and exercises, you will learn how these operations are performed in MongoDB. Also, you will understand how queries are executed in MongoDB.

In contrast to traditional SQL, which is used for querying, MongoDB uses its own JSON-like query language to retrieve information from the stored data.

After the successful installation of MongoDB, as explained in Chapter 5, you will navigate to the directory C:\practicalmongodb\bin\. This folder has all of the executables for running MongoDB.

The MongoDB shell can be started by executing the mongo executable.

The first step is always to start the database server. Open the command prompt (by running it as administrator) and issue the command CD \.

Next, run the command C:\practicalmongodb\bin\mongod.exe. (If the installation is in some other folder, the path will change accordingly. For the examples in this chapter, the installation is in the C:\practicalmongodb folder.) This will start the database server.

```
C:\>c:\practicalmongodb\bin\mongod.exe
2015-07-06T02:29:24.501-0700 I CONTROL  Hotfix KB2731284 or later update is insalled, no
need to zero-out data files
2015-07-06T02:29:24.522-0700 I JOURNAL  [initandlisten] journal dir=c:\data\db\ournal
.......................................................
2015-07-06T02:29:24.575-0700 I CONTROL  [initandlisten] MongoDB starting : pid=384
port=27017 dbpath=c:\data\db\ 64-bit host=ANC09
```

© Shakuntala Gupta Edward, Navin Sabharwal 2015
S.G. Edward and N. Sabharwal, *Practical MongoDB*, DOI 10.1007/978-1-4842-0647-8_6

```
2015-07-06T02:29:24.575-0700 I CONTROL  [initandlisten] targetMinOS: Windows 7/windows
Server 2008 R2
2015-07-06T02:29:24.575-0700 I CONTROL  [initandlisten] db version v3.0.4
2015-07-06T02:29:24.575-0700 I CONTROL  [initandlisten] OpenSSL version: OpenSSL1.0.1j-fips
19 Mar 2015
2015-07-06T02:29:24.575-0700 I CONTROL  [initandlisten] build info: windows sys
getwindowsversion(major=6, minor=1, build=7601, platform=2, service_pack='Service Pack 1')
BOOST_LIB_VERSION=1_49
2015-07-06T02:29:24.575-0700 I CONTROL  [initandlisten] allocator: system
2015-07-06T02:29:24.575-0700 I CONTROL  [initandlisten] options: {}
2015-07-06T02:29:24.584-0700 I NETWORK  [initandlisten] waiting for connections on port 27017
```

MongoDB by default listens for any incoming connections on port 27017 of the localhost interface.

Now that the database server is started, you can start issuing commands to the server using the mongo shell.

Before you look at the mongo shell, let's briefly look at how to use the import/export tool to import and export data in and out of the MongoDB database.

First, create a CSV file to hold the records of students with the following structure:

```
Name, Gender, Class, Score, Age.
```

Sample data of the CSV is shown in Figure 6-1.

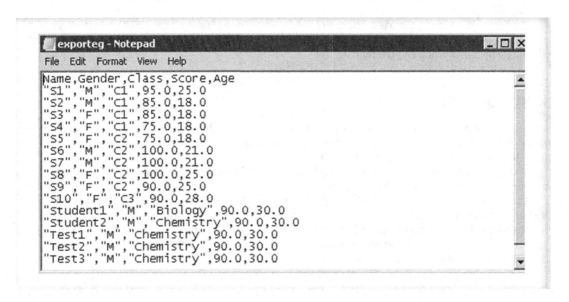

Figure 6-1. *Sample CSV file*

Next, import the data from the MongoDB database to a new collection in order to look at how the import tool works.

Open the command prompt by *running it as an administrator*. The following command is used to get help on the import command:

```
C:\>c:\practicalmongodb\bin\mongoimport.exe --help
Import CSV, TSV or JSON data into MongoDB.
When importing JSON documents, each document must be a separate line of the input file.
Example:
  mongoimport --host myhost --db my_cms --collection docs < mydocfile.json
....
C:\>
```

Issue the following command to import the data from the file exporteg.csv to a new collection called importeg in the MyDB database:

```
C:\>c:\practicalmongodb\bin\mongoimport.exe --host localhost --db mydb --collection
importeg --type csv --file c:\exporteg.csv --headerline
2015-07-06T01:53:23.537-0700     connected to: localhost
2015-07-06T01:53:23.608-0700     imported 15 documents
```

In order to validate whether the collection is created and the data is imported, you connect to the database (which is localhost in this case) using mongo shell, and you issue commands to validate whether the collection exists or not.

To start the mongo shell, run command prompt as administrator and issue the command C:\PracticalMongoDB\bin\mongo.exe (the path will vary based on the installation folder; in this example, the folder is C:\PracticalMongoDB\), and press Enter.

This by default connects to the localhost database server which is listening on port 27017.

```
C:\>c:\practicalmongodb\bin\mongo.exe
MongoDB shell version: 3.0.4
connecting to: test
> use mydb
switched to db mydb
> show collections
importeg
system.indexes
> db.importeg.find()
{ "_id" : ObjectId("5450af58c770b7161eefd31d"), "Name" : "S1", "Gender" : "M",
"Class" : "C1", "Score" : 95, "Age" : 25 }
.......

{ "_id" : ObjectId("5450af59c770b7161eefd31e"), "Name" : "S2", "Gender" : "M",
"Class" : "C1", "Score" : 85, "Age" : 18 }
>
```

In brief, what you are doing here is

1. Connecting to the mongo shell

2. Switching to your database, which is MyDB in this case

3. Checking for the collections that exist in the MyDB database using show collections.

4. Checking the count of the collection that you imported using the import tool.

5. Finally, executing the find() command to check for the data in the new collection.

To connect to different hosts and ports, -host and -port can be used along with the command.
As you can see in Figure 6-1, by default the database test is used for context.
At any point in time, executing the db command will show the current database to which the shell is connected:

```
> db
test
>
```

To display all the database names, you can run the show dbs command. Executing this command will list all of the databases for the connected server.

```
> show dbs
```

At any point, help can be accesses using the help() command.

```
> help
        db.help()                   help on db methods
        db.mycoll.help()            help on collection methods
        sh.help()                   sharding helpers
        rs.help()                   replica set helpers
        help admin                  administrative help
        help connect                connecting to a db help
        help keys                   key shortcuts
        help misc                   misc things to know
        help mr                     mapreduce
        show dbs                    show database names
        show collections           show collections in current database
        show users                  show users in current database
.............
        exit                        quit the mongo shell
```

As shown above, if you need help on any of the methods of db or collection, you can use db.help() or db.<CollectionName>.help(). For example, if you need help on the db command, execute db.help().

```
> db.help()
DB methods:
        db.addUser(userDocument)
...
        db.shutdownServer()
        db.stats()
        db.version() current version of the server
>
```

Until now you have been using the default test db. The command use <newdbname> can be used to switch to a new database.

```
> use mydb
switched to db mydb
```

Before you start your exploration, let's first briefly look at MongoDB terminology and concepts corresponding to SQL terminology and concepts. This is summarized in Table 6-1.

Table 6-1. SQL and MongoDB Terminology

SQL	MongoDB
Database	Database
Table	Collection
Row	Document
Column	Field
Index	Index
Joins within table	Embedding and referencing
Primary Key: A column or set of columns can be specified	Primary Key: Automatically set to _id field

Let's start your exploration of the options for querying in MongoDB. Switch to the MYDBPOC database.

```
> use mydbpoc
switched to db mydbpoc
>
```

This switches the context from test to MYDBPOC. The same can be confirmed using the db command.

```
> db
mydbpoc
>
```

Although the context is switched to MYDBPOC, the database name will not appear if the show dbs command is issued because MongoDB doesn't create a database until data is inserted into the database. This is in keeping with MongoDB's dynamic approach to data facilitating, dynamic namespace allocation, and a simplified and accelerated development process. If you issue the show dbs command at this point, it will not list the MYDBPOC database in the list of databases because the database is not created until data is inserted into the database.

The following example assumes a polymorphic collection named users which contains documents of the following two prototypes:

```
{
_id: ObjectID(),
FName: "First Name",
LName: "Last Name",
Age: 30, Gender: "M",
Country: "Country"
}
and
```

```
{
_id: ObjectID(),
Name: "Full Name",
Age: 30,
Gender: "M",
Country: "Country"
}
and
{
_id: ObjectID(), Name: "Full Name", Age: 30 }
```

Create and Insert

You will now look at how databases and collections are created. As explained earlier, the documents in MongoDB are in the JSON format.

First, by issuing the db command you will confirm that the context is the mydbpoc database.

```
> db
mydbpoc
>
```

Now you'll see how to create documents.

The first document complies with the first prototype whereas the second document complies with the second prototype. You have created two documents named *user1* and *user2.*

```
> user1 = {FName: "Test", LName: "User", Age:30, Gender: "M", Country: "US"}
{
        "FName" : "Test",
        "LName" : "User",
        "Age" : 30,
        "Gender" : "M",
        "Country" : "US"
}
> user2 = {Name: "Test User", Age:45, Gender: "F", Country: "US"}
{ "Name" : "Test User", "Age" : 45, "Gender" : "F", "Country" : "US" }
>
```

You will next add both these documents (*user1* and *user2)* to the users collection in the following order of operations:

```
> db.users.insert(user1)
> db.users.insert(user2)
>
```

The above operation will not only insert the two documents to the users collection but it will also create the collection as well as the database. The same can be verified using the show collections and show dbs commands.

As mentioned, show dbs will display the list of databases.

```
> show dbs
admin     0.078GB
local     0.078GB
mydb      0.078GB
mydbproc  0.078GB
```

And show collections will display the list of collection in the current database.

```
> show collections
system.indexes
users
>
```

Along with the collection users, the system.indexes collection also gets displayed. This system.indexes collection is created by default when the database is created. It manages the information of all the indexes of all collections within the database.

Executing the command db.users.find() will display the documents in the users collection.

```
> db.users.find()
{ "_id" : ObjectId("5450c048199484c9a4d26b0a"), "FName" : "Test", "LName" : "User",
"Age" : 30, "Gender": "M", "Country" : "US" }
{ "_id" : ObjectId("5450c05d199484c9a4d26b0b"), "Name" : "Test", User", "Age" : 45,
"Gender" : "F", "Country" : "US" }

>
```

You can see that the two documents you created are displayed. In addition to the fields you added to the document, there's an additional _id field that is generated for all of the documents.

All documents must have a unique __id field. If not explicitly specified by you, the same will be auto-assigned as a unique object ID by MongoDB, as shown in the example above.

You didn't explicitly insert an _id field but when you use the find() command to display the documents you can see an _id field associated with each document.

The reason behind this is by default an index is created on the __id field, which can be validated by issuing the find command on the system.indexes collection.

```
>db.system.indexes.find()
{ "v" : 1, "key" : { "_id" : 1 }, "ns" : "mydbpoc.users", "name" : "_id_" }
>
```

New indexes can be added or removed from the collection using the ensureIndex() and dropIndex() commands. We will cover this later in this chapter. By default, an index is created on the _id field of all collections. *This default index cannot be dropped.*

Explicitly Creating Collections

In the above example, the first insert operation implicitly created the collection. However, the user can also explicitly create a collection before executing the insert statement.

```
db.createCollection("users")
```

Inserting Documents Using Loop

Documents can also be added to the collection using a *for* loop. The following code inserts users using *for*.

```
> for(var i=1; i<=20; i++) db.users.insert({"Name" : "Test User" + i, "Age": 10+i,
"Gender" : "F", "Country" : "India"})
>
```

In order to verify that the insert is successful, run the `find` command on the collection.

```
> db.users.find()
{ "_id" : ObjectId("52f48cf474f8fdcfcae84f79"), "FName" : "Test", "LName" : "User",
"Age" : 30, "Gender" : "M", "Country" : "US" }
{ "_id" : ObjectId("52f48cfb74f8fdcfcae84f7a"), "Name" : "Test User", "Age" : 45
, "Gender" : "F", "Country" : "US" }
................
{ "_id" : ObjectId("52f48eeb74f8fdcfcae84f8c"), "Name" : "Test User18", "Age" :
28, "Gender" : "F", "Country" : "India" }
Type "it" for more
>
```

Users appear in the collection. Before you go any further, let's understand the *"Type "it" for more"* statement.

The `find` command returns a cursor to the result set. Instead of displaying all documents(which can be thousands or millions of results) in one go on the screen, the cursor displays first 20 documents and waits for the request to iterate (*it*) to display the next 20 and so on until all of the result set is displayed.

The resulting cursor can also be assigned to a variable and then programmatically it can be iterated over using a *while* loop. The cursor object can also be manipulated as an array.

In your case, if you type *"it"* and press Enter, the following will appear:

```
> it
{ "_id" : ObjectId("52f48eeb74f8fdcfcae84f8d"), "Name" : "Test User19", "Age" :
29, "Gender" : "F", "Country" : "India" }
{ "_id" : ObjectId("52f48eeb74f8fdcfcae84f8e"), "Name" : "Test User20", "Age" :
30, "Gender" : "F", "Country" : "India" }
>
```

Since only two documents were remaining, it displays the remaining two documents.

Inserting by Explicitly Specifying _id

In the previous examples of insert, the _id field was not specified, so it was implicitly added. In the following example, you will see how to explicitly specify the _id field when inserting the documents within a collection.

While explicitly specifying the _id field, you have to keep in mind the uniqueness of the field; otherwise the insert will fail.

The following command explicitly specifies the _id field:

```
> db.users.insert({"_id":10, "Name": "explicit id"})
```

The insert operation creates the following document in the users collection:

```
{ "_id" : 10, "Name" : "explicit id" }
```

This can be confirmed by issuing the following command:

```
>db.users.find()
```

Update

In this section, you will explore the update() command, which is used to update the documents in a collection.

The update() method updates a single document by default. If you need to update all documents that match the selection criteria, you can do so by setting the multi option as true.

Let's begin by updating the values of existing columns. The $set operator will be used for updating the records.

The following command updates the country to UK for all female users:

```
> db.users.update({"Gender":"F"}, {$set:{"Country":"UK"}})
```

To check whether the update has happened, issue a find command to check all the female users.

```
> db.users.find({"Gender":"F"})
{ "_id" : ObjectId("52f48cfb74f8fdcfcae84f7a"), "Name" : "Test User", "Age" : 45
, "Gender" : "F", "Country" : "UK" }
{ "_id" : ObjectId("52f48eeb74f8fdcfcae84f7b"), "Name" : "Test User1", "Age" : 11,
"Gender" : "F", "Country" : "India" }
{ "_id" : ObjectId("52f48eeb74f8fdcfcae84f7c"), "Name" : "Test User2", "Age" : 12,
"Gender" : "F", "Country" : "India" }
..................
Type "it" for more
>
```

If you check the output, you will see that only the first document record is updated, which is the default behavior of update since no multi option was specified.

Now let's change the update command and include the multi option:

```
>db.users.update({"Gender":"F"},{$set:{"Country":"UK"}},{multi:true})
>
```

Issue the find command again to check whether the country has been updated for all the female employees or not. Issuing the find command will return the following output:

```
> db.users.find({"Gender":"F"})
{ "_id" : ObjectId("52f48cfb74f8fdcfcae84f7a"), "Name" : "Test User", "Age" : 45,
"Gender" : "F", "Country" : "UK" }
..............
Type "it" for more
>
```

61

As you can see, the country is updated to UK for all records that matched the criteria.

When working in a real-world application, you may come across a schema evolution where you might end up adding or removing fields from the documents. Let's see how to perform these alterations in the MongoDB database.

The update() operations can be used at the document level, which helps in updating either a single document or set of documents within a collection.

Next, let's look at how to add new fields to the documents. In order to add fields to the document, use the update() command with the $set operator and the multi option.

If you use a field name with $set, which is non-existent, then the field will be added to the documents. The following command will add the field company to all the documents:

```
> db.users.update({},{$set:{"Company":"TestComp"}},{multi:true})
>
```

Issuing find command against the user's collection, you will find the new field added to all documents.

```
> db.users.find()
{ "Age" : 30, "Company" : "TestComp", "Country" : "US", "FName" : "Test", "Gender" : "M",
"LName" : "User", "_id" : ObjectId("52f48cf474f8fdcfcae84f79") }
{ "Age" : 45, "Company" : "TestComp", "Country" : "UK", "Gender" : "F", "Name" : "Test
User", "_id" : ObjectId("52f48cfb74f8fdcfcae84f7a") }
{ "Age" : 11, "Company" : "TestComp", "Country" : "UK", "Gender" : "F", ....................
Type "it" for more
>
```

If you execute the update() command with fields existing in the document, it will update the field's value; however, if the field is not present in the document, then the field will be added to the documents.

You will next see how to use the same update() command with the $unset operator to remove fields from the documents.

The following command will remove the field Company from all the documents:

```
> db.users.update({},{$unset:{"Company":""}},{multi:true})
>
```

This can be checked by issuing the find() command against the Users collection. You can see that the Company field has been deleted from the documents.

```
> db.users.find()
{ "Age" : 30, "Country" : "US", "FName" : "Test", "Gender" : "M", "LName" : "User", "_id" :
ObjectId("52f48cf474f8fdcfcae84f79") }
.............
Type "it" for more
```

Delete

To delete documents in a collection, use the remove () method. If you specify a selection criterion, only the documents meeting the criteria will be deleted. If no criteria is specified, all of the documents will be deleted.

The following command will delete the documents where *Gender = 'M'*:

```
> db.users.remove({"Gender":"M"})
>
```

The same can be verified by issuing the find() command on Users:

```
> db.users.find({"Gender":"M"})
>
```

No documents are returned.
The following command will delete all documents:

```
> db.users.remove({})
> db.users.find()
>
```

As you can see, no documents are returned.
Finally, if you want to drop the collection, the following command will drop the collection:

```
> db.users.drop()
true
>
```

In order to validate whether the collection is dropped or not, issue the show collections command.

```
> show collections
system.indexes
>
```

As you can see, the collection name is not displayed, confirming that the collection has been removed from the database.

Having covered the basic Create, Update, and Delete operations, the next section will show you how to perform Read operations.

Read

In this part of the chapter, you will look at various examples illustrating the querying functionality available as part of MongoDB that enables you to read the stored data from the database.

In order to start with basic querying, first create the users collection and insert data following the insert command.

```
> user1 = {FName: "Test", LName: "User", Age:30, Gender: "M", Country: "US"}
{
        "FName" : "Test",
        "LName" : "User",
        "Age" : 30,
        "Gender" : "M",
        "Country" : "US"
}
```

```
> user2 = {Name: "Test User", Age:45, Gender: "F", Country: "US"}
{ "Name" : "Test User", "Age" : 45, "Gender" : "F", "Country" : "US" }
> db.users.insert(user1)
> db.users.insert(user2)
> for(var i=1; i<=20; i++) db.users.insert({"Name" : "Test User" + i, "Age": 10+i,
"Gender" : "F", "Country" : "India"})
```

Now let's start with basic querying. The find() command is used to retrieve data from the database. Firing a find() command returns all the documents within the collection.

```
> db.users.find()
{ "_id" : ObjectId("52f4a823958073ea07e15070"), "FName" : "Test", "LName" : "User",
"Age" : 30, "Gender" : "M", "Country" : "US" }
{ "_id" : ObjectId("52f4a826958073ea07e15071"), "Name" : "Test User", "Age" : 45,
"Gender" : "F", "Country" : "US" }
......
{ "_id" : ObjectId("52f4a83f958073ea07e15083"), "Name" : "Test User18", "Age" :28,
"Gender" : "F", "Country" : "India" }
Type "it" for more
>
```

Query Documents

A rich query system is provided by MongoDB. Query documents can be passed as a parameter to the find() method to filter documents within a collection.

A query document is specified within open "{" and closed "}" curly braces. A query document is matched against all of the documents in the collection before returning the result set.

Using the find() command without any query document or an empty query document such as find({}) returns all the documents within the collection.

A query document can contain selectors and projectors.

A selector is like a where condition in SQL or a filter that is used to filter out the results.

A projector is like the select condition or the selection list that is used to display the data fields.

Selector

You will now see how to use the selector. The following command will return all the female users:

```
> db.users.find({"Gender":"F"})
{ "_id" : ObjectId("52f4a826958073ea07e15071"), "Name" : "Test User", "Age" : 45,
"Gender" : "F", "Country" : "US" }
.............
{ "_id" : ObjectId("52f4a83f958073ea07e15084"), "Name" : "Test User19", "Age" :29,
"Gender" : "F", "Country" : "India" }
Type "it" for more
>
```

Let's step it up a notch. MongoDB also supports operators that merge different conditions together in order to refine your search on the basis of your requirements.

Let's refine the above query to now look for female users from India. The following command will return the same:

```
> db.users.find({"Gender":"F", $or: [{"Country":"India"}]})
{ "_id" : ObjectId("52f4a83f958073ea07e15072"), "Name" : "Test User1", "Age" : 11,
"Gender" : "F", "Country" : "India" }
...........
{ "_id" : ObjectId("52f4a83f958073ea07e15085"), "Name" : "Test User20", "Age" :30,
"Gender" : "F", "Country" : "India" }
>
```

Next, if you want to find all female users who belong to either India or US, execute the following command:

```
>db.users.find({"Gender":"F",$or:[{"Country":"India"},{"Country":"US"}]})
{ "_id" : ObjectId("52f4a826958073ea07e15071"), "Name" : "Test User", "Age" : 45,
"Gender" : "F", "Country" : "US" }
.............
{ "_id" : ObjectId("52f4a83f958073ea07e15084"), "Name" : "Test User19", "Age" :29,
"Gender" : "F", "Country" : "India" }
Type "it" for more
```

For aggregation requirements, the aggregate functions need to be used. Next, you'll learn how to use the count() function for aggregation.

In the above example, instead of displaying the documents, you want to find out a count of female users who stay in either India or the US. So execute the following command:

```
>db.users.find({"Gender":"F",$or:[{"Country":"India"}, {"Country":"US"}]}).count()
21
>
```

If you want to find a count of users irrespective of any selectors, execute the following command:

```
> db.users.find().count()
22
>
```

Projector

You have seen how to use selectors to filter out documents within the collection. In the above example, the find() command returns all fields of the documents matching the selector.

Let's add a projector to the query document where, in addition to the selector, you will also mention specific details or fields that need to be displayed.

Suppose you want to display the first name and age of all female employees. In this case, along with the selector, a projector is also used.

Execute the following command to return the desired result set:

```
> db.users.find({"Gender":"F"}, {"Name":1,"Age":1})
{ "_id" : ObjectId("52f4a826958073ea07e15071"), "Name" : "Test User", "Age" : 45 }
..........
Type "it" for more
>
```

sort()

In MongoDB, the sort order is specified as follows: 1 for ascending and -1 for descending sort.

If in the above example you want to sort the records by ascending order of *age*, you execute the following command:

```
>db.users.find({"Gender":"F"}, {"Name":1,"Age":1}).sort({"Age":1})
{ "_id" : ObjectId("52f4a83f958073ea07e15072"), "Name" : "Test User1", "Age" : 11 }
{ "_id" : ObjectId("52f4a83f958073ea07e15073"), "Name" : "Test User2", "Age" : 12 }
{ "_id" : ObjectId("52f4a83f958073ea07e15074"), "Name" : "Test User3", "Age" : 13 }
..............
{ "_id" : ObjectId("52f4a83f958073ea07e15085"), "Name" : "Test User20", "Age" :30 }
Type "it" for more
```

If you want to display the records in descending order by *name* and ascending order by *age*, you execute the following command:

```
>db.users.find({"Gender":"F"},{"Name":1,"Age":1}).sort({"Name":-1,"Age":1})
{ "_id" : ObjectId("52f4a83f958073ea07e1507a"), "Name" : "Test User9", "Age" : 19 }
............
{ "_id" : ObjectId("52f4a83f958073ea07e15072"), "Name" : "Test User1", "Age" : 11 }
Type "it" for more
```

limit()

You will now look at how you can limit the records in your result set. For example, in huge collections with thousands of documents, if you want to return only five matching documents, the `limit` command is used, which enables you to do exactly that.

Returning to your previous query of female users who live in either India or US, say you want to limit the result set and return only two users. The following command needs to be executed:

```
>db.users.find({"Gender":"F",$or:[{"Country":"India"},{"Country":"US"}]}).limit(2)
{ "_id" : ObjectId("52f4a826958073ea07e15071"), "Name" : "Test User", "Age" : 45,
"Gender" : "F", "Country" : "US" }
{ "_id" : ObjectId("52f4a83f958073ea07e15072"), "Name" : "Test User1", "Age" : 11,
"Gender" : "F", "Country" : "India" }
```

skip()

If the requirement is to skip the first two records and return the third and fourth user, the `skip` command is used. The following command needs to be executed:

```
>db.users.find({"Gender":"F",$or:[{"Country":"India"}, {"Country":"US"}]}).limit(2).skip(2)
{ "_id" : ObjectId("52f4a83f958073ea07e15073"), "Name" : "Test User2", "Age" : 12,
"Gender" : "F", "Country" : "India" }
{ "_id" : ObjectId("52f4a83f958073ea07e15074"), "Name" : "Test User3", "Age" : 13,
"Gender" : "F", "Country" : "India" }
>
```

findOne()

Similar to find() is the findOne() command. The findOne() method can take the same parameters as find(), but rather then returning a cursor, it returns a single document. Say you want to return one female user who stays in either India or US. This can be achieved using the following command:

```
> db.users.findOne({"Gender":"F"}, {"Name":1,"Age":1})
{
        "_id" : ObjectId("52f4a826958073ea07e15071"),
        "Name" : "Test User",
        "Age" : 45
}
>
```

Similarly, if you want to return the first record irrespective of any selector in that case, you can use findOne() and it will return the first document in the collection.

```
> db.users.findOne()
{
        "_id" : ObjectId("52f4a823958073ea07e15070"),
        "FName" : "Test",
        "LName" : "User",
        "Age" : 30,
        "Gender" : "M",
        "Country" : "US"}
```

Using Cursor

When the find() method is used, MongoDB returns the results of the query as a cursor object. In order to display the result, the mongo shell iterates over the returned cursor.

MongoDB enables the users to work with the Cursor object of the find method. In the next example, you will see how to store the cursor object in a variable and manipulate it using a *while* loop.

Say you want to return all the users in the US. In order to do so, you created a variable, assigned the output of find() to the variable, which is a cursor, and then using the *while* loop you iterate and print the output.

The code snippet is as follows:

```
> var c = db.users.find({"Country":"US"})
> while(c.hasNext()) printjson(c.next())
{
        "_id" : ObjectId("52f4a823958073ea07e15070"),
        "FName" : "Test",
        "LName" : "User",
        "Age" : 30,
        "Gender" : "M",
        "Country" : "US"
}
```

```
{
        "_id" : ObjectId("52f4a826958073ea07e15071"),
        "Name" : "Test User",
        "Age" : 45,
        "Gender" : "F",
        "Country" : "US"
}
>
```

The next() function returns the next document. The hasNext() function returns true if a document exists, and printjson() renders the output in JSON format.

The variable to which the cursor object is assigned can also be manipulated as an array. If, instead of looping through the variable, you want to display the document at array index 1, you can run the following command:

```
> var c = db.users.find({"Country":"US"})
> printjson(c[1])
{
        "_id" : ObjectId("52f4a826958073ea07e15071"),
        "Name" : "Test User",
....    "Gender" : "F",
      "Country" : "US"}
>
```

explain()

The explain() function can be used to see what steps the MongoDB database is running while executing a query. Starting from version 3.0, the output format of the function and the parameter that is passed to the function have changed. It takes an optional parameter called verbose, which determines what the explain output should look like. The following are the verbosity modes: allPlansExecution, executionStats, and queryPlanner. The default verbosity mode is queryPlanner, which means if nothing is specified, it defaults to queryPlanner.

The following code covers the steps executed when filtering on the username field:

```
> db.users.find({"Name":"Test User"}).explain("allPlansExecution")

"queryPlanner" : {
        "plannerVersion" : 1,
        "namespace" : "mydbproc.users",
        "indexFilterSet" : false,
        "parsedQuery" : {
                "$and" : [ ]
        },
        "winningPlan" : {
                "stage" : "COLLSCAN",
                "filter" : {
                        "$and" : [ ]
                },
                "direction" : "forward"
        },
        "rejectedPlans" : [ ]
},
```

```
"executionStats" : {
        "executionSuccess" : true,
        "nReturned" : 20,
        "executionTimeMillis" : 0,
        "totalKeysExamined" : 0,
        "totalDocsExamined" : 20,
        "executionStages" : {
                "stage" : "COLLSCAN",
                "filter" : {
                        "$and" : [ ]
                },
                "nReturned" : 20,
                "executionTimeMillisEstimate" : 0,
                "works" : 22,
                "advanced" : 20,
                "needTime" : 1,
                "needFetch" : 0,
                "saveState" : 0,
                "restoreState" : 0,
                "isEOF" : 1,
                "invalidates" : 0,
                "direction" : "forward",
                "docsExamined" : 20
        },
        "allPlansExecution" : [ ]
},
"serverInfo" : {
        "host" : " ANOC9",
        "port" : 27017,
        "version" : "3.0.4",
        "gitVersion" : "534b5a3f9d10f00cd27737fbcd951032248b5952"
},
"ok" : 1
```

As you can see, the explain() output returns information regarding queryPlanner, executionStats, and serverInfo. As highlighted above, the information the output returns depends on the verbosity mode selected.

You have seen how to perform basic querying, sorting, limiting, etc. You also saw how to manipulate the result set using a *while* loop or as an array. In the next section, you will take a look at indexes and how you can use them in your queries.

Using Indexes

Indexes are used to provide high performance read operations for queries that are used frequently. By default, whenever a collection is created and documents are added to it, an index is created on the _id field of the document.

In this section, you will look at how different types of indexes can be created. Let's begin by inserting 1 million documents using *for* loop in a new collection called testindx.

```
>for(i=0;i<1000000;i++){db.testindx.insert({"Name":"user"+i,"Age":Math.floor(Math.
random()*120)})}
```

Next, issue the find() command to fetch a *Name* with value of *user101*. Run the explain() command to check what steps MongoDB is executing in order to return the result set.

```
> db.testindx.find({"Name":"user101"}).explain("allPlansExecution")

{
        "queryPlanner" : {
                "plannerVersion" : 1,
                "namespace" : "mydbproc.testindx",
                "indexFilterSet" : false,
                "parsedQuery" : {
                        "Name" : {
                                "$eq" : "user101"
                        }
                },
                "winningPlan" : {
                        "stage" : "COLLSCAN",
                        "filter" : {
                                "Name" : {
                                        "$eq" : "user101"
                                }
                        },
                        "direction" : "forward"
                },
                "rejectedPlans" : [ ]
        },
        "executionStats" : {
                "executionSuccess" : true,
                "nReturned" : 1,
                "executionTimeMillis" : 645,
                "totalKeysExamined" : 0,
                "totalDocsExamined" : 1000000,
                "executionStages" : {
                        "stage" : "COLLSCAN",
                        "filter" : {
                                "Name" : {
                                        "$eq" : "user101"
                                }
                        },
                        "nReturned" : 1,
                        "executionTimeMillisEstimate" : 20,
                        "works" : 1000002,
                        "advanced" : 1,
                        "needTime" : 1000000,
                        "needFetch" : 0,
                        "saveState" : 7812,
                        "restoreState" : 7812,
                        "isEOF" : 1,
                        "invalidates" : 0,
```

```
                    "direction" : "forward",
                    "docsExamined" : 1000000
                },
                "allPlansExecution" : [ ]
        },
        "serverInfo" : {
                "host" : " ANOC9",
                "port" : 27017,
                "version" : "3.0.4",
                "gitVersion" : "534b5a3f9d10f00cd27737fbcd951032248b5952"
        },
        "ok" : 1
```

As you can see, the database scanned the entire table. This has a significant performance impact and it is happening because there are no indexes.

Single Key Index

Let's create an index on the Name field of the document. Use ensureIndex() to create the index.

```
> db.testindx.ensureIndex({"Name":1})
```

The index creation will take few minutes depending on the server and the collection size.

Let's run the same query that you ran earlier with explain() to check what the steps the database is executing post index creation. Check the n, nscanned, and millis fields in the output.

```
>db.testindx.find({"Name":"user101"}).explain("allPathsExecution")

{
        "queryPlanner" : {
                "plannerVersion" : 1,
                "namespace" : "mydbproc.testindx",
                "indexFilterSet" : false,
                "parsedQuery" : {
                        "Name" : {
                                "$eq" : "user101"
                        }
                },
                "winningPlan" : {
                        "stage" : "FETCH",
                        "inputStage" : {
                                "stage" : "IXSCAN",
                                "keyPattern" : {
                                        "Name" : 1
                                },
                                "indexName" : "Name_1",
                                "isMultiKey" : false,
                                "direction" : "forward",
```

```
                                  "indexBounds" : {
                                          "Name" : [
                                                  "[\"user101\", \"user101\"]"
                                          ]
                                  }
                          }
                  },
                  "rejectedPlans" : [ ]
          },
          "executionStats" : {
                  "executionSuccess" : true,
                  "nReturned" : 1,
                  "executionTimeMillis" : 0,
                  "totalKeysExamined" : 1,
                  "totalDocsExamined" : 1,
                  "executionStages" : {
                          "stage" : "FETCH",
                          "nReturned" : 1,
                          "executionTimeMillisEstimate" : 0,
                          "works" : 2,
                          "advanced" : 1,
                          "needTime" : 0,
                          "needFetch" : 0,
                          "saveState" : 0,
                          "restoreState" : 0,
                          "isEOF" : 1,
                          "invalidates" : 0,
                          "docsExamined" : 1,
                          "alreadyHasObj" : 0,
                          "inputStage" : {
                                  "stage" : "IXSCAN",
                                  "nReturned" : 1,
                                  "executionTimeMillisEstimate" : 0,
                                  "works" : 2,
                                  "advanced" : 1,
                                  "needTime" : 0,
                                  "needFetch" : 0,
                                  "saveState" : 0,
                                  "restoreState" : 0,
                                  "isEOF" : 1,
                                  "invalidates" : 0,
                                  "keyPattern" : {
                                          "Name" : 1
                                  },
                                  "indexName" : "Name_1",
                                  "isMultiKey" : false,
                                  "direction" : "forward",
                                  "indexBounds" : {
                                          "Name" : [
                                                  "[\"user101\", \"user101\"]"
                                          ]
                                  },
```

```
                          "keysExamined" : 1,
                          "dupsTested" : 0,
                          "dupsDropped" : 0,
                          "seenInvalidated" : 0,
                          "matchTested" : 0
                       }
               },
               "allPlansExecution" : [ ]
       },
       "serverInfo" : {
               "host" : "ANOC9",
               "port" : 27017,
               "version" : "3.0.4",
               "gitVersion" : "534b5a3f9d10f00cd27737fbcd951032248b5952"
       },
       "ok" : 1
}
>
```

As you can see in the results, there is no table scan. The index creation makes a significant difference in the query execution time.

Compound Index

When creating an index, you should keep in mind that the index covers most of your queries. If you sometimes query only the Name field and at times you query both the Name and the Age field, creating a compound index on the Name and Age fields will be more beneficial than an index that is created on either of the fields because the compound index will cover both queries.

The following command creates a compound index on fields Name and Age of the collection testindx.

```
> db.testindx.ensureIndex({"Name":1, "Age": 1})
```

Compound indexes help MongoDB execute queries with multiple clauses more efficiently. When creating a compound index, it is also very important to keep in mind that the fields that will be used for exact matches (e.g. Name: "S1") come first, followed by fields that are used in ranges (e.g. Age: {"$gt":20}).

Hence the above index will be beneficial for the following query:

```
>db.testindx.find({"Name": "user5","Age":{"$gt":25}}).explain("allPlansExecution")

{
        "queryPlanner" : {
                "plannerVersion" : 1,
                "namespace" : "mydbproc.testindx",
                "indexFilterSet" : false,
                "parsedQuery" : {
                        "$and" : [
                                {
                                        "Name" : {
                                                "$eq" : "user5"
                                        }
                                },
```

```
                         {
                                 "Age" : {
                                         "$gt" : 25
                                 }
                         }
                 ]
        },
        "winningPlan" : {
                "stage" : "KEEP_MUTATIONS",
                "inputStage" : {
                        "stage" : "FETCH",
                        "filter" : {
                                "Age" : {
                                        "$gt" : 25
                                }
                        },
                        ............................
                        "indexBounds" : {
                                "Name" : [
                                        "[\"user5\", \"user5\"
        },
        "rejectedPlans" : [
                {
                        "stage" : "FETCH",
.....................................................
                                "indexName" : "Name_1_Age_1",
                                "isMultiKey" : false,
                                "direction" : "forward",
.....................................................
    "executionStats" : {
        "executionSuccess" : true,
        "nReturned" : 1,
        "executionTimeMillis" : 0,
        "totalKeysExamined" : 1,
        "totalDocsExamined" : 1,
.....................................................
                "inputStage" : {
                        "stage" : "FETCH",
                        "filter" : {
                                "Age" : {
                                        "$gt" : 25
                                }
                        },
                        "nReturned" : 1,
                        "executionTimeMillisEstimate" : 0,
                        "works" : 2,
                        "advanced" : 1,
        "allPlansExecution" : [
                {
                        "nReturned" : 1,
                        "executionTimeMillisEstimate" : 0,
```

```
                                "totalKeysExamined" : 1,
                                "totalDocsExamined" : 1,
                                "executionStages" : {
..............................................................
        "serverInfo" : {
                "host" : " ANOC9",
                "port" : 27017,
                "version" : "3.0.4",
                "gitVersion" : "534b5a3f9d10f00cd27737fbcd951032248b5952"
        },
        "ok" : 1
}
>
```

Support for sort Operations

In MongoDB, a sort operation that uses an indexed field to sort documents provides the greatest performance.

As in other databases, indexes in MongoDB have an order due to this. If an index is used to access documents, it returns results in the same order as the index.

A compound index needs to be created when sorting on multiple fields. In a compound index, the output can be in the sorted order of either an index prefix or the full index.

The index prefix is a subset of the compound index, which contains one or more fields from the start of the index.

For example, the following are the index prefix of the compound index: { x:1, y: 1, z: 1}.

The sort operation can be on any of the combinations of index prefix like {x: 1}, {x: 1, y: 1}.

A compound index can only help with sorting if it is a prefix of the sort.

For example, a compound index on Age, Name, and Class, like

```
> db.testindx.ensureIndex({"Age": 1, "Name": 1, "Class": 1})
```

will be useful for the following queries:

```
> db.testindx.find().sort({"Age":1})
> db.testindx.find().sort({"Age":1,"Name":1})
> db.testindx.find().sort({"Age":1,"Name":1, "Class":1})
```

The above index won't be of much help in the following query:

```
> db.testindx.find().sort({"Gender":1, "Age":1, "Name": 1})
```

You can diagnose how MongoDB is processing a query by using the explain() command.

Unique Index

Creating index on a field doesn't ensure uniqueness, so if an index is created on the Name field, then two or more documents can have the same names. However, if uniqueness is one of the constraints that needs to be enabled, the unique property needs to be set to *true* when creating the index.

First, let's drop the existing indexes.

```
>db.testindx.dropIndexes()
```

The following command will create a unique index on the Name field of the testindx collection:

```
> db.testindx.ensureIndex({"Name":1},{"unique":true})
```

Now if you try to insert duplicate names in the collection as shown below, MongoDB returns an error and does not allow insertion of duplicate records:

```
> db.testindx.insert({"Name":"uniquename"})
> db.testindx.insert({"Name":"uniquename"})
"E11000 duplicate key error index: mydbpoc.testindx.$Name_1 dup key: { : "uniquename" }"
```

If you check the collection, you'll see that only the first uniquename was stored.

```
> db.testindx.find({"Name":"uniquename"})
{ "_id" : ObjectId("52f4b3c3958073ea07f092ca"), "Name" : "uniquename" }
>
```

Uniqueness can be enabled for compound indexes also, which means that although individual fields can have duplicate values, the combination will always be unique.

For example, if you have a unique index on {"name":1, "age":1},

```
> db.testindx.ensureIndex({"Name":1, "Age":1},{"unique":true})
>
```

then the following inserts will be permissible:

```
> db.testindx.insert({"Name":"usercit"})
> db.testindx.insert({"Name":"usercit", "Age":30})
```

However, if you execute

```
> db.testindx.insert({"Name":"usercit", "Age":30})
```

it'll throw an error like

```
E11000 duplicate key error index: mydbpoc.testindx.$Name_1_Age_1
dup key: { : "usercit", : 30.0 }
```

You may create the collection and insert the documents first and then create an index on the collection. If you create a unique index on the collection that might have duplicate values in the fields on which the index is being created, the index creation will fail.

To cater to this scenario, MongoDB provides a dropDups option. The dropDups option saves the first document found and remove any subsequent documents with duplicate values.

The following command will create a unique index on the name field and will delete any duplicate documents:

```
>db.testindx.ensureIndex({"Name":1},{"unique":true, "dropDups":true})
>
```

system.indexes

Whenever you create a database, by default a `system.indexes` collection is created. All of the information about a database's indexes is stored in the `system.indexes` collection. This is a reserved collection, so you cannot modify its documents or remove documents from it. You can manipulate it only through `ensureIndex` and the `dropIndexes` database commands.

Whenever an index is created, its meta information can be seen in `system.indexes`. The following command can be used to fetch all the index information about the mentioned collection:

```
db.collectionName.getIndexes()
```

For example, the following command will return all indexes created on the `testindx` collection:

```
> db.testindx.getIndexes()
```

dropIndex

The `dropIndex` command is used to remove the index.

The following command will remove the `Name` field index from the `testindx` collection:

```
> db.testindx.dropIndex({"Name":1})
{ "nIndexesWas" : 3, "ok" : 1 }
>
```

reIndex

When you have performed a number of insertions and deletions on the collection, you may have to rebuild the indexes so that the index can be used optimally. The `reIndex` command is used to rebuild the indexes.

The following command rebuilds all the indexes of a collection. It will first drop the indexes, including the default index on the `_id` field, and then it will rebuild the indexes.

```
db.collectionname.reIndex()
```

The following command rebuilds the indexes of the `testindx` collection:

```
> db.testindx.reIndex()
{
        "nIndexesWas" : 2,
        "msg" : "indexes dropped for collection",
        "nIndexes" : 2,
        ..............
        "ok" : 1
}
>
```

We will be discussing in detail the different types of indexes available in MongoDB in the next chapter.

How Indexing Works

MongoDB stores indexes in a *BTree* structure, so range queries are automatically supported.

If multiple selection criteria are used in a query, MongoDB tries to find the best single index to select a candidate set. After that, it sequentially iterates through the set to evaluate the other criteria.

When the query is executed for the first time, MongoDB creates multiple execution plans for each index that is available for the query. It lets the plans execute within certain number of ticks in turns, until the plan that executes the fastest finishes. The result is then returned to the system, which remembers the index that was used by the fastest execution plan.

For subsequent queries, the remembered index will be used until some certain number of updates has happened within the collection. After the updating limit is crossed, the system will again follow the process to find out the best index that is applicable at that time.

The reevaluation of the query plans will happen when either of the following events has occurred:

- The collection receives 1,000 write operations.

- An index is added or dropped.

- A restart of the mongod process happens.

- A reindexing for rebuilding the index happens.

If you want to override MongoDB's default index selection, the same can be done using the `hint()` method.

The index filter is introduced in version 2.6. It is made of indexes that an optimizer will evaluate for a query, including the query, projections, and the sorting. MongoDB will use the index as provided by the index filter and will ignore the `hint()`.

Before version 2.6, at any point in time MongoDB uses only one index, so you need to ensure that composite indexes exist to match your queries better. This can be done by checking the sort and search criteria of the queries.

Index intersection is introduced in version 2.6. It enables intersection of indexes for fulfilling queries with compound conditions where part of condition is fulfilled by one index and the other part is fulfilled by the other index.

In general, an index intersection is made up of two indexes; however, multiple index intersections can be used for resolving a query. This capability provides better optimization.

As in other databases, index maintenance has a cost attached. Every operation that changes the collection (such as creation, updating, or deletion) has an overhead because the indexes also need to be updated. To maintain an optimal balance, you need to periodically check the effectiveness of having an index that can be measured by the ratio of reads and writes you are doing on the system. Identify the less-used indexes and delete them.

Stepping Beyond the Basics

This section will cover advanced querying using conditional operators and regular expressions in the selector part. Each of these operators and regular expressions provides you with more control over the queries you write and consequently over the information you can fetch from the MongoDB database.

Using Conditional Operators

Conditional operators enable you to have more control over the data you are trying to extract from the database. In this section, you will be focusing on the following operators: $lt, $lte, $gt, $gte, $in, $nin, and $not.

The following example assumes a collection named Students that contains the following types of documents:

```
{
_id: ObjectID(),
Name: "Full Name",
Age: 30,
Gender: "M",
Class: "C1",
Score: 95
}
```

You will first create the collection and insert few sample documents.

```
>db.students.insert({Name:"S1",Age:25,Gender:"M",Class:"C1",Score:95})
>db.students.insert({Name:"S2",Age:18,Gender:"M",Class:"C1",Score:85})
>db.students.insert({Name:"S3",Age:18,Gender:"F",Class:"C1",Score:85})
>db.students.insert({Name:"S4",Age:18,Gender:"F",Class:"C1",Score:75})
>db.students.insert({Name:"S5",Age:18,Gender:"F",Class:"C2",Score:75})
>db.students.insert({Name:"S6",Age:21,Gender:"M",Class:"C2",Score:100})
>db.students.insert({Name:"S7",Age:21,Gender:"M",Class:"C2",Score:100})
>db.students.insert({Name:"S8",Age:25,Gender:"F",Class:"C2",Score:100})
>db.students.insert({Name:"S9",Age:25,Gender:"F",Class:"C2",Score:90})
>db.students.insert({Name:"S10",Age:28,Gender:"F",Class:"C3",Score:90})
> db.students.find()
{ "_id" : ObjectId("52f874faa13cd6a65998734d"), "Name" : "S1", "Age" : 25, "Gender" : "M",
"Class" : "C1", "Score" : 95 }
......................
{ "_id" : ObjectId("52f8758da13cd6a659987356"), "Name" : "S10", "Age" : 28, "Gender" : "F",
"Class" : "C3", "Score" : 90 }
>
```

$lt and $lte

Let's start with the $lt and $lte operators. They stand for *"less than"* and *"less than or equal to,"* respectively.

If you want to find *all students who are younger than 25* (Age < 25), you can execute the following find with a selector:

```
> db.students.find({"Age":{"$lt":25}})
{ "_id" : ObjectId("52f8750ca13cd6a65998734e"), "Name" : "S2", "Age" : 18, "Gender" : "M",
"Class" : "C1", "Score" : 85 }
...........................
{ "_id" : ObjectId("52f87556a13cd6a659987353"), "Name" : "S7", "Age" : 21, "Gender" : "M",
"Class" : "C2", "Score" : 100 }
>
```

If you want to find out *all students who are older than 25* (Age <= 25), execute the following:

```
> db.students.find({"Age":{"$lte":25}})
{ "_id" : ObjectId("52f874faa13cd6a65998734d"), "Name" : "S1", "Age" : 25, "Gender" : "M",
"Class" : "C1", "Score" : 95 }
.....................
{ "_id" : ObjectId("52f87578a13cd6a659987355"), "Name" : "S9", "Age" : 25, "Gender" : "F",
"Class" : "C2", "Score" : 90 }
>
```

$gt and $gte

The $gt and $gte operators stand for *"greater than"* and *"greater than or equal to,"* respectively.

Let's find out *all of the students with Age > 25*. This can be achieved by executing the following command:

```
> db.students.find({"Age":{"$gt":25}})
{ "_id" : ObjectId("52f8758da13cd6a659987356"), "Name" : "S10", "Age" : 28, "Gender" : "F",
"Class" : "C3", "Score" : 90 }
>
```

If you change the above example to return *students with Age >= 25,* then the command is

```
> db.students.find({"Age":{"$gte":25}})
{ "_id" : ObjectId("52f874faa13cd6a65998734d"), "Name" : "S1", "Age" : 25, "Gender" : "M",
"Class" : "C1", "Score" : 95 }
...................................
{ "_id" : ObjectId("52f8758da13cd6a659987356"), "Name" : "S10", "Age" : 28, "Gender" : "F",
"Class" : "C3", "Score" : 90 }
>
```

$in and $nin

Let's find *all students who belong to either class C1 or C2*. The command for the same is

```
> db.students.find({"Class":{"$in":["C1","C2"]}})
{ "_id" : ObjectId("52f874faa13cd6a65998734d"), "Name" : "S1", "Age" : 25, "Gender" : "M",
"Class" : "C1", "Score" : 95 }
..............................
{ "_id" : ObjectId("52f87578a13cd6a659987355"), "Name" : "S9", "Age" : 25, "Gender" : "F",
"Class" : "C2", "Score" : 90 }
>
```

The inverse of this can be returned by using $nin.

Let's next find *students who don't belong to class C1 or C2*. The command is

```
> db.students.find({"Class":{"$nin":["C1","C2"]}})
{ "_id" : ObjectId("52f8758da13cd6a659987356"), "Name" : "S10", "Age" : 28, "Gender" : "F",
"Class" : "C3", "Score" : 90 }
>
```

Let's next see how you can combine all of the above operators and write a query. Say you want to *find out all students whose gender is either "M" or they belong to class "C1" or 'C2" and whose age is greater than or equal to 25*. This can be achieved by executing the following command:

```
>db.students.find({$or:[{"Gender":"M","Class":{"$in":["C1","C2"]}}], "Age":{"$gte":25}})
{ "_id" : ObjectId("52f874faa13cd6a65998734d"), "Name" : "S1", "Age" : 25, "Gender" : "M",
"Class" : "C1", "Score" : 95 }
>
```

Regular Expressions

In this section, you will look at how to use regular expressions. Regular expressions are useful in scenarios where you want to *find students with name starting with "A"*.

In order to understand this, let's add three or four more students with different names.

```
> db.students.insert({Name:"Student1", Age:30, Gender:"M", Class: "Biology", Score:90})
> db.students.insert({Name:"Student2", Age:30, Gender:"M", Class: "Chemistry", Score:90})
> db.students.insert({Name:"Test1", Age:30, Gender:"M", Class: "Chemistry", Score:90})
> db.students.insert({Name:"Test2", Age:30, Gender:"M", Class: "Chemistry", Score:90})
> db.students.insert({Name:"Test3", Age:30, Gender:"M", Class: "Chemistry", Score:90})
>
```

Say you want to *find all students with names starting with "St" or "Te" and whose class begins with "Che"*. The same can be filtered using regular expressions, like so:

```
> db.students.find({"Name":/(St|Te)*/i, "Class":/(Che)/i})
{ "_id" : ObjectId("52f89ecae451bb7a56e59086"), "Name" : "Student2", "Age" : 30,
"Gender" : "M", "Class" : "Chemistry", "Score" : 90 }
........................
{ "_id" : ObjectId("52f89f06e451bb7a56e59089"), "Name" : "Test3", "Age" : 30,
"Gender" : "M", "Class" : "Chemistry", "Score" : 90 }
>
```

In order to understand how the regular expression works, let's take the query "Name":/(St|Te)*/i.

//**i** indicates that the regex is case insensitive.

(St|Te)* means the Name string must start with either "St" or "Te".

The * at the end means it will match anything after that.

When you put everything together, you are doing a case insensitive match of names that have either "St" or "Te" at the beginning of them. In the regex for the *Class* also the same Regex is issued.

Next, let's complicate the query a bit. Let's combine it with the operators covered above.

Fetch Students with names as student1, student2 and who are male students with age >=25. The command for this is as follows:

```
>db.students.find({"Name":/(student*)/i,"Age":{"$gte":25},"Gender":"M"})
{ "_id" : ObjectId("52f89eb1e451bb7a56e59085"), "Name" : "Student1", "Age" : 30,
 "Gender" : "M", "Class" : "Biology", "Score" : 90 }
{ "_id" : ObjectId("52f89ecae451bb7a56e59086"), "Name" : "Student2", "Age" : 30,
 "Gender" : "M", "Class" : "Chemistry", "Score" : 90 }
```

MapReduce

The MapReduce framework enables division of the task, which in this case is data aggregation across a cluster of computers in order to reduce the time it takes to aggregate the data set. It consists of two parts: Map and Reduce.

Here's a more specific description: MapReduce is a framework that is used to process problems that are highly distributable across enormous datasets and are run using multiple nodes. If all the nodes have the same hardware, these nodes are collectively referred as a cluster; otherwise, it's referred as a grid. This processing can occur on structured data (data stored in a database) and unstructured data (data stored in a file system).

- "Map": In this step, the node that is acting as the master takes the input parameter and divides the big problem into multiple small sub-problems. These sub-problems are then distributed across the worker nodes. The worker nodes might further divide the problem into sub-problems. This leads to a multi-level tree structure. The worker nodes will then work on the sub-problems within them and return the answer back to the master node.

- "Reduce": In this step, all the sub-problems' answers are available with the master node, which then combines all the answers and produce the final output, which is the answer to the big problem you were trying to solve.

In order to understand how it works, let's consider a small example where you will *find out the number of male and female students* in your collection.

This involves the following steps: first you create the map and reduce functions and then you call the mapReduce function and pass the necessary arguments.

Let's start by defining the map function:

```
> var map = function(){emit(this.Gender,1);};
>
```

This step takes as input the document and based on the Gender field it emits documents of the type {"F", 1} or {"M", 1}.

Next, you create the reduce function:

```
> var reduce = function(key, value){return Array.sum(value);};
>
```

This will group the documents emitted by the map function on the key field, which in your example is Gender, and will return the sum of values, which in the above example is emitted as "1". The output of the reduce function defined above is a *gender-wise count*.

Finally, you put them together using the mapReduce function, like so:

```
> db.students.mapReduce(map, reduce, {out: "mapreducecount1"})
{
        "result" : "mapreducecount1",
        "timeMillis" : 29,
        "counts" : {
                "input" : 15,
                "emit" : 15,
                "reduce" : 2,
                "output" : 2
        },
        "ok" : 1,
}
>
```

This actually is applying the map, reduce function, which you defined on the students collection. The final result is stored in a new collection called mapreducecount1.

In order to vet it, run the find() command on the mapreducecount1 collection, as shown:

```
> db.mapreducecount1.find()
{ "_id" : "F", "value" : 6 }
{ "_id" : "M", "value" : 9 }
>
```

Here's one more example to explain the workings of MapReduce. Let's use MapReduce to *find out a class-wise average score*. As you saw in the above example, you need to first create the map function and then the reduce function and finally you combine them to store the output in a collection in your database. The code snippet is

```
> var map_1 = function(){emit(this.Class,this.Score);};
> var reduce_1 = function(key, value){return Array.avg(value);};
>db.students.mapReduce(map_1,reduce_1, {out:"MR_ClassAvg_1"})
{
        "result" : "MR_ClassAvg_1",
        "timeMillis" : 4,
        "counts" : {
                "input" : 15,   "emit" : 15,
                "reduce" : 3 ,   "output" : 5
        },
        "ok" : 1,
}

> db.MR_ClassAvg_1.find()
{ "_id" : "Biology", "value" : 90 }
{ "_id" : "C1", "value" : 85 }
{ "_id" : "C2", "value" : 93 }
{ "_id" : "C3", "value" : 90 }
{ "_id" : "Chemistry", "value" : 90 }
>
```

The first step is to define the map function, which loops through the collection documents and returns output as {"Class": Score}, for example {"C1":95}. The second step does a grouping on the class and computes the average of the scores for that class. The third step combines the results; it defines the collection to which the map, reduce function needs to be applied and finally it defines where to store the output, which in this case is a new collection called MR_ClassAvg_1.

In the last step, you use find in order to check the resulting output.

aggregate()

The previous section introduced the MapReduce function. In this section, you will get a glimpse of the aggregation framework of MongoDB.

The aggregation framework enables you find out the aggregate value without using the MapReduce function. Performance-wise, the aggregation framework is faster than the MapReduce function. You always need to keep in mind that MapReduce is meant for batch approach and not for real-time analysis.

You will next depict the above two discussed outputs using the aggregate function. First, the output was to *find the count of male and female students*. This can be achieved by executing the following command:

```
> db.students.aggregate({$group:{_id:"$Gender", totalStudent: {$sum: 1}}})
{ "_id" : "F", "totalStudent" : 6 }
{ "_id" : "M", "totalStudent" : 9 }
>
```

Similarly, in order to *find out the class-wise average score*, the following command can be executed:

```
> db.students.aggregate({$group:{_id:"$Class", AvgScore: {$avg: "$Score"}}})
{ "_id" : "Biology", "AvgScore" : 90 }
{ "_id" : "C3", "AvgScore" : 90 }
{ "_id" : "Chemistry", "AvgScore" : 90 }
{ "_id" : "C2", "AvgScore" : 93 }
{ "_id" : "C1", "AvgScore" : 85 }
>
```

Designing an Application's Data Model

In this section, you will look at how to design the data model for an application. The MongoDB database provides two options for designing a data model: the user can either embed related objects within one another, or it can reference each other using ID. In this section, you will explore these options.

In order to understand these options, you will design a blogging application and demonstrate the usage of the two options.

A typical blog application consists of the following scenarios:

You have people posting blogs on different subjects. In addition to the subject categorization, different tags can also be used. As an example, if the category is politics and the post talks about a politician, then that politician's name can be added as a tag to the post. This helps users find posts related to their interests quickly and also lets them link related posts together.

The people viewing the blog can comment on the blog posts.

Relational Data Modeling and Normalization

Before jumping into MongoDB's approach, let's take a little detour into how you would model this in a relational database such as SQL.

In relational databases, the data modelling typically progresses by defining the tables and gradually removing data redundancy to achieve a normal form.

What Is a Normal Form?

In relational databases, a normal form typically begins by creating tables as per the application requirement and then gradually removing redundancy to achieve the highest normal form, which is also termed the third normal form or 3NF.In order to understand this better, let's put the blogging application data in tabular form. The initial data is shown in Figure 6-2.

Author	Posts	Category	Tag	Comments	Commenter

Figure 6-2. *Blogging application initial data*

This data is actually in the first normal form. You will have lots of redundancy because you can have multiple comments against the posts and multiple tags can be associated with the post. The problem with redundancy, of course, is that it introduces the possibility of inconsistency, where various copies of the same data may have different values. To remove this redundancy, you need to further normalize the data by splitting it into multiple tables. As part of this step, you must identify a *key* column that uniquely identifies each row in the table so that you can create links between the tables. The above scenarios when modeled using the 3NF normal forms will look like the RDBMs diagram shown in Figure 6-3.

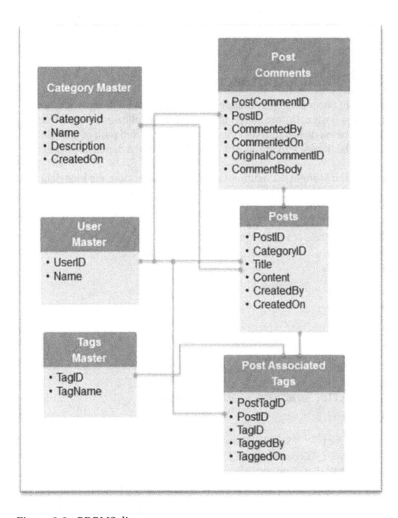

Figure 6-3. *RDBMS diagram*

85

In this case, you have a data model that is free of redundancy, allowing you to update it without having to worry about updating multiple rows. In particular, you no longer need to worry about *inconsistency* in the data model.

The Problem with Normal Forms

As mentioned, the nice thing about normalization is that it allows for easy updating without any redundancy (i.e. it helps keep the data consistent). Updating a user name means updating the name in the Users table.

However, a problem arises when you try to get the data back *out*. For instance, to find all tags and comments associated with posts by a specific user, the relational database programmer uses a JOIN. By using a JOIN, the database returns all data as per the application screen design, but the real problem is what operation the database performs to get that result set.

Generally, any RDBMS reads from a disk and does a seek, which takes well over 99% of the time spent reading a row. When it comes to disk access, random seeks are the enemy. The reason why this is so important in this context is because JOINs typically require random seeks. The JOIN operation is one of the most expensive operations within a relational database. Additionally, if you end up needing to scale your database to multiple servers, you introduce the problem of generating a *distributed join*, a complex and generally slow operation.

MongoDB Document Data Model Approach

As you know, in MongoDB, data is stored in *documents*. Fortunately for us as application designers, this opens up some new possibilities in schema design. Unfortunately for us, it also complicates our schema design process. Now when faced with a schema design problem there's no longer a fixed path of normalized database design, as there is with relational databases. In MongoDB, the schema design depends on the problem you are trying to solve.

If you have to model the above using the MongoDB document model, you might store the blog data in a document as follows:

```
{
            "_id" : ObjectId("509d27069cc1ae293b36928d"),
            "title" : "Sample title",
            "body" : "Sample text.",
            "tags" : [
                    "Tag1",
                    "Tag2",
                    "Tag3",
                    "Tag4"
            ],
            "created_date" : ISODate("2015-07-06T12:41:39.110Z"),
            "author" : "Author 1",
            "category_id" : ObjectId("509d29709cc1ae293b369295"),
            "comments" : [
                    {
                            "subject" : "Sample comment",
                            "body" : "Comment Body",
                            "author " : "author 2",
                            "created_date":ISODate("2015-07-06T13:34:23.929Z")
                    }
            ]}
```

As you can see, you have embedded the comments and tags within a single document only. Alternatively, you could "normalize" the model a bit by referencing the comments and tags by the _id field:

```
// Authors document:
{
"_id": ObjectId("509d280e9cc1ae293b36928e "),
"name": "Author 1",}
// Tags document:
{
"_id": ObjectId("509d35349cc1ae293b369299"),
"TagName": "Tag1",.....}
// Comments document:
{
"_id": ObjectId("509d359a9cc1ae293b3692a0"),
"Author": ObjectId("508d27069cc1ae293b36928d"),
.......
"created_date" : ISODate("2015-07-06T13:34:59.336Z")
}
//Category Document
{
"_id": ObjectId("509d29709cc1ae293b369295"),
"Category": "Catgeory1"......
}
//Posts Document
        {
                "_id" : ObjectId("509d27069cc1ae293b36928d"),
                "title" : "Sample title","body" : "Sample text.",
                "tags" : [       ObjectId("509d35349cc1ae293b369299"),
                        ObjectId("509d35349cc1ae293b36929c")
                ],
                "created_date" : ISODate("2015-07-06T13:41:39.110Z"),
                "author_id" : ObjectId("509d280e9cc1ae293b36928e"),
                "category_id" : ObjectId("509d29709cc1ae293b369295"),
                "comments" : [
                        ObjectId("509d359a9cc1ae293b3692a0"),
                                ]}
```

The remainder of this chapter is devoted to identifying which solution will work in your context (i.e. whether to use referencing or whether to embed).

Embedding

In this section, you will see if embedding will have a positive impact on the performance. Embedding can be useful when you want to fetch some set of data and display it on the screen, such as a page that displays comments associated with the blog; in this case the comments can be embedded in the *Blogs* document.

The benefit of this approach is that since MongoDB stores the documents contiguously on disk, all the related data can be fetched in a single seek.

Apart from this, since JOINs are not supported and you used referencing in this case, the application might do something like the following to fetch the comments data associated with the blog.

1. Fetch the associated `comments _id` from the *blogs* document.

2. Fetch the *comments* document based on the `comments_id` found in the first step.

If you take this approach, which is referencing, not only does the database have to do multiple seeks to find your data, but additional latency is introduced into the lookup since it now takes *two* round trips to the database to retrieve your data.

If the application frequently accesses the comments data along with the blogs, then almost certainly embedding the comments within the *blog* documents will have a positive impact on the performance.

Another concern that weighs in favor of embedding is the desire for *atomicity* and *isolation* in writing data. MongoDB is designed without multi-documents transactions. In MongoDB, the atomicity of the operation is provided only at a single document level so data that needs to be updated together atomically needs to be placed together in a single document.

When you update data in your database, you must ensure that your update either succeeds or fails entirely, never having a "partial success," and that no other database reader ever sees an incomplete write operation.

Referencing

You have seen that embedding is the approach that will provide the best performance in many cases; it also provides data consistency guarantees. However, in some cases, a more normalized model works better in MongoDB.

One reason for having multiple collections and adding references is the increased flexibility it gives when querying the data. Let's understand this with the blogging example mentioned above.

You saw how to use embedded schema, which will work very well when displaying all the data together on a single page (i.e. the page that displays the blog post followed by all of the associated comments).

Now suppose you have a requirement to search for the comments posted by a particular user. The query (using this embedded schema) would be as follows:

```
db.posts.find({'comments.author': 'author2'},{'comments': 1})
```

The result of this query, then, would be documents of the following form:

```
{
                "_id" : ObjectId("509d27069cc1ae293b36928d"),
                "comments" : [          {
                            "subject" : "Sample Comment 1 ",
                            "body" : "Comment1 Body.",
                            "author_id" : "author2",
                            "created_date" : ISODate("2015-07-06T13:34:23.929Z")}...]
        }
                "_id" : ObjectId("509d27069cc1ae293b36928d"),
                "comments" : [
                        {
                            "subject" : "Sample Comment 2",
                            "body" : "Comments Body.",
                            "author_id" : "author2",
                            "created_date" : ISODate("2015-07-06T13:34:23.929Z")
                        }...]}
```

The major drawback to this approach is that you get back *much* more data than you actually need. In particular, you can't ask for just author2's comments; you have to ask for posts that author2 has commented on, which includes all of the other comments on those posts as well. This data will require further filtering within the application code.

On the other hand, suppose you decide to use a normalized schema. In this case you will have three documents: "Authors," "Posts," and "Comments."

The "Authors" document will have Author-specific content such as Name, Age, Gender, etc., and the "Posts" document will have posts-specific details such as post creation time, author of the post, actual content, and the subject of the post.

The "Comments" document will have the post's comments such as CommentedOn date time, created by author, and the text of the comment. This is depicted as follows:

```
// Authors document:
{
"_id": ObjectId("508d280e9cc1ae293b36928e "),
"name": "Jenny",
..........
}
//Posts Document
        {
                "_id" : ObjectId("508d27069cc1ae293b36928d"),.....................
        }
// Comments document:
{
"_id": ObjectId("508d359a9cc1ae293b3692a0"),
"Author": ObjectId("508d27069cc1ae293b36928d"),
 "created_date" : ISODate("2015-07-06T13:34:59.336Z"),
"Post_id": ObjectId("508d27069cc1ae293b36928d"),
..........
}
```

In this scenario, the query to find the comments by "author2" can be fulfilled by a simple find() *on the comments collection*:

```
db.comments.find({"author": "author2"})
```

In general, if your application's query pattern is well known, and data tends to be accessed in only one way, an embedded approach works well. Alternatively, if your application may query data in many different ways, or you are not able to anticipate the patterns in which data may be queried, a more "normalized" approach may be better.

For instance, in the above schema, you will be able to sort the comments or return a more restricted set of comments using the *limit, skip* operators. In the embedded case, you're stuck retrieving all the comments in the same order in which they are stored in the post.

Another factor that may weigh in favor of using document references is when you have one-to-many relationships.

For instance, a popular blog with a large amount of reader engagement may have hundreds or even thousands of comments for a given post. In this case, embedding carries significant penalties with it:

- **Effect on read performance**: As the document size increases, it will occupy more memory. The problem with memory is that a MongoDB database caches frequently accessed documents in memory, and the larger the documents become, the lesser the probability of them fitting into memory. This will lead to more page faults while retrieving the documents, which will lead to random disk I/O, which will further slow down the performance.

- **Effect on update performance**: As the size increases and an update operation is performed on such documents to append data, eventually MongoDB is going to need to move the document to an area with more space available. This movement, when it happens, *significantly* slows update performance.

Apart from this, MongoDB documents have a hard size limit of 16MB. Although this is something to be aware of, you will usually run into problems due to memory pressure and document copying well before you reach the 16MB size limit.

One final factor that weighs in favor of using document references is the case of many-to-many or M:N relationships.

For instance, in the above example, there are tags. Each blog can have multiple tags and each tag can be associated to multiple blog entries.

One approach to implement the blogs-tags M:N relationship is to have the following three collections:

- The Tags collection, which will store the tags details

- The Blogs collection, which will have blogs details

- A third collection, called Tag-To-Blog Mapping, which will map between the tags and the blogs

This approach is similar to the one in relational databases, but this will negatively impact the application's performance because the queries will end up doing a lot of application-level "joins."

Alternatively, you can use the embedding model where you embed the tags within the blogs document, but this will lead to data duplication. Although this will simplify the read operation a bit, it will increase the complexity of the update operation, because while updating a tag detail, the user needs to ensure that the updated tag is updated at each and every place where it has been embedded in other blog documents.

Hence for many-to-many joins, a compromise approach is often best, embedding a list of _id values rather than the full document:

```
// Tags document:
{
"_id": ObjectId("508d35349cc1ae293b369299"),
"TagName": "Tag1",
..........
}
// Posts document with Tag IDs added as References
//Posts Document
        {               "_id" : ObjectId("508d27069cc1ae293b36928d"),
            "tags" : [
                    ObjectId("509d35349cc1ae293b369299"),
                    ObjectId("509d35349cc1ae293b36929a"),
                    ObjectId("509d35349cc1ae293b36929b"),
                    ObjectId("509d35349cc1ae293b36929c")
            ],....................................
        }
```

Although querying will be a bit complicated, you no longer need to worry about updating a tag everywhere.

In summary, schema design in MongoDB is one of the very early decisions that you need to make, and it is dependent on the application requirements and queries.

As you have seen, when you need to access the data together or you need to make atomic updates, embedding will have a positive impact. However, if you need more flexibility while querying or if you have a many-to-many relationships, using references is a good choice.

Ultimately, the decision depends on the access patterns of your application, and there are no hard-and-fast rules in MongoDB. In the next section, you will learn about various data modelling considerations.

Decisions of Data Modelling

This involves deciding how to structure the documents so that the data is modeled effectively. An important point to decide is whether you need to embed the data or use references to the data (i.e. whether to use embedding or referencing).

This point is best demonstrated with an example. Suppose you have a book review site which has authors and books as well as reviews with threaded comments.

Now the question is how to structure the collections. The decision depends on the number of comments expected on per book and how frequently the read vs. write operations will be performed.

Operational Considerations

In addition to the way the elements interact with each other (i.e. whether to store the documents in an embedded manner or use references), a number of other operational factors are important when designing a data model for the application. These factors are covered in the following sections.

Data Lifecycle Management

This feature needs to be used if your application has datasets that need to be persisted in the database only for a limited time period.

Say you need to retain the data related to the review and comments for a month. This feature can be taken into consideration.

This is implemented by using the Time to Live (TTL) feature of the collection. The TTL feature of the collection ensures that the documents are expired after a period of time.

Additionally, if the application requirement is to work with only the recently inserted documents, using capped collections will help optimize the performance.

Indexes

Indexes can be created to support commonly used queries to increase the performance. By default, an index is created by MongoDB on the _id field.

The following are a few points to consider when creating indexes:

- At least 8KB of data space is required by each index.

- For write operations, an index addition has some negative performance impact. Hence for collections with heavy writes, indexes might be expensive because for each insert, the keys must be added to all the indexes.

- Indexes are beneficial for collections with heavy read operations such as where the proportion of read-to-write operations is high. The un-indexed read operations are not affected by an index.

Sharding

One of the important factors when designing the application model is whether to partition the data or not. This is implemented using sharding in MongoDB.

Sharding is also referred as partitioning of data. In MongoDB, a collection is partitioned with its documents distributed across cluster of machines, which are referred as shards. This can have a significant impact on the performance. We will discuss sharding more in Chapter tk.

A Large Number of Collections

The design considerations for having multiple collections vs. storing data in a single collection are the following:

- There is no performance penalty in choosing multiple collections for storing data.

- Having distinct collections for different types of data can have performance improvements in high-throughput batch processing applications.

When you are designing models that have a large number of collections, you need to take into consideration the following behaviors:

- A certain minimum overhead of few kilobytes is associated with each collection.

- At least 8KB of data space is required by each index, including the _id index.

You know by now that the metadata for each database is stored in the <database>.ns file. Each collection and index has its own entry in the namespace file, so you need to consider the limits_on_the_size_ of_namespace files when deciding to implement a large number of collections.

Growth of the Document

Few updates, such as pushing an element to an array, adding new fields, etc., can lead to an increase in the document size, which can lead to the movement of the document from one slot to another in order to fit in the document. This process of document relocation is both resource and time consuming. Although MongoDB provides padding to minimize the relocation occurrences, you may need to handle the document growth manually.

Summary

In this chapter you learned the basic CRUD operations plus advanced querying capabilities. You also examined the two ways of storing and retrieving data: embedding and referencing.

In the following chapter, you will learn about the MongoDB architecture, its core components, and features.

CHAPTER 7

MongoDB Architecture

"MongoDB architecture covers the deep-dive architectural concepts of MongoDB."

In this chapter, you will learn about the MongoDB architecture, especially core processes and tools, standalone deployment, sharding concepts, replication concepts, and production deployment.

Core Processes

The core components in the MongoDB package are

- **mongod**, which is the core database process
- **mongos**, which is the controller and query router for sharded clusters
- **mongo**, which is the interactive MongoDB shell

These components are available as applications under the bin folder. Let's discuss these components in detail.

mongod

The primary daemon in a MongoDB system is known as mongod. This daemon handles all the data requests, manages the data format, and performs operations for background management.

When a mongod is run without any arguments, it connects to the default data directory, which is C:\data\db or /data/db, and default port 27017, where it listens for socket connections.

It's important to ensure that the data directory exists and you have write permissions to the directory before the mongod process is started.

If the directory doesn't exist or you don't have write permissions on the directory, the start of this process will fail. If the default port 27017 is not available, the server will fail to start.

mongod also has a HTTP server which listens on a port 1000 higher than the default port, so if you started the mongod with the default port 27017, in this case the HTTP server will be on port 28017 and will be accessible using the URL http://localhost:28017. This basic HTTP server provides administrative information about the database.

© Shakuntala Gupta Edward, Navin Sabharwal 2015
S.G. Edward and N. Sabharwal, *Practical MongoDB*, DOI 10.1007/978-1-4842-0647-8_7

mongo

mongo provides an interactive JavaScript interface for the developer to test queries and operations directly on the database and for the system administrators to manage the database. This is all done via the command line. When the mongo shell is started, it will connect to the default database called test. This database connection value is assigned to global variable db.

As a developer or administrator you need to change the database from test to your database post the first connection is made. You can do this by using <databasename>.

mongos

mongos is used in MongoDB sharding. It acts as a routing service that processes queries from the application layer and determines where in the sharded cluster the requested data is located.

We will discuss mongos in more detail in the sharding section. Right now you can think of mongos as the process that routes the queries to the correct server holding the data.

MongoDB Tools

Apart from the core services, there are various tools that are available as part of the MongoDB installation:

- **mongodump**: This utility is used as part of an effective backup strategy. It creates a binary export of the database contents.

- **mongorestore**: The binary database dump created by the mongodump utility is imported to a new or an existing database using the mongorestore utility.

- **bsondump**: This utility converts the BSON files into human-readable formats such as JSON and CSV. For example, this utility can be used to read the output file generated by mongodump.

- **mongoimport, mongoexport**: mongoimport provides a method for taking data in JSON, CSV, or TSV formats and importing it into a mongod instance. mongoexport provides a method to export data from a mongod instance into JSON, CSV, or TSV formats.

- **mongostat, mongotop, mongosniff**: These utilities provide diagnostic information related to the current operation of a mongod instance.

Standalone Deployment

Standalone deployment is used for development purpose; it doesn't ensure any redundancy of data and it doesn't ensure recovery in case of failures. So it's not recommended for use in production environment. Standalone deployment has the following components: a single mongod and a client connecting to the mongod, as shown in Figure 7-1.

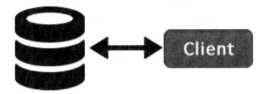

Figure 7-1. *Standalone deployment*

MongoDB uses sharding and replication to provide a highly available system by distributing and duplicating the data. In the coming sections, you will look at sharding and replication. Following that you'll look at the recommended production deployment architecture.

Replication

In a standalone deployment, if the mongod is not available, you risk losing all the data, which is not acceptable in a production environment. Replication is used to offer safety against such kind of data loss.

Replication provides for data redundancy by replicating data on different nodes, thereby providing protection of data in case of node failure. Replication provides high availability in a MongoDB deployment.

Replication also simplifies certain administrative tasks where the routine tasks such as backups can be offloaded to the replica copies, freeing the main copy to handle the important application requests.

In some scenarios, it can also help in scaling the reads by enabling the client to read from the different copies of data.

In this section, you will learn how replication works in MongoDB and its various components. There are two types of replication supported in MongoDB: traditional master/slave replication and replica set.

Master/Slave Replication

In MongoDB, the traditional master/slave replication is available but it is recommended only for more than 50 node replications. The preferred replication approach is replica sets, which we will explain later. In this type of replication, there is one master and a number of slaves that replicate the data from the master. The only advantage with this type of replication is that there's no restriction on the number of slaves within a cluster. However, thousands of slaves will overburden the master node, so in practical scenarios it's better to have less than dozen slaves. In addition, this type of replication doesn't automate failover and provides less redundancy.

In a basic master/slave setup, you have two types of mongod instances: one instance is in the master mode and the remaining are in the slave mode, as shown in Figure 7-2. Since the slaves are replicating from the master, all slaves need to be aware of the master's address.

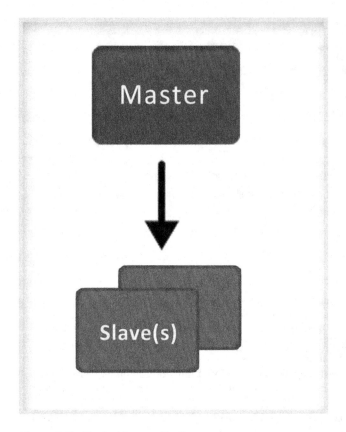

Figure 7-2. *Master/slave replication*

The master node maintains a capped collection (oplog) that stores an ordered history of logical writes to the database.

The slaves replicate the data using this oplog collection. Since the oplog is a capped collection, if the slave's state is far behind the master's state, the slave may become out of sync. In that scenario, the replication will stop and manual intervention will be needed to re-establish the replication.

There are two main reasons behind a slave becoming out of sync:

- The slave shuts down or stops and restarts later. During this time, the oplog may have deleted the log of operations required to be applied on the slave.

- The slave is slow in executing the updates that are available from the master.

Replica Set

The replica set is a sophisticated form of the traditional master-slave replication and is a recommended method in MongoDB deployments.

Replica sets are basically a type of master-slave replication but they provide automatic failover. A replica set has one master, which is termed as primary, and multiple slaves, which are termed as secondary in the replica set context; however, unlike master-slave replication, there's no one node that is fixed to be primary in the replica set.

If a master goes down in replica set, automatically one of the slave nodes is promoted to the master. The clients start connecting to the new master, and both data and application will remain available. In a replica set, this failover happens in an automated fashion. We will explain the details of how this process happens later.

The primary node is selected through an election mechanism. If the primary goes down, the selected node will be chosen as the primary node.

Figure 7-3 shows how a two-member replica set failover happens. Let's discuss the various steps that happen for a two-member replica set in failover.

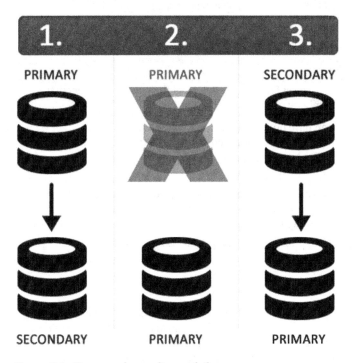

Figure 7-3. *Two-member replica set failover*

1. The primary goes down, and the secondary is promoted as primary.

2. The original primary comes up, it acts as slave, and becomes the secondary node.

The points to be noted are

- A replica set is a mongod's cluster, which replicates among one another and ensures automatic failover.

- In the replica set, one mongod will be the primary member and the others will be secondary members.

- The primary member is elected by the members of the replica set. All writes are directed to the primary member whereas the secondary members replicate from the primary asynchronously using oplog.

- The secondary's data sets reflect the primary data sets, enabling them to be promoted to primary in case of unavailability of the current primary.

Replica set replication has a limitation on the number of members. Prior to version 3.0, the limit was 12 but this has been changed to 50 in version 3.0. So now replica set replication can have maximum of 50 members only, and at any given point of time in a 50-member replica set, only 7 can participate in a vote. We will explain the voting concept in a replica set in detail.

Starting from Version 3.0, replica set members can use different storage engines. For example, the WiredTiger storage engine might be used by the secondary members whereas the MMAPv1 engine could be used by the primary. In the coming sections, you will look at the different storage engines available with MongoDB.

Primary and Secondary Members

Before you move ahead and look at how the replica set functions, let's look at the type of members that a replica set can have. There are two types of members: primary members and secondary members.

- **Primary member**: A replica set can have only one primary, which is elected by the voting nodes in the replica set. Any node with associated priority as 1 can be elected as a primary. The client redirects all the write operations to the primary member, which is then later replicated to the secondary members.

- **Secondary member:** A normal secondary member holds the copy of the data. The secondary member can vote and also can be a candidate for being promoted to primary in case of failover of the current primary.

In addition to this, a replica set can have other types of secondary members.

Types of Secondary Members

Priority 0 members are secondary members that maintain the primary's data copy but can never become a primary in case of a failover. Apart from that, they function as a normal secondary node, and they can participate in voting and can accept read requests. The Priority 0 members are created by setting the priority to 0.

Such types of members are specifically useful for the following reasons:

1. They can serve as a cold standby.

2. In replica sets with varied hardware or geographic distribution, this configuration ensures that only the qualified members get elected as primary.

3. In a replica set that spans multiple data centers across network partitioning, this configuration can help ensure that the main data center has the eligible primary. This is used to ensure that the failover is quick.

Hidden members are 0-priority members that are hidden from the client applications. Like the 0-priority members, this member also maintains a copy of the primary's data, cannot become the primary, and can participate in the voting, but unlike 0-priotiy members, it can't serve any read requests or receive any traffic beyond what replication requires. A node can be set as hidden member by setting the hidden property to true. In a replica set, these members can be dedicated for reporting needs or backups.

Delayed members are secondary members that replicate data with a delay from the primary's oplog. This helps to recover from human errors, such as accidentally dropped databases or errors that were caused by unsuccessful application upgrades.

When deciding on the delay time, consider your maintenance period and the size of the oplog. The delay time should be either equal to or greater than the maintenance window and the oplog size should be set in a manner to ensure that no operations are lost while replicating.

Note that since the delayed members will not have up-to-date data as the primary node, the priority should be set to 0 so that they cannot become primary. Also, the hidden property should be true in order to avoid any read requests.

Arbiters are secondary members that do not hold a copy of the primary's data, so they can never become the primary. They are solely used as member for participating in voting. This enables the replica set to have an uneven number of nodes without incurring any replication cost which arises with data replication.

Non-voting members hold the primary's data copy, they can accept client read operations, and they can also become the primary, but they cannot vote in an election.

The voting ability of a member can be disabled by setting its votes to 0. By default every member has one vote. Say you have a replica set with seven members. Using the following commands in mongo shell, the votes for fourth, fifth, and sixth member are set to 0:

```
cfg_1 = rs.conf()
cfg_1.members[3].votes = 0
cfg_1.members[4].votes = 0
cfg_1.members[5].votes = 0
rs.reconfig(cfg_1)
```

Although this setting allows the fourth, fifth, and sixth members to be elected as primary, when voting their votes will not be counted. They become non-voting members, which means they can stand for election but cannot vote themselves.

You will see how the members can be configured later in this chapter.

Elections

In this section, you will look at the process of election for selecting a primary member. In order to get elected, a server need to not just have the majority but needs to have majority of the total votes.

If there are X servers with each server having 1 vote, then a server can become primary only when it has at least $[(X/2) + 1]$ votes.

If a server gets the required number of votes or more, then it will become primary.

The primary that went down still remains part of the set; when it is up, it will act as a secondary server until the time it gets a majority of votes again.

The complication with this type of voting system is that you cannot have just two nodes acting as master and slave. In this scenario, you will have total of two votes, and to become a master, a node will need the majority of votes, which will be both of the votes in this case. If one of the servers goes down, the other server will end up having one vote out of two, and it will never be promoted as master, so it will remain a slave.

In case of network partitioning, the master will lose the majority of votes since it will have only its own one vote and it'll be demoted to slave and the node that is acting as slave will also remain a slave in the absence of the majority of the votes. You will end up having two slaves until both servers reach each other again.

A replica set has number of ways to avoid such situations. The simplest way is to use an arbiter to help resolve such conflicts. It's very lightweight and is just a voter, so it can run on either of the servers itself.

Let's now see how the above scenario will change with the use of an arbiter. Let's first consider the network partitioning scenario. If you have a master, a slave, and an arbiter, each has one vote, totalling three votes. If a network partition occurs with the master and arbiter in one data center and the slave in another data center, the master will remain master since it will still have the majority of votes.

If the master fails with no network partitioning, the slave can be promoted to master because it will have two votes (slave + arbiter).

This three-server setup provides a robust failover deployment.

Example - Working of Election Process in More Details

This section will explain how the election happens.

Let's assume you have a replica set with the following three members: A1, B1, and C1. Each member exchanges a heartbeat request with the other members every few seconds. The members respond with their current situation information to such requests. A1 sends out heartbeat request to B1 and C1. B1 and C1 respond with their current situation information, such as the state they are in (primary or secondary), their current clock time, their eligibility to be promoted as primary, and so on. A1 receives all this information's and updates its "map" of the set, which maintains information such as the members changed state, members that have gone down or come up, and the round trip time.

While updating the A1's map changes, it will check a few things depending on its state:

- If A1 is primary and one of the members has gone down, then it will ensure that it's still able to reach the majority of the set. If it's not able to do so, it will demote itself to secondary state.

  Demotions: There's a problem when A1 undergoes a demotion. By default in MongoDB writes are fire-and-forget (i.e. the client issues the writes but doesn't wait for a response). If an application is doing the default writes when the primary is stepping down, it will never realize that the writes are actually not happening and might end up losing data. Hence it's recommended to use safe writes. In this scenario, when the primary is stepping down, it closes all its client connections, which will result in socket errors to the clients. The client libraries then need to recheck who the new primary is and will be saved from losing their write operations data.

- If A1 is a secondary and if the map has not changed, it will occasionally check whether it should elect itself.

  The first task A1 will do is run a sanity check where it will check answers to few question such as, Does A1 think it's already primary? Does another member think its primary? Is A1 not eligible for election? If it can't answer any of the basic questions, A1 will continue idling as is; otherwise, it will proceed with the election process:

  - A1 sends a message to the other members of the set, which in this case are B1 and C1, saying "I am planning to become a primary. Please suggest"

  - When B1 and C1 receive the message, they will check the view around them. They will run through a big list of sanity checks, such as, Is there any other node that can be primary? Does A1 have the most recent data or is there any other node that has the most recent data? If all the checks seem ok, they send a "go-ahead" message; however, if any of the checks fail, a "stop election" message is sent.

  - If any of the members send a "stop election" reply, the election is cancelled and A1 remains a secondary member.

  - If the "go-ahead" is received from all, A1 goes to the election process final phase.

In the second (final) phase,

- A1 resends a message declaring its candidacy for the election to the remaining members.

- Members B1 and C1 do a final check to ensure that all the answers still hold true as before.

- If yes, A1 is allowed to take its election lock, which prevents its voting capabilities for 30 seconds and sends back a vote.

- If any of the checks fail to hold true, a veto is sent.

- If any veto is received, the election stops.

- If no one vetoes and A1 gets a majority of the votes, it becomes a primary.

The election is affected by the priority settings. A 0 priority member can never become a primary.

Data Replication Process

Let's look at how the data replication works. The members of a replica set replicate data continuously. Every member, including the primary member, maintains an oplog. An oplog is a capped collection where the members maintain a record of all the operations that are performed on the data set.

The secondary members copy the primary member's oplog and apply all the operations in an asynchronous manner.

Oplog

Oplog stands for the operation log. An oplog is a capped collection where all the operations that modify the data are recorded.

The oplog is maintained in a special database, namely `local` in the collection `oplog.$main`. Every operation is maintained as a document, where each document corresponds to one operation that is performed on the master server. The document contains various keys, including the following keys:

- `ts`: This stores the timestamp when the operations are performed. It's an internal type and is composed of a 4-byte timestamp and a 4-byte incrementing counter.

- `op`: This stores information about the type of operation performed. The value is stored as 1-byte code (e.g. it will store an "I" for an insert operation).

- `ns`: This key stores the collection namespace on which the operation was performed.

- `o`: This key specifies the operation that is performed. In case of an insert, this will store the document to insert.

Only operations that change the data are maintained in the oplog because it's a mechanism for ensuring that the secondary node data is in sync with the primary node data.

The operations that are stored in the oplog are transformed so that they remain idempotent, which means that even if it's applied multiple times on the secondary, the secondary node data will remain consistent. Since the oplog is a capped collection, with every new addition of an operation, the oldest operations are automatically moved out. This is done to ensure that it does not grow beyond a pre-set bound, which is the oplog size.

Depending on the OS, whenever the replica set member first starts up, the oplog is created of a default size by MongoDB.

By default in MongoDB, available free space or 5% is used for the oplog on Windows and 64-bit Linux instances. If the size is lower than 1GB, then 1GB of space is allocated by MongoDB.

Although the default size is sufficient in most cases, you can use the -oplogsize option to specify the oplog size in MB when starting the server.

If you have the following workload, there might be a requirement of reconsidering the oplog size:

- **Updates to multiple documents simultaneously:** Since the operations need to be translated into operations that are idempotent, this scenario might end up requiring great deal of oplog size.

- **Deletes and insertions happening at the same rate involving same amount of data:** In this scenario, although the database size will not increase, the operations translation into an idempotent operation can lead to a bigger oplog.

- **Large number of in-place updates:** Although these updates will not change the database size, the recording of updates as idempotent operations in the oplog can lead to a bigger oplog.

Initial Sync and Replication

Initial sync is done when the member is in either of the following two cases:

1. The node has started for the first time (i.e. it's a new node and has no data).

2. The node has become stale, where the primary has overwritten the oplog and the node has not replicated the data. In this case, the data will be removed.

In both cases, the initial sync involves the following steps:

1. First, all databases are cloned.

2. Using oplog of the source node, the changes are applied to its dataset.

3. Finally, the indexes are built on all the collections.

Post the initial sync, the replica set members continuously replicate the changes in order to be up-to-date.

Most of the synchronization happens from the primary, but chained replication can be enabled where the sync happens from a secondary only (i.e. the sync targets are changed based on the ping time and state of other member's replication).

Syncing – Normal Operation

In normal operations, the secondary chooses a member from where it will sync its data, and then the operations are pulled from the chosen source's oplog collection (local.oplog.rs).

Once the operation (op) is get, the secondary does the following:

1. It first applies the op to its data copy.

2. Then it writes the op to its local oplog.

3. Once the op is written to the oplog, it requests the next op.

Suppose it crashes between step 1 and step 2, and then it comes back again. In this scenario, it'll assume the operation has not been performed and will re-apply it.

Since oplog ops are idempotent, the same operation can be applied any number of times, and every time the result document will be same.

> If you have the following doc
>
> {I:11}
>
> an increment operation is performed on the same, such as
>
> {$inc:{I:1}} on the primary
>
> In this case the following will be stored in the primary oplog:
>
> {I:12}.

This will be replicated by the secondaries. So the value remains the same even if the log is applied multiple times.

Starting Up

When a node is started, it checks its local collection to find out the `lastOpTimeWritten`. This is the time of the latest op that was applied on the secondary.

The following shell helper can be used to find the latest op in the shell:

```
> rs.debug.getLastOpWritten()
```

The output returns a field named `ts`, which depicts the last op time.

If a member starts up and finds the `ts` entry, it starts by choosing a target to sync from and it will start syncing as in a normal operation. However, if no entry is found, the node will begin the initial sync process.

Whom to Sync From?

In this section, you will look at how the source is chosen to sync from. As of 2.0, based on the average ping time servers automatically sync from the "nearest" node.

When you bring up a new node, it sends heartbeats to all nodes and monitors the response time. Based on the data received, it then decides the member to sync from using the following algorithm:

```
for each healthy member Loop:
    if state is Primary
        add the member to possible sync target set
    if member's lastOpTimeWritten is greater then the local lastOpTime Written
add the member to possible sync target set
Set sync_from  = MIN (PING TIME to members of sync target set)

Note: A "healthy member" can be thought of as a "normal" primary or secondary member.
```

In version 2.0, the slave's delayed nodes were debatably included in "healthy" nodes. Starting from version 2.2, delayed nodes and hidden nodes are excluded from the "healthy" nodes.

Running the following command will show the server that is chosen as the source for syncing:

```
db.adminCommand({replSetGetStatus:1})
```

The output field of `syncingTo` is present only on secondary nodes and provides information on the node from which it is syncing.

Making Writes Work with Chaining Slaves

You have seen that the above algorithm for choosing a source to sync from implies that slave chaining is semi-automatic. When a server is started, it'll most probably choose a server within the same data center to sync from, thus reducing the WAN traffic.

However, this will never lead to a loop because the nodes will sync only from a secondary that has a latest value of lastOpTimeWritten which is greater than its own. You will never end up in a scenario where N1 is syncing from N2 *and* N2 is syncing from N1. It will always be either N1 is syncing from N2 *or* N2 is syncing from N1.

In this section, you will see how w (write operation) works with slave chaining. If N1 is syncing from N2, which is further syncing from N3, in this case how N3 will know that until which point N1 is synced to.

When N1 starts its sync from N2, a special "handshake" message is sent, which intimates to N2 that N1 will be syncing from its oplog. Since N2 is not primary, it will forward the message to the node it is syncing from (i.e. it opens a connection to N3 pretending to be N1). By the end of the above step, N2 has two connections that are opened with N3: one connection for itself and the other for N1.

Whenever an op request is made by N1 to N2, the op is sent by N2 from its oplog and a dummy request is forwarded on the link of N1 to N3, as shown in Figure 7-4.

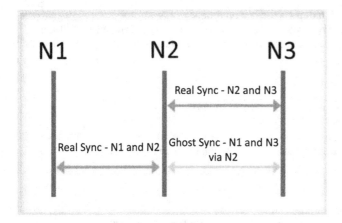

Figure 7-4. *Writes via chaining slaves*

Although this minimizes network traffic, it increases the absolute time for the write to reach to all of the members.

Failover

In this section, you will look at how primary and secondary member failovers are handled in replica sets. All members of a replica set are connected to each other. As shown in Figure 7-5, they exchange a heartbeat message amongst each other.

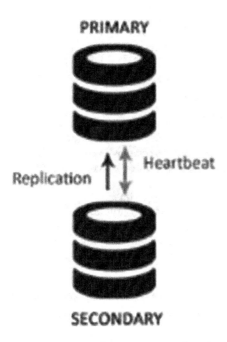

Figure 7-5. *Heartbeat message exchange*

Hence a node with missing heartbeat is considered as crashed.

If the Node Is a Secondary Node

If the node is a secondary node, it will be removed from the membership of the replica set. In the future, when it recovers, it can re-join. Once it re-joins, it needs to update the latest changes.

1. If the down period is small, it connects to the primary and catches up with the latest updates.

2. However, if the down period is lengthy, the secondary server will need to resync with primary where it deletes all its data and does an initial sync as if it's a new server.

If the Node Is the Primary Node

If the node is a primary node, in this scenario if the majority of the members of the original replica sets are able to connect to each other, a new primary will be elected by these nodes, which is in accordance with the automatic failover capability of the replica set.

The election process will be initiated by any node that cannot reach the primary.

The new primary is elected by majority of the replica set nodes. Arbiters can be used to break ties in scenarios such as when network partitioning splits the participating nodes into two halves and the majority cannot be reached.

The node with the highest priority will be the new primary. If you have more than one node with same priority, the data freshness can be used for breaking ties.

The primary node uses a heartbeat to track how many nodes are visible to it. If the number of visible nodes falls below the majority, the primary automatically falls back to the secondary state. This scenario prevents the primary from functioning when it's separated by a network partition.

Rollbacks

In scenario of a primary node change, the data on the new primary is assumed to be the latest data in the system. When the former primary joins back, any operation that is applied on it will also be rolled back. Then it will be synced with the new primary.

The rollback operation reverts all the write operations that were not replicated across the replica set. This is done in order to maintain database consistency across the replica set.

When connecting to the new primary, all nodes go through a resync process to ensure the rollback is accomplished. The nodes look through the operation that is not there on the new primary, and then they query the new primary to return an updated copy of the documents that were affected by the operations. The nodes are in the process of resyncing and are said to be recovering; until the process is complete, they will not be eligible for primary election.

This happens very rarely, and if it happens, it is often due to network partition with replication lag where the secondaries cannot keep up with the operation's throughput on the former primary.

It needs to be noted that if the write operations replicate to other members before the primary steps down, and those members are accessible to majority of the nodes of the replica set, the rollback does not occur.

The rollback data is written to a BSON file with filenames such as <database>.<collection>. <timestamp>.bson in the database's dbpath directory.

The administrator can decide to either ignore or apply the rollback data. Applying the rollback data can only begin when all the nodes are in sync with the new primary and have rolled back to a consistent state.

The content of the rollback files can be read using Bsondump, which then need to be manually applied to the new primary using mongorestore.

There is no method to handle rollback situations automatically for MongoDB. Therefore manual intervention is required to apply rollback data. While applying the rollback, it's vital to ensure that these are replicated to either all or at least some of the members in the set so that in case of any failover rollbacks can be avoided.

Consistency

You have seen that the replica set members keep on replicating data among each other by reading the oplog. How is the consistency of data maintained? In this section, you will look at how MongoDB ensures that you always access consistent data.

In MongoDB, although the reads can be routed to the secondaries, the writes are always routed to the primary, eradicating the scenario where two nodes are simultaneously trying to update the same data set. The data set on the primary node is always consistent.

If the read requests are routed to the primary node, it will always see the up-to-date changes, which means the read operations are always consistent with the last write operations.

However, if the application has changed the read preference to read from secondaries, there might be a probability of user not seeing the latest changes or seeing previous states. This is because the writes are replicated asynchronously on the secondaries.

This behavior is characterized as eventual consistency, which means that although the secondary's state is not consistent with the primary node state, it will eventually become consistent over time.

There is no way that reads from the secondary can be guaranteed to be consistent, except by issuing write concerns to ensure that writes succeed on all members before the operation is actually marked successful. We will be discussing write concerns in a while.

Possible Replication Deployment

The architecture you chose to deploy a replica set affects its capability and capacity. In this section, you will look at few strategies that you need to be aware of while deciding on the architecture. We will also be discussing the deployment architecture.

1. **Odd number of members**: This should be done in order to ensure that there is no tie when electing a primary. If the number of nodes is even, then an arbiter can be used to ensure that the total nodes participating in election is odd, as shown in Figure 7-6.

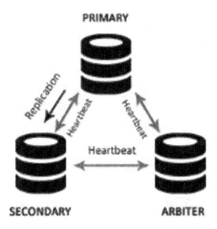

Figure 7-6. *Members replica set with primary, secondary, and arbiter*

2. **Replica set fault tolerance** is the count of members, which can go down but still the replica set has enough members to elect a primary in case of any failure. Table 7-1 indicates the relationship between the member count in the replica set and its fault tolerance. Fault tolerance should be considered when deciding on the number of members.

Table 7-1. *Replica Set Fault Tolerance*

Number of Members	Majority Required for Electing a Primary	Fault Tolerance
3	2	1
4	3	1
5	3	2
6	4	2

3. If the application has **specific dedicated requirements**, such as for reporting or backups, then delayed or hidden members can be considered as part of the replica set, as shown in Figure 7-7.

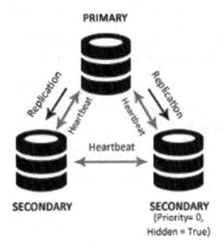

Figure 7-7. *Members replica set with primary, secondary, and hidden members*

4. If the **application is read-heavy**, the read can be distributed across secondaries. As the requirement increases, more nodes can be added to increase the data duplication; this can have a positive impact on the read throughput.

5. The **members should be distributed geographically** in order to cater to main data center failure. As shown in Figure 7-8, the members that are kept at a geographically different location other than the main data center can have priority set as 0, so that they cannot be elected as primary and can act as a standby only.

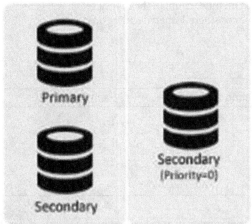

Figure 7-8. *Members replica set with primary, secondary, and a priority 0 member distributed across the data center*

6. When **replica set members are distributed** across data centers, network partitioning can prevent data centers from communicating with each other. In order to ensure a majority in the case of network partitioning, it keeps a majority of the members in one location.

Scaling Reads

Although the primary purpose of the secondaries is to ensure data availability in case of downtime of the primary node, there are other valid use cases for secondaries. They can be used dedicatedly to perform backup operations or data processing jobs or to scale out reads. One of the ways to scale reads is to issue the read queries against the secondary nodes; by doing so the workload on the master is reduced.

One important point that you need to consider when using secondaries for scaling read operations is that in MongoDB the replication is asynchronous, which means if any write or update operation is performed on the master's data, the secondary data will be momentarily out-of-date. If the application in question is read-heavy and is accessed over a network and does not need up-to-date data, the secondaries can be used to scale out the read in order to provide a good read throughput. Although by default the read requests are routed to the primary node, the requests can be distributed over secondary nodes by specifying the **read preferences**. Figure 7-9 depicts the default read preference.

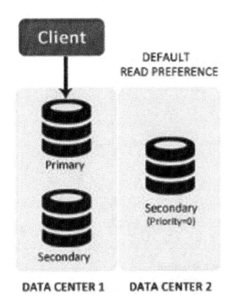

Figure 7-9. *Default read preference*

The following are ideal use cases whereby routing the reads on secondary node can help gain a significant improvement in the read throughput and can also help reduce the latency:

1. **Applications that are geographically distributed**: In such cases, you can have a replica set that is distributed across geographies. The read preferences should be set to read from the **nearest** secondary node. This helps in reducing the latency that is caused when reading over network and this improves the read performance. See Figure 7-10.

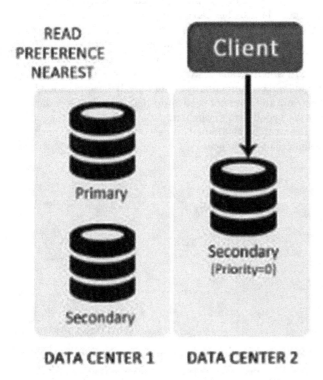

Figure 7-10. *Read Preference – Nearest*

2. If the application always requires up-to-date data, it uses the option `primaryPreferred`, which in normal circumstances will always read from the primary node, but in case of emergency will route the read to secondaries. This is useful during failovers. See Figure 7-11.

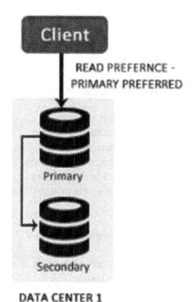

Figure 7-11. *Read Preference – primaryPreferred*

3. If you have an application that supports two types of operations, the first operation is the main workload that involves reading and doing some processing on the data, whereas the second operation generates reports using the data. In such a scenario, you can have the reporting reads directed to the secondaries.

MongoDB supports the following read preference modes:

- **primary**: This is the default mode. All the read requests are routed to the primary node.

- **primaryPreferred**: In normal circumstances the reads will be from primary but in an emergency such as a primary not available, reads will be from the secondary nodes.

- **secondary**: Reads from the secondary members.

- **secondaryPreferred**: Reads from secondary members. If secondaries are unavailable, then read from the primary.

- **nearest**: Reads from the nearest replica set member.

In addition to scaling reads, the second ideal use case for using secondaries is to offload intensive processing, aggregating, and administration tasks in order to avoid degrading the primary's performance. Blocking operations can be performed on the secondary without ever affecting the primary node's performance.

Application Write Concerns

When the client application interacts with MongoDB, it is generally not aware whether the database is on standalone deployment or is deployed as a replica set. However, when dealing with replica sets, the client should be aware of **write concern** and **read concern**.

Since a replica set duplicates the data and stores it across multiple nodes, these two concerns give a client application the flexibility to enforce data consistency across nodes while performing read or write operations.

Using a write concern enables the application to get a success or failure response from MongoDB.

When used in a replica set deployment of MongoDB, the write concern sends a confirmation from the server to the application that the write has succeeded on the primary node. However, this can be configured so that the write concern returns success only when the write is replicated to all the nodes maintaining the data.

In practical scenario, this isn't feasible because it will reduce the write performance. Ideally the client can ensure, using a write concern, that the data is replicated to one more node in addition to the primary, so that the data is not lost even if the primary steps down.

The write concern returns an object that indicates either error or no error.

The w option ensures that the write has been replicated to the specified number of members. Either a number or a majority can be specified as the value of the w option.

If a number is specified, the write replicates to that many number of nodes before returning success. If a majority is specified, the write is replicated to a majority of members before returning the result.

Figure 7-12 shows how a write happens with w: 2.

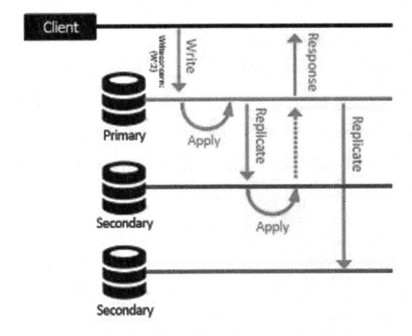

Figure 7-12. writeConcern

If while specifying number the number is greater than the nodes that actually hold the data, the command will keep on waiting until the members are available. In order to avoid this indefinite wait time, wtimeout should also be used along with w, which will ensure that it will wait for the specified time period, and if the write has not succeeded by that time, it will time out.

How Writes Happen with Write Concern

In order to ensure that the written data is present on say at least two members, issue the following command:

```
>db.testprod.insert({i:"test", q: 50, t: "B"}, {writeConcern: {w:2}})
```

In order to understand how this command will be executed, say you have two members, one named primary and the other named secondary, and it is syncing its data from the primary.

But how will the primary know the point at which the secondary is synced? Since the primary's oplog is queried by the secondary for op results to be applied, if the secondary requests an op written at say **t** time, it implies to the primary that the secondary has replicated all ops written before **t**.

The following are the steps that a write concern takes.

1. The write operation is directed to the primary.

2. The operation is written to the oplog of primary with ts depicting the time of operation.

3. A w: 2 is issued, so the write operation needs to be written to one more server before it's marked successful.

4. The secondary queries the primary's oplog for the op, and it applies the op.

5. Next, the secondary sends a request to the primary requesting for ops with ts greater than t.

6. At this point, the primary sends an update that the operation until t has been applied by the secondary as it's requesting for ops with {ts: {$gt: t}}.

7. The writeConcern finds that a write has occurred on both the primary and secondary, satisfying the w: 2 criteria, and the command returns success.

Implementing Advanced Clustering with Replica Sets

Having learned the architecture and inner workings of replica sets, you will now focus on administration and usage of replica sets. You will be focusing on the following:

1. Setting up a replica set.

2. Removing a server.

3. Adding a server.

4. Adding an arbiter.

5. Inspecting the status.

6. Forcing a new election of a primary.

7. Using the web interface to inspect the status of the replica set.

The following examples assume a replica set named testset that has the configuration shown in Table 7-2.

Table 7-2. *Replica Set Configuration*

Member	Daemon	Host:Port	Data File Path
Active_Member_1	Mongod	[hostname]:27021	C:\db1\active1\data
Active_Member_2	Mongod	[hostname]:27022	C:\db1\active2\data
Passive_Member_1	Mongod	[hostname]:27023	C:\db1\passive1\data

The hostname used in the above table can be found out using the following command:

```
C:\>hostname
ANOC9
C:\>
```

In the following examples, the [*hostname*] need to be substituted with the value that the *hostname* command returns on your system. In our case, the value returned is ANOC9, which is used in the following examples.

Use the default (MMAPv1) storage engine in the following implementation.

Setting Up a Replica Set

In order to get the replica set up and running, you need to make all the active members up and running.

The first step is to start the first active member. Open a terminal window and create the data directory:

```
C:\>mkdir C:\db1\active1\data
C:\>
```

Connect to the mongod:

```
c:\practicalmongodb\bin>mongod --dbpath C:\db1\active1\data --port 27021 --replSet
testset/ANOC9:27021 -rest

2015-07-13T23:48:40.543-0700 I CONTROL  ** WARNING: --rest is specified without --httpinterface,
2015-07-13T23:48:40.543-0700 I CONTROL  **    enabling http interface
2015-07-13T23:48:40.543-0700 I CONTROL  Hotfix KB2731284 or later update is installed, no
                                         need to zero-out data files
2015-07-13T23:48:40.563-0700 I JOURNAL  [initandlisten] journal dir=C:\db1\active1\data\journal
2015-07-13T23:48:40.564-0700 I JOURNAL  [initandlisten] recover : no journal files present,
                                                         no recovery needed
...............................         port=27021 dbpath=C:\db1\active1\data 64-bit
                                         host=ANOC9
2015-07-13T23:48:40.614-0700 I CONTROL  [initandlisten] targetMinOS: Windows 7/Windows
                                                         Server 2008 R2
2015-07-13T23:48:40.615-0700 I CONTROL  [initandlisten] db version v3.0.4
```

As you can see, the –replSet option specifies the name of the replica set the instance is joining and the name of one more member of the set, which in the above example is Active_Member_2.

Although you have only specified one member in the above example, multiple members can be provided by specifying comma-separated addresses like so:

```
mongod -dbpath C:\db1\active1\data -port 27021 -replset
testset/[hostname]:27022,[hostname]:27023 --rest
```

In the next step, you get the second active member up and running. Create the data directory for the second active member in a new terminal window.

```
C:\>mkdir C:\db1\active2\data
C:\>
```

Connect to mongod:

```
c:\ practicalmongodb \bin>mongod --dbpath C:\db1\active2\data --port 27022 -replSet
testset/ANOC9:27021 -rest
2015-07-13T00:39:11.599-0700 I CONTROL  ** WARNING: --rest is specified without --httpinterface,
2015-07-13T00:39:11.599-0700 I CONTROL  **            enabling http interface
2015-07-13T00:39:11.604-0700 I CONTROL  Hotfix KB2731284 or later update is installed, no
                                         need to zero-out data files
2015-07-13T00:39:11.615-0700 I JOURNAL  [initandlisten] journal dir=C:\db1\active2\data\journal
2015-07-13T00:39:11.615-0700 I JOURNAL  [initandlisten] recover : no journal files present,
                                                        no recovery needed
2015-07-13T00:39:11.664-0700 I JOURNAL  [durability] Durability thread started
2015-07-13T00:39:11.664-0700 I JOURNAL  [journal writer] Journal writer thread started
                                         rs.initiate() in the shell -- if that is not already done
```

Finally, you need to start the passive member. Open a separate window and create the data directory for the passive member.

```
C:\>mkdir C:\db1\passive1\data
C:\>
```

Connect to mongod:

```
c:\ practicalmongodb \bin>mongod --dbpath C:\db1\passive1\data --port 27023 --replSet
testset/ ANOC9:27021 -rest
2015-07-13T05:11:43.746-0700 I CONTROL  Hotfix KB2731284 or later update is installed, no
                                         need to zero-out data files
2015-07-13T05:11:43.757-0700 I JOURNAL  [initandlisten] journal dir=C:\db1\passive1\data\journal
2015-07-13T05:11:43.808-0700 I CONTROL  [initandlisten] MongoDB starting : pid=620 port=27019
                                         dbpath=C:\db1\passive1\data 64-bit host= ANOC9
......................................................................................
2015-07-13T05:11:43.812-0700 I CONTROL  [initandlisten] options: { net: { http:
{ RESTInterfaceEnabled: true, enabled: true }, port: 27019 }, replication: { re
lSet: "testset/ ANOC9:27017" }, storage: { dbPath: "C:\db1\passive1\data" }
```

In the preceding examples, the --rest option is used to activate a REST interface on port +1000. Activating REST enables you to inspect the replica set status using web interface.

By the end of the above steps, you have three servers that are up and running and are communicating with each other; however the replica set is still not initialized. In the next step, you initialize the replica set and instruct each member about their responsibilities and roles.

In order to initialize the replica set, you connect to one of the servers. In this example, it is the first server, which is running on port 27021.

Open a new command prompt and connect to the mongo interface for the first server:

```
C:\>cd c:\practicalmongodb\bin
c:\practicalmongodb\bin>mongo ANOC9 --port 27021
MongoDB shell version: 3.0.4
connecting to: ANOC9:27021/test
>
```

Next, switch to the admin database.

```
> use admin
switched to db admin
>
```

Next, a configuration data structure is set up, which mentions server wise roles:

```
>cfg = {
... _id: 'testset',
... members: [
... {_id:0, host: 'ANOC9:27021'},
... {_id:1, host: 'ANOC9:27022'},
... {_id:2, host: 'ANOC9:27023', priority:0}
... ]
... }
{        "_id" : "testset",
        "members" : [
                {
                        "_id" : 0,
                        "host" : "ANOC9:27021"
                },
..........
                {
                        "_id" : 2,
                        "host" : "ANOC9:27023",
                        "priority" : 0
                } ]}>
```

With this step the replicas set structure is configured.

You have used 0 priority when defining the role for the passive member. This means that the member cannot be promoted to primary.

The next command initiates the replica set:

```
> rs.initiate(cfg)
{ "ok" : 1}
```

Let's now view the replica set status in order to vet that it's set up correctly:

```
testset:PRIMARY> rs.status()
{
     "set" : "testset",
"date" : ISODate("2015-07-13T04:32:46.222Z")
     "myState" : 1,
"members" : [
        {
                "_id" : 0,
..........................
testset:PRIMARY>
```

The output indicates that all is OK. The replica set is now successfully configured and initialized.

Let's see how you can determine the primary node. In order to do so, connect to any of the members and issue the following and verify the primary:

```
testset:PRIMARY> db.isMaster()
{
       "setName" : "testset",
       "setVersion" : 1,
       "ismaster" : true,
       "primary" : " ANOC9:27021",
       "me" : "ANOC9:27021",
       .........................................
       "localTime" : ISODate("2015-07-13T04:36:52.365Z"),
       .............................................................
       "ok" : 1
}testset:PRIMARY>
```

Removing a Server

In this example, you will remove the secondary active member from the set. Let's connect to the secondary member mongo instance. Open a new command prompt, like so:

```
C:\>cd c:\practicalmongodb\bin
c:\practicalmongodb\bin>mongo ANOC9 --port 27022
MongoDB shell version: 3.0.4
connecting to: 127.0.0.1:27022/ANOC9
testset:SECONDARY>

Issue the following command to shut down the instance:
testset:SECONDARY> use admin
switched to db admin
testset:SECONDARY> db.shutdownServer()
2015-07-13T21:48:59.009-0700 I NETWORK  DBClientCursor::init call() failed server should be down...
```

Next, you need to connect to the primary member mongo console and execute the following to remove the member:

```
testset:PRIMARY> use admin
switched to db admin
testset:PRIMARY> rs.remove("ANOC9:27022")
{ "ok" : 1 }
testset:PRIMARY>
```

In order to vet whether the member is removed or not you can issue the rs.status() command.

Adding a Server

You will next add a new active member to the replica set. As with other members, you begin by opening a new command prompt and creating the data directory first:

```
C:\>mkdir C:\db1\active3\data
C:\>
```

Next, you start the mongod using the following command:

```
c:\practicalmongodb\bin>mongod --dbpath C:\db1\active3\data --port 27024 --replSet testset/
ANOC9:27021 --rest
..........
```

You have the new mongod running, so now you need to add this to the replica set. For this you connect to the primary's mongo console:

```
C:\>c:\practicalmongodb\bin\mongo.exe --port 27021
MongoDB shell version: 3.0.4
connecting to: 127.0.0.1:27021/test
testset:PRIMARY>
```

Next, you switch to admin db:

```
testset:PRIMARY> use admin
switched to db admin
testset:PRIMARY>
```

Finally, the following command needs to be issued to add the new mongod to the replica set:

```
testset:PRIMARY> rs.add("ANOC9:27024")
{ "ok" : 1 }
```

The replica set status can be checked to vet whether the new active member is added or not using rs.status().

Adding an Arbiter to a Replica Set

In this example, you will add an arbiter member to the set. As with the other members, you begin by creating the data directory for the MongoDB instance:

```
C:\>mkdir c:\db1\arbiter\data
C:\>
```

You next start the mongod using the following command:

```
c:\practicalmongodb\bin>mongod --dbpath c:\db1\arbiter\data --port 30000 --replSet testset/
ANOC9:27021 --rest
2015-07-13T22:05:10.205-0700 I CONTROL  [initandlisten] MongoDB starting : pid=3700
port=30000 dbpath=c:\db1\arbiter\data 64-bit host=ANOC9
.......................................................
```

Connect to the primary's mongo console, switch to the admin db, and add the newly created mongod as an arbiter to the replica set:

```
C:\>c:\practicalmongodb\bin\mongo.exe --port 27021
MongoDB shell version: 3.0.4
connecting to: 127.0.0.1:27021/test
testset:PRIMARY> use admin
switched to db admin

testset:PRIMARY> rs.addArb("ANOC9:30000")
{ "ok" : 1 }
testset:PRIMARY>
```

Whether the step is successful or not can be verified using rs.status().

Inspecting the Status Using rs.status()

We have been referring to rs.status() throughout the examples above to check the replica set status. In this section, you will learn what this command is all about.

It enables you to check the status of the member whose console they are connected to and also enables them to view its role within the replica set.

The following command is issued from the primary's mongo console:

```
testset:PRIMARY> rs.status()
{
     "set" : "testset",
"date" : ISODate("2015-07-13T22:15:46.222Z")
     "myState" : 1,
"members" : [
        {
                "_id" : 0,
.........................
        "ok" : 1
testset:PRIMARY>
```

The **myState** field's value indicates the status of the member and it can have the values shown in Table 7-3.

Table 7-3. Replica Set Status

myState	Description
0	Phase 1, starting up
1	Primary member
2	Secondary member
3	Recovering state
4	Fatal error state
5	Phase 2, Starting up
6	Unknown state
7	Arbiter member
8	Down or unreachable
9	This state is reached when a write operation is rolled back by the secondary after transitioning from primary.
10	Members enter this state when removed from the replica set.

Hence the above command returns myState value as 1, which indicates that this is the primary member.

Forcing a New Election

The current primary server can be forced to step down using the rs.stepDown () command. This force starts the election for a new primary.

This command is useful in the following scenarios:

1. When you are simulating the impact of a primary failure, forcing the cluster to fail over. This lets you test how your application responds in such a scenario.

2. When the primary server needs to be offline. This is done for either a maintenance activity or for upgrading or to investigating the server.

3. When a diagnostic process need to be run against the data structures.

The following is the output of the command when run against the testset replica set:

```
testset:PRIMARY> rs.stepDown()
2015-07-13T22:52:32.000-0700 I NETWORK  DBClientCursor::init call() failed
2015-07-13T22:52:32.005-0700 E QUERY    Error: error doing query: failed
2015-07-13T22:52:32.009-0700 I NETWORK  trying reconnect to 127.0.0.1:27021 (127.0.0.1) failed
2015-07-13T22:52:32.011-0700 I NETWORK  reconnect 127.0.0.1:27021 (127.0.0.1) ok
                                        testset:SECONDARY>
```

After execution of the command the prompt changed from testset:PRIMARY to testset:SECONDARY. rs.status() can be used to check whether the stepDown () is successful or not.

Please note the myState value it returns is 2 now, which means the "Member is operating as secondary."

Inspecting Status of the Replica Set Using a Web Interface

A web-based console is maintained by MongoDB for viewing the system status. In your example, the console can be accessed via `http://localhost:28021`.

By default the web interface port number is set to X+1000 where X is the mongod instance port number. In this chapter's example, since the primary instance is on 27021, the web interface is on port 28021.

Figure 7-13 shows a link to the replica set status. Clicking the link takes you to the replica set dashboard shown in Figure 7-14.

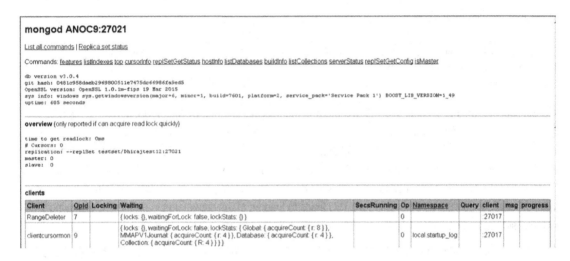

Figure 7-13. Web interface

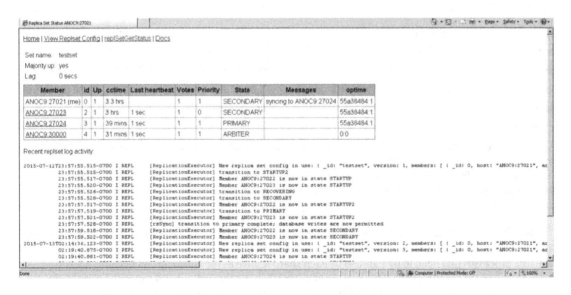

Figure 7-14. Replica set status report

Sharding

You saw in the previous section how replica sets in MongoDB are used to duplicate the data in order to protect against any adversity and to distribute the read load in order to increase the read efficiency.

MongoDB uses memory extensively for low latency database operations. When you compare the speed of reading data from memory to reading data from disk, reading from memory is approximately 100,000 times faster than reading from the disk.

In MongoDB, ideally the working set should fit in memory. The working set consists of the most frequently accessed data and indexes.

A page fault happens when data which is not there in memory is accessed by MongoDB. If there's free memory available, the OS will directly load the requested page into memory; however, in the absence of free memory, the page in memory is written to the disk and then the requested page is loaded in the memory, slowing down the process. Few operations accidentally purge large portion of the working set from the memory, leading to an adverse effect on the performance. One example is a query scanning through all documents of a database where the size exceeds the server memory. This leads to loading of the documents in memory and moving the working set out to disk.

Ensuring you have defined the appropriate index coverage for your queries during the schema design phase of the project will minimize the risk of this happening. The MongoDB explain operation can be used to provide information on your query plan and the indexes used.

MongoDB's serverStatus command returns a workingSet document that provides an estimate of the instance's working set size. The Operations team can track how many pages the instance accessed over a given period of time and the elapsed time between the working set's oldest and newest document. Tracking all these metrics, it's possible to detect when the working set will be hitting the current memory limit, so proactive actions can be taken to ensure the system is scaled well enough to handle that.

In MongoDB, the scaling is handled by scaling out the data horizontally (i.e. partitioning the data across multiple commodity servers), which is also called sharding (horizontal scaling).

Sharding addresses the challenges of scaling to support large data sets and high throughput by horizontally dividing the datasets across servers where each server is responsible for handling its part of data and no one server is burdened. These servers are also called shards.

Every shard is an independent database. All the shards collectively make up a single logical database.

Sharding reduces the operations count handled by each shard. For example, when data is inserted, only the shards responsible for storing those records need to be accessed.

The processes that need to be handled by each shard reduce as the cluster grows because the subset of data that the shard holds reduces. This leads to an increase in the throughput and capacity horizontally.

Let's assume you have a database that is 1TB in size. If the number of shards is 4, you will have approximately 265GB of data handled by each shard, whereas if the number of shards is increased to 40, only 25GB of data will be held on each shard.

Figure 7-15 depicts how a collection that is sharded will appear when distributed across three shards.

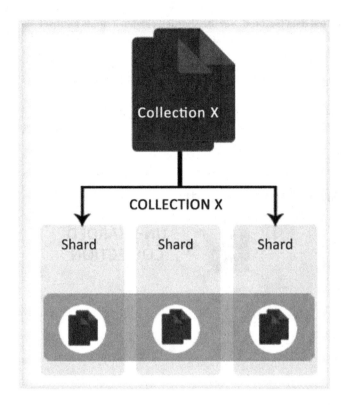

Figure 7-15. *Sharded collection across three shards*

Although sharding is a compelling and powerful feature, it has significant infrastructure requirements and it increases the complexity of the overall deployment. So you need to understand the scenarios where you might consider using sharding.

Use sharding in the following instances:

- The size of the dataset is huge and it has started challenging the capacity of a single system.

- Since memory is used by MongoDB for quickly fetching data, it becomes important to scale out when the active work set limits are set to reach.

- If the application is write-intensive, sharding can be used to spread the writes across multiple servers.

Sharding Components

You will next look at the components that enable sharding in MongoDB. Sharding is enabled in MongoDB via sharded clusters.

The following are the components of a sharded cluster:

- Shards

- mongos

- Config servers

The shard is the component where the actual data is stored. For the sharded cluster, it holds a subset of data and can either be a mongod or a replica set. All shard's data combined together forms the complete dataset for the sharded cluster.

Sharding is enabled per collection basis, so there might be collections that are not sharded. In every sharded cluster there's a primary shard where all the unsharded collections are placed in addition to the sharded collection data.

When deploying a sharded cluster, by default the first shard becomes the primary shard although it's configurable. See Figure 7-16.

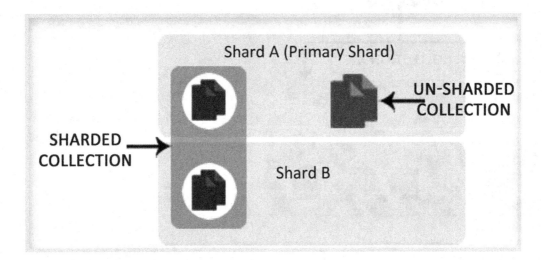

Figure 7-16. *Primary shard*

Config servers are special mongods that hold the sharded cluster's metadata. This metadata depicts the sharded system state and organization.

The config server stores data for a single sharded cluster. The config servers should be available for the proper functioning of the cluster.

One config server can lead to a cluster's single point of failure. For production deployment it's recommended to have at least three config servers, so that the cluster keeps functioning even if one config server is not accessible.

A config server stores the data in the config database, which enables routing of the client requests to the respective data. This database should not be updated.

MongoDB writes data to the config server only when the data distribution has changed for balancing the cluster.

The mongos act as the routers. They are responsible for routing the read and write request from the application to the shards.

An application interacting with a mongo database need not worry about how the data is stored internally on the shards. For them, it's transparent because it's only the mongos they interact with. The mongos, in turn, route the reads and writes to the shards.

The mongos cache the metadata from config server so that for every read and write request they don't overburden the config server.

However, in the following cases, the data is read from the config server:

- Either an existing mongos has restarted or a new mongos has started for the first time.

- Migration of chunks. We will explain chunk migration in detail later.

Data Distribution Process

You will next look at how the data is distributed among the shards for the collections where sharding is enabled. In MongoDB, the data is sharded or distributed at the collection level. The collection is partitioned by the shard key.

Shard Key

Any indexed single/compound field that exists within all documents of the collection can be a shard key. You specify that this is the field basis which the documents of the collection need to be distributed. Internally, MongoDB divides the documents based on the value of the field into chunks and distributes them across the shards.

There are two ways MongoDB enables distribution of the data: range-based partitioning and hash-based partitioning.

Range-Based Partitioning

In range-based partitioning, the shard key values are divided into ranges. Say you consider a `timestamp` field as the shard key. In this way of partitioning, the values are considered as a straight line starting from a Min value to Max value where Min is the starting period (say, 01/01/1970) and Max is the end period (say, 12/31/9999). Every document in the collection will have timestamp value within this range only, and it will represent some point on the line.

Based on the number of shards available, the line will be divided into ranges, and documents will be distributed based on them.

In this scheme of partitioning, shown in Figure 7-17, the documents where the values of the shard key are nearby are likely to fall on the same shard. This can significantly improve the performance of the range queries.

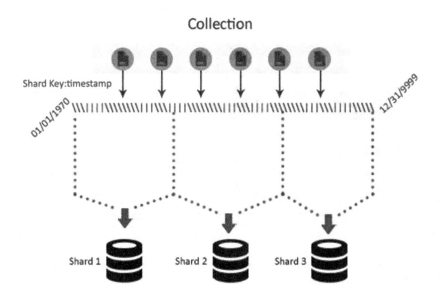

Figure 7-17. *Range-based partitioning*

However, the disadvantage is that it can lead to uneven distribution of data, overloading one of the shards, which may end up receiving majority of the requests, whereas the other shards remain underloaded, so the system will not scale properly.

Hash-Based Partitioning

In hash-based partitioning, the data is distributed on the basis of the hash value of the shard field. If selected, this will lead to a more random distribution compared to range-based partitioning.

It's unlikely that the documents with close shard key will be part of the same chunk. For example, for ranges based on the hash of the _id field, there will be a straight line of hash values, which will again be partitioned on basis of the number of shards. On the basis of the hash values, the documents will lie in either of the shards. See Figure 7-18.

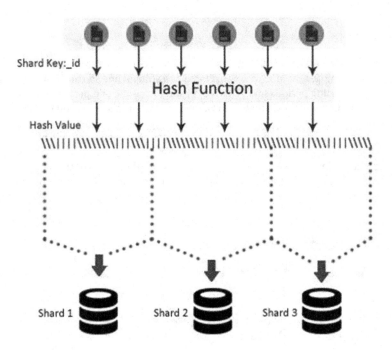

Figure 7-18. *Hash-based partitioning*

In contrast to range-based partitioning, this ensures that the data is evenly distributed, but it happens at the cost of efficient range queries.

Chunks

The data is moved between the shards in form of chunks. The shard key range is further partitioned into sub-ranges, which are also termed as chunks. See Figure 7-19.

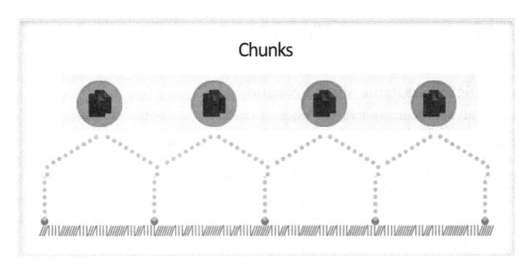

Figure 7-19. *Chunks*

For a sharded cluster, 64MB is the default chunk size. In most situations, this is an apt size for chunk slitting and migration.

Let's discuss the execution of sharding and chunks with an example. Say you have a blog posts collection which is sharded on the field date. This implies that the collection will be split up on the basis of the date field values. Let's assume further that you have three shards. In this scenario the data might be distributed across shards as follows:

Shard #1: Beginning of time up to July 2009

Shard #2: August 2009 to December 2009

Shard #3: January 2010 to through the end of time

In order to retrieve documents from January 1, 2010 until today, the query is sent to mongos. In this scenario,

1. The client queries mongos.

2. The mongos know which shards have the data, so mongos sends the queries to Shard #3.

3. Shard #3 executes the query and returns the results to mongos.

4. Mongos combines the data received from various shards, which in this case is Shard #3 only, and returns the final result back to the client.

The application doesn't need to be sharding-aware. It can query the mongos as though it's a normal mongod.

Let's consider another scenario where you insert a new document. The new document has today's date. The sequences of events are as follows:

1. The document is sent to the mongos.

2. Mongos checks the date and on basis of that, sends the document to Shard #3.

3. Shard #3 inserts the document.

From a client's point of view, this is again identical to a single server setup.

Role of ConfigServers in the Above Scenario

Consider a scenario where you start getting insert requests for millions of documents with the date of September 2009. In this case, Shard #2 begins to get overloaded.

The config server steps in once it realizes that Shard #2 is becoming too big. It will split the data on the shard and start migrating it to other shards. After the migration is completed, it sends the updated status to the mongos. So now Shard #2 has data from August 2009 until September 18, 2009 and Shard #3 contains data from September 19, 2009 until the end of time.

When a new shard is added to the cluster, it's the config server's responsibility to figure out what to do with it. The data may need to be immediately migrated to the new shard, or the new shard may need to be in reserve for some time. In summary, the config servers are the brains. Whenever any data is moved around, the config servers let the mongos know about the final configuration so that the mongos can continue doing proper routing.

Data Balancing Process

You will next look at how the cluster is kept balanced (i.e. how MongoDB ensures that all the shards are equally loaded).

The addition of new data or modification of existing data, or the addition or removal of servers, can lead to imbalance in the data distribution, which means either one shard is overloaded with more chunks and the other shards have less number of chunks, or it can lead to an increase in the chunk size, which is significantly greater than the other chunks.

MongoDB ensures balance with the following background processes:

- Chunk splitting
- Balancer

Chunk Splitting

Chunk splitting is one of the processes that ensures the chunks are of the specified size. As you have seen, a shard key is chosen and it is used to identify how the documents will be distributed across the shards. The documents are further grouped into chunks of 64MB (default and is configurable) and are stored in the shards based on the range it is hosting.

If the size of the chunk changes due to an insert or update operation, and exceeds the default chunk size, then the chunk is split into two smaller chunks by the mongos. See Figure 7-20.

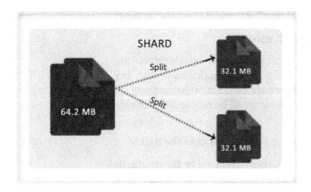

Figure 7-20. *Chunk splitting*

This process keeps the chunks within a shard of the specified size or lesser than that (i.e. it ensures that the chunks are of the configured size).

Insert and update operations trigger splits. The split operation leads to modification of the data in the config server as the metadata is modified. Although splits don't lead to migration of data, this operation can lead to an unbalance of the cluster with one shard having more chunks compared to another.

Balancer

Balancer is the background process that is used to ensure that all of the shards are equally loaded or are in a balanced state. This process manages chunk migrations.

Splitting of the chunk can cause imbalance. The addition or removal of documents can also lead to a cluster imbalance. In a cluster imbalance, balancer is used, which is the process of distributing data evenly.

When you have a shard with more chunks as compared to other shards, then the chunks balancing is done automatically by MongoDB across the shards. This process is transparent to the application and to you.

Any of the mongos within the cluster can initiate the balancer process. They do so by acquiring a lock on the config database of the config server, as balancer involves migration of chunks from one shard to another, which can lead to a change in the metadata, which will lead to change in the config server database. The balancer process can have huge impact on the database performance, so it can either

1. Be configured to start the migration only when the migration threshold has reached. The migration threshold is the difference in the number of maximum and minimum chunks on the shards. Threshold is shown in Table 7-4.

Table 7-4. *Migration Threshold*

Number of Chunks	Migration Threshold
< 20	2
21-80	4
>80	8

2. Or it can be scheduled to run in a time period that will not impact the production traffic.

The balancer migrates one chunk at a time (see Figure 7-21) and follows these steps:

1. The moveChunk command is sent to the source shard.

2. An internal moveChunk command is started on the source where it creates the copy of the documents within the chunk and queues it. In the meantime, any operations for that chunk are routed to the source by the mongos because the config database is not yet changed and the source will be responsible for serving any read/write request on that chunk.

3. The destination shard starts receiving the copy of the data from the source.

4. Once all of the documents in the chunks have been received by the destination shard, the synchronization process is initiated to ensure that all changes that have happened to the data while migration are updated at the destination shard.

5. Once the synchronization is completed, the next step is to update the metadata with the chunk's new location in the config database. This activity is done by the destination shard that connects to the config database and carries out the necessary updates.

6. Post successful completion of all the above, the document copy that is maintained at the source shard is deleted.

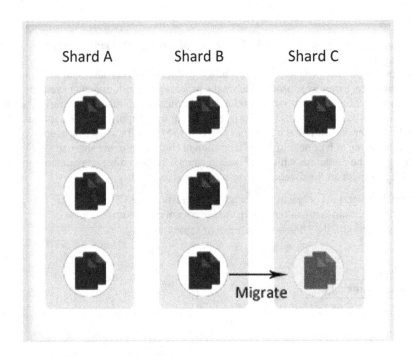

Figure 7-21. *Chunk migration*

If in the meanwhile the balancer needs additional chunk migration from the source shard, it can start with the new migration without even waiting for the deletion step to finish for the current migration.

In case of any error during the migration process, the process is aborted by the balancer, leaving the chunks on the original shard. On successful completion of the process, the chunk data is removed from the original shard by MongoDB.

Addition or removal of shards can also lead to cluster imbalance. When a new shard is added, data migration to the shard is started immediately. However, it takes time for the cluster to be balanced.

When a shard is removed, the balancer ensures that the data is migrated to the other shards and the metadata information is updated. Post completion of the two activities, the shard is removed safely.

Operations

You will next look at how the read and write operations are performed on the sharded cluster. As mentioned, the config servers maintain the cluster metadata. This data is stored in the config database. This data of the config database is used by the mongos to service the application read and write requests.

The data is cached by the mongos instances, which is then used for routing write and read operations to the shards. This way the config servers are not overburdened.

The mongos will only read from the config servers in the following scenarios:

- The mongos has started for first time or

- An existing mongos has restarted or

- After chunk migration when the mongos needs to update its cached metadata with the new cluster metadata.

Whenever any operation is issued, the first step that the mongos need to do is to identify the shards that will be serving the request. Since the shard key is used to distribute data across the sharded cluster, if the operation is using the shard key field, then based on that specific shards can be targeted.

If the shard key is employeeid, the following things can happen:

1. If the find query contains the employeeid field, then to satiate the query, only specific shards will be targeted by the mongos.

2. If a single update operation uses employeeid for updating the document, the request will be routed to the shard holding that employee data.

However, if the operation is not using the shard key, then the request is broadcast to all the shards. Generally a multi-update or remove operation is targeted across the cluster.

While querying the data, there might be scenarios where in addition to identifying the shards and getting the data from them, the mongos might need to work on the data returned from various shards before sending the final output to the client.

Say an application has issued a find() request with sort(). In this scenario, the mongos will pass the $orderby option to the shards. The shards will fetch the data from their data set and will send the result in an ordered manner. Once the mongos has all the shard's sorted data, it will perform an incremental merge sort on the entire data and then return the final output to the client.

Similar to sort are the aggregation functions such as limit(), skip(), etc., which require mongos to perform operations post receiving the data from the shards and before returning the final result set to the client.

The mongos consumes minimal system resources and has no persistent state. So if the application requirement is a simple find () queries that can be solely met by the shards and needs no manipulation at the mongos level, you can run the mongos on the same system where your application servers are running.

Implementing Sharding

In this section, you will learn to configure sharding in one machine on a Windows platform.

You will keep the example simple by using only two shards. In this configuration, you will be using the services listed in Table 7-5.

Table 7-5. *Sharding Cluster Configuration*

Component	Type	Port	Datafile path
Shard Controller	Mongos	27021	-
Config Server	Mongod	27022	C:\db1\config\data
Shard0	Mongod	27023	C:\db1\shard1\data
Shard1	Mongod	27024	C:\db1\shard2\data

You will be focusing on the following:

1. Setting up a sharded cluster.

2. Creating a database and collection, and enable sharding on the collection.

3. Using the import command to load data in the sharded collection.

4. Distributed data amongst the shards.

5. Adding and removing shards from the cluster and checking how data is distributed automatically.

Setting the Shard Cluster

In order to set up the cluster, the first step is to set up the configuration server. Enter the following code in a new terminal window to create the data directory for the config server and start the mongod:

```
C:\> mkdir C:\db1\config\data
C:\>CD C:\practicalmongodb\bin
C:\ practicalmongodb\bin>mongod --port 27022 --dbpath C:\db1\config\data --configsvr

2015-07-13T23:02:41.982-0700 I JOURNAL  [journal writer] Journal writer thread started
2015-07-13T23:02:41.984-0700 I CONTROL  [initandlisten] MongoDB starting : pid=3084
port=27022 dbpath=C:\db1\config\data master=1 64-bit host=ANOC9
.....................................
2015-07-13T23:02:42.066-0700 I REPL     [initandlisten] ******
2015-07-13T03:02:42.067-0700 I NETWORK  [initandlisten] waiting for connections on port 27022
```

Next, start the mongos. Type the following in a new terminal window:

```
C:\>cd c:\practicalmongodb\bin
c:\practicalmongodb\bin>mongos --configdb localhost:27022 --port 27021 --chunkSize 1
2015-07-13T23:06:07.246-0700 W SHARDING running with 1 config server should be done only for
testing purposes and is not recommended for production
........................................................
2015-07-13T23:09:07.464-0700 I SHARDING [Balancer] distributed lock 'balancer/
ANOC9:27021:1429783567:41' unlocked
```

You now have the shard controller (i.e. the mongos) up and running.

If you switch to the window where the config server has been started, you will find a registration of the shard server to the config server.

In this example you have used chunk size of 1MB. Note that this is not ideal in a real-life scenario since the size is less than 4MB (a document's maximum size). However, this is just for demonstration purpose since this creates the necessary amount of chunks without loading a large amount of data. The chunkSize is 128MB by default unless otherwise specified.

Next, bring up the shard servers, Shard0 and Shard1.

Open a fresh terminal window. Create the data directory for the first shard and start the mongod:

```
C:\>mkdir C:\db1\shard0\data
C:\>cd c:\practicalmongodb\bin
c:\practicalmongodb\bin>mongod --port 27023 --dbpath c:\db1\shard0\data –shardsvr
2015-07-13T23:14:58.076-0700 I CONTROL  [initandlisten] MongoDB starting : pid=1996
port=27023 dbpath=c:\db1\shard0\data 64-bit host=ANOC9
.........................................................
2015-07-13T23:14:58.158-0700 I NETWORK  [initandlisten] waiting for connections on port 27023
```

Open fresh terminal window. Create the data directory for the second shard and start the mongod:

```
C:\>mkdir c:\db1\shard1\data
C:\>cd c:\practicalmongodb\bin
c:\practicalmongodb\bin>mongod --port 27024 --dbpath C:\db1\shard1\data --shardsvr
2015-07-13T23:17:01.704-0700 I CONTROL  [initandlisten] MongoDB starting : pid=3672
port=27024 dbpath=C:\db1\shard1\data 64-bit host=ANOC9
2015-07-13T23:17:01.704-0700 I NETWORK  [initandlisten] waiting for connections on port 27024
```

All the servers relevant for the setup are up and running by the end of the above step. The next step is to add the shards information to the shard controller.

The mongos appears as a complete MongoDB instance to the application in spite of actually not being a full instance. The mongo shell can be used to connect to the mongos to perform any operation on it.

Open the mongos mongo console:

```
C:\>cd c:\practicalmongodb\bin
c:\ practicalmongodb\bin>mongo localhost:27021
MongoDB shell version: 3.0.4
connecting to: localhost:27021/test
mongos>
```

Switch to the admin database:

```
mongos> use admin
switched to db admin
mongos>
```

Add the shards information by running the following commands:

```
mongos> db.runCommand({addshard:"localhost:27023",allowLocal:true})
{ "shardAdded" : "shard0000", "ok" : 1 }
mongos> db.runCommand({addshard:"localhost:27024",allowLocal:true})
{ "shardAdded" : "shard0001", "ok" : 1 }
mongos>
```

This activates the two shard servers.
The next command checks the shards:

```
mongos> db.runCommand({listshards:1})
{
        "shards" : [
                {
                        "_id" : "shard0000",
                        "host" : "localhost:27023"
                },              {
                        "_id" : "shard0001",
                        "host" : "localhost:27024"
                }
        ],        "ok" : 1}
```

Creating a Database and Shard Collection

In order to continue further with the example, you will create a database named testdb and a collection named testcollection, which you will be sharding on the key testkey.

Connect to the mongos console and issue the following command to get the database:

```
mongos> testdb=db.getSisterDB("testdb")
testdb
```

Next, enabling sharding at database level for testdb:

```
mongos> db.runCommand({enableSharding system: "testdb"})
{ "ok" : 1 }
mongos>
```

Next, specify the collection that needs to be sharded and the key on which the collection will be sharded:

```
mongos> db.runCommand({shardcollection: "testdb.testcollection", key: {testkey:1}})
{ "collectionsharded" : "testdb.testcollection", "ok" : 1 }
mongos>
```

With the completion of the above steps you now have a sharded cluster set up with all components up and running. You have also created a database and enabled sharding on the collection.

Next, import data into the collection so that you can check the data distribution on the shards.

You will be using the import command to load data in the testcollection. Connect to a new terminal window and execute the following:

```
C:\>cd C:\practicalmongodb\bin
C:\practicalmongodb\bin>mongoimport --host ANOC9 --port 27021 --db testdb --collection
testcollection --type csv --file c:\mongoimport.csv --headerline
2015-07-13T23:17:39.101-0700    connected to: ANOC9:27021
2015-07-13T23:17:42.298-0700    [###############.........] testdb.testcollection 1.1 MB/1.9 MB (59.6%)
2015-07-13T23:17:44.781-0700    imported 100000 documents
```

The mongoimport.csv consists of two fields. The first is the testkey, which is a randomly generated number. The second field is a text field; it is used to ensure that the documents occupy a sufficient number of chunks, making it feasible to use the sharding mechanism.

This inserts 100,000 objects in the collection.

In order to vet whether the records are inserted or not, connect to the mongo console of the mongos and issue the following command:

```
C:\Windows\system32>cd c:\practicalmongodb\bin
c:\practicalmongodb\bin>mongo localhost:27021
MongoDB shell version: 3.0.4
connecting to: localhost:27021/test
mongos> use testdb
switched to db testdb
mongos> db.testcollection.count()
100000
mongos>
```

Next, connect to the consoles of the two shards (Shard0 and Shard1) and look at how the data is distributed. Open a new terminal window and connect to Shard0's console:

```
C:\>cd C:\practicalmongodb\bin
C:\ practicalmongodb\bin>mongo localhost:27023
MongoDB shell version: 3.0.4
connecting to: localhost:27023/test
```

Switch to testdb and issue the count() command to check number of documents on the shard:

```
> use testdb
switched to db testdb
> db.testcollection.count()
57998
```

Next, open a new terminal window, connect to Shard1's console, and follow the steps as above (i.e. switch to testdb and check the count of testcollection collection):

```
C:\>cd c:\practicalmongodb\bin
c:\practicalmongodb\bin>mongo localhost:27024
MongoDB shell version: 3.0.4
connecting to: localhost:27024/test
> use testdb
switched to db testdb
> db.testcollection.count()
42002
>
```

You might see a difference in the document's number in each shard when you run the above command for some time. When the documents are loaded, all of the chunks are placed on one shard by the mongos. In time the shard set is rebalanced by distributing the chunks evenly across all the shards.

Adding a New Shard

You have a sharded cluster set up and you also have sharded a collection and looked at how the data is distributed amongst the shards. Next, you'll add a new shard to the cluster so that the load is spread out a little more.

You will be repeating the steps mentioned above. Begin by creating a data directory for the new shard in a new terminal window:

```
c:\>mkdir c:\db1\shard2\data
```

Next, start the mongod at port 27025:

```
c:\>cd c:\practicalmongodb\bin
c:\ practicalmongodb\bin>mongod --port 27025 --dbpath C:\db1\shard2\data --shardsvr
2015-07-13T23:25:49.103-0700 I CONTROL  [initandlisten] MongoDB starting : pid=3744
port=27025 dbpath=C:\db1\shard2\data 64-bit host=ANOC9
..............................
2015-07-13T23:25:49.183-0700 I NETWORK  [initandlisten] waiting for connections on port 27025
```

Next, the new shard server will be added to the shard cluster. In order to configure it, open the mongos mongo console in a new terminal window:

```
C:\>cd c:\practicalmongodb\bin
c:\practicalmongodb\bin>mongo localhost:27021
MongoDB shell version: 3.0.4
connecting to: localhost:27021/test
mongos>
```

Switch to the admin database and run the addshard command. This command adds the shard server to the sharded cluster.

```
mongos> use admin
switched to db admin
mongos> db.runCommand({addshard: "localhost:27025", allowlocal: true})
{ "shardAdded" : "shard0002", "ok" : 1 }
mongos>
```

In order to vet whether the addition is successful or not, run the listshards command:

```
mongos> db.runCommand({listshards:1})
{
        "shards" : [
                {
                        "_id" : "shard0000",
                        "host" : "localhost:27023"
                },
```

```
        {
                "_id" : "shard0001",
                "host" : "localhost:27024"
        },
        {

                "_id" : "shard0002",
                "host" : "localhost:27025"

        }
    ],
    "ok" : 1
}
```

Next, check how the testcollection data is distributed. Connect to the new shard's console in a new terminal window:

```
C:\>cd c:\practicalmongodb\bin
c:\practicalmongodb\bin>mongo localhost:27025
MongoDB shell version: 3.0.4
connecting to: localhost:27025/test
```

Switch to testdb and check the collections listed on the shard:

```
> use testdb
switched to db testdb
> show collections
system.indexes
testcollection
```

Issue a testcollection.count command three times:

```
> db.testcollection.count()
6928
> db.testcollection.count()
12928
> db.testcollection.count()
16928
```

Interestingly, the number of items in the collection is slowly going up. The mongos is rebalancing the cluster.

With time, the chunks will be migrated from the shard servers Shard0 and Shard1 to the newly added shard server, Shard2, so that the data is evenly distributed across all the servers. Post completion of this process the config server metadata is updated. This is an automatic process and it happens even if there's no new data addition in the testcollection. This is one of the important factors you need to consider when deciding on the chunk size.

If the value of chunkSize is very large, you will end up having less even data distribution. The data is more evenly distributed when the chunkSize is smaller.

Removing a Shard

In the following example, you will see how to remove a shard server. For this example, you will be removing the server you added in the above example.

In order to initiate the process, you need to log on to the mongos console, switch to the admin db, and execute the following command to remove the shard from the shard cluster:

```
C:\>cd c:\practicalmongodb\bin
c:\practicalmongodb\bin>mongo localhost:27021
MongoDB shell version: 3.0.4
connecting to: localhost:27021/test
mongos> use admin
switched to db admin
mongos> db.runCommand({removeShard: "localhost:27025"})
{
        "msg" : "draining started successfully",
        "state" : "started",
        "shard" : "shard0002",
        "ok" : 1
}
mongos>
```

As you can see, the removeShard command returns a message. One of the message fields is state, which indicates the process state. The message also states that the draining process has started. This is indicated by the field msg.

You can reissue the removeShard command to check the progress:

```
mongos> db.runCommand({removeShard: "localhost:27025"})
{
        "msg" : "draining ongoing",
        "state" : "ongoing",
        "remaining" : {
                "chunks" : NumberLong(2),
                "dbs" : NumberLong(0)
        },
        "ok" : 1
}
mongos>
```

The response tells you the number of chunks and databases that still need to be drained from the server. If you reissue the command and the process is terminated, the output of the command will depict the same.

```
mongos> db.runCommand({removeShard: "localhost:27025"})
{
        "msg" : "removeshard completed successfully",
        "state" : "completed",
        "shard" : "shard0002",
        "ok" : 1
}
mongos>
```

You can use the listshards to vet whether removeShard was successful or not.

As you can see, the data is successfully migrated to the other shards, so you can delete the storage files and terminate the Shard2 mongod process.

This ability to modify the shard cluster without going offline is one of the critical components of MongoDB, which enables it to support highly available, highly scalable, large capacity data stores.

Listing the Sharded Cluster Status

The printShardingStatus() command gives lots of insight into the sharding system internals.

```
mongos> db.printShardingStatus()
--- Sharding Status ---
  sharding version: {
        "_id" : 1,
        "version" : 3,
        "minCompatibleVersion" : 5,
        "currentVersion" : 6,
        "clusterId" : ObjectId("52fb7a8647e47c5884749a1a")
}
  shards:
        {  "_id" : "shard0000",  "host" : "localhost:27023" }
        {  "_id" : "shard0001",  "host" : "localhost:27024" }
balancer:
        Currently enabled:  yes
        Currently running:  no
        Failed balancer rounds in last 5 attempts:  0
        Migration Results for the last 24 hours:
                17 : Success
  databases:
        {  "_id" : "admin",  "partitioned" : false,  "primary" : "config" }
        {  "_id" : "testdb",  "partitioned" : true,  "primary" : "shard0000" }
        ...............
```

The output lists the following:

- All of the shard servers of the shard cluster

- The configurations of each sharded database/collection

- All of the chunks of the sharded dataset

Important information that can be obtained from the above command is the sharding keys range, which is associated with each chunk. This also shows where specific chunks are stored (on which shard server). The output can be used to analyse the shard server's keys and chunks distribution.

Controlling Collection Distribution (Tag-Based Sharding)

In the previous section, you saw how data distribution happens. In this section, you will learn about tag-based sharding. This feature was introduced in version 2.2.0.

Tagging gives operators control over which collections go to which shard.

In order to understand tag-based sharding, let's set up a sharded cluster. You will be using the shard cluster created above. For this example, you need three shards, so you will add Shard2 again to the cluster.

Prerequisite

You will start the cluster first. Just to reiterate, follow these steps.

1. Start the config server. Enter the following command in a new terminal window (if it's not already running):

    ```
    C:\> mkdir C:\db1\config\data
    C:\>cd c:\practicalmongodb\bin
    C:\practicalmongodb\bin>mongod --port 27022 --dbpath C:\db\config\data --configsvr
    ```

2. Start the mongos. Enter the following command in a new terminal window (if it's not already running):

    ```
    C:\>cd c:\practicalmongodb\bin
    c:\practicalmongodb\bin>mongos --configdb localhost:27022 --port 27021
    ```

3. You will start the shard servers next.

Start Shard0. Enter the following command in a new terminal window (if it's not already running):

```
C:\>cd c:\practicalmongodb\bin
c:\practicalmongodb\bin>mongod --port 27023 --dbpath c:\db1\shard0\data --shardsvr
```

Start Shard1. Enter the following command in a new terminal window (if it's not already running):

```
C:\>cd c:\practicalmongodb\bin
C:\practicalmongodb\bin>mongod --port 27024 --dbpath c:\db1\shard1\data –shardsvr
```

Start Shard2. Enter the following command in a new terminal window (if it's not already running):

```
C:\>cd c:\practicalmongodb\bin
c:\practicalmongodb\bin>mongod --port 27025 --dbpath c:\db1\shard2\data –shardsvr
```

Since you have removed Shard2 from the sharded cluster in the earlier example, you must add Shard2 to the sharded cluster because for this example you need three shards.

In order to do so, you need to connect to the mongos. Enter the following commands:

```
C:\Windows\system32>cd c:\practicalmongodb\bin
c:\practicalmongodb\bin>mongo localhost:27021
MongoDB shell version: 3.0.4
connecting to: localhost:27021/test
mongos>
```

Before the shard is added to the cluster you need to delete the testdb database:

```
mongos> use testdb
switched to db testdb
mongos> db.dropDatabase()
{ "dropped" : "testdb", "ok" : 1 }
mongos>
```

Next, add the Shard2 shard using the following steps:

```
mongos> use admin
switched to db admin
mongos> db.runCommand({addshard: "localhost:27025", allowlocal: true})
{ "shardAdded" : "shard0002", "ok" : 1 }
mongos>
```

If you try adding the removed shard without removing the testdb database, it will give the following error:

```
mongos>db.runCommand({addshard: "localhost:27025", allowlocal: true})
{
        "ok" : 0,
        "errmsg" : "can't add shard localhost:27025 because a local database 'testdb' exists
        in another shard0000:localhost:27023"}
```

In order to ensure that all the three shards are present in the cluster, run the following command:

```
mongos> db.runCommand({listshards:1})
{
        "shards" : [
                {
                        "_id" : "shard0000",
                        "host" : "localhost:27023"
                },      {
                        "_id" : "shard0001",
                        "host" : "localhost:27024"
                },      {
                        "_id" : "shard0002",
                        "host" : "localhost:27025"
                }
        ],      "ok" : 1}
```

Tagging

By the end of the above steps you have your sharded cluster with a config server, three shards, and a mongos up and running. Next, connect to the mongos at 30999 port and configdb at 27022 in a new terminal window:

```
C:\ >cd c:\practicalmongodb\bin
c:\ practicalmongodb\bin>mongos --port 30999 --configdb localhost:27022
2015-07-13T23:24:39.674-0700 W SHARDING running with 1 config server should be done only for
testing purposes and is not recommended for production
.................................
2015-07-13T23:24:39.931-0700 I SHARDING [Balancer] distributed lock 'balancer /ANOC9:30999:
1429851279:41' unlocked..
```

Next, start a new terminal window, connect to the mongos, and enable sharding on the collections:

```
C:\ >cd c:\practicalmongodb\bin
c:\practicalmongodb\bin>mongo localhost:27021
MongoDB shell version: 3.0.4
connecting to: localhost:27021/test
mongos> show dbs
admin    (empty)
config   0.016GB
testdb   0.078GB
mongos> conn=new Mongo("localhost:30999")
connection to localhost:30999
mongos> db=conn.getDB("movies")
movies
mongos> sh.enableSharding("movies")
{ "ok" : 1 }
mongos> sh.shardCollection("movies.drama", {originality:1})
{ "collectionsharded" : "movies.hindi", "ok" : 1 }
mongos> sh.shardCollection("movies.action", {distribution:1})
{ "collectionsharded" : "movies.action", "ok" : 1 }
mongos> sh.shardCollection("movies.comedy", {collections:1})
{ "collectionsharded" : "movies.comedy", "ok" : 1 }
mongos>
```

The steps are as follows:

1. Connect to the mongos console.

2. View the running databases connected to the mongos instance running at port 30999.

3. Get reference to the database movies.

4. Enable sharding of the database movies.

5. Shard the collection movies.drama by shard key originality.

6. Shard the collection movies.action by shard key distribution.

7. Shard the collection movies.comedy by shard key collections.

Next, insert some data in the collections, using the following sequence of commands:

```
mongos>for(var i=0;i<100000;i++){db.drama.insert({originality:Math.random(), count:i,
time:new Date()});}
mongos>for(var i=0;i<100000;i++){db.action.insert({distribution:Math.random(),
count:i, time:new Date()});}
mongos>for(var i=0;i<100000;i++) {db.comedy.insert({collections:Math.random(), count:i,
time:new Date()});}
mongos>
```

By the end of the above step you have three shards and three collections with sharding enabled on the collections. Next you will see how data is distributed across the shards.

Switch to configdb:

```
mongos> use config
switched to db config
mongos>
```

You can use chunks.find to look at how the chunks are distributed:

```
mongos> db.chunks.find({ns:"movies.drama"}, {shard:1, _id:0}).sort({shard:1})
{ "shard" : "shard0000" }
{ "shard" : "shard0000" }
{ "shard" : "shard0000" }
{ "shard" : "shard0000" }
{ "shard" : "shard0001" }
{ "shard" : "shard0001" }
{ "shard" : "shard0001" }
{ "shard" : "shard0002" }
{ "shard" : "shard0002" }
{ "shard" : "shard0002" }
mongos> db.chunks.find({ns:"movies.action"}, {shard:1, _id:0}).sort({shard:1})
{ "shard" : "shard0000" }
{ "shard" : "shard0000" }
{ "shard" : "shard0000" }
{ "shard" : "shard0000" }
{ "shard" : "shard0000" }
{ "shard" : "shard0001" }
{ "shard" : "shard0001" }
{ "shard" : "shard0001" }
{ "shard" : "shard0001" }
{ "shard" : "shard0002" }
{ "shard" : "shard0002" }
{ "shard" : "shard0002" }
{ "shard" : "shard0002" }
mongos> db.chunks.find({ns:"movies.comedy"}, {shard:1, _id:0}).sort({shard:1})
{ "shard" : "shard0000" }
{ "shard" : "shard0000" }
{ "shard" : "shard0000" }
{ "shard" : "shard0000" }
{ "shard" : "shard0001" }
```

```
{ "shard" : "shard0001" }
{ "shard" : "shard0001" }
{ "shard" : "shard0002" }
{ "shard" : "shard0002" }
{ "shard" : "shard0002" }
mongos>
```

As you can see, the chunks are pretty evenly spread out amongst the shards. See Figure 7-22.

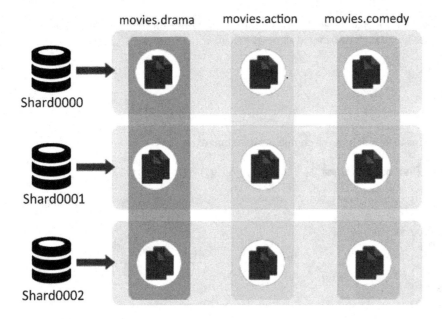

movies.drama   movies.action   movies.comedy

Shard0000

Shard0001

Shard0002

Figure 7-22. *Distribution without tagging*

Next, you will use tags to separate the collections. The intent of this is to have one collection per shard (i.e. your goal is to have the chunk distribution shown in Table 7-6).

Table 7-6. *Chunk Distribution*

Collection Chunks	On Shard
movies.drama	Shard0000
movies.action	Shard0001
movies.comedy	Shard0002

A **tag** describes the shard's property, which can be anything. Hence you might tag a shard as "slow" or "fast" or "rack space" or "west coast."

In the following example, you will tag the shards as belonging to each of the collection:

```
mongos> sh.addShardTag("shard0000", "dramas")
mongos> sh.addShardTag("shard0001", "actions")
mongos> sh.addShardTag("shard0002", "comedies")
mongos>
```

This signifies the following:

- Put the chunks tagged "dramas" on shard0000.

- Put the chunks tagged "actions" on shard0001.

- And put the chunks tagged "comedies" on shard0002.

Next, you will create rules to tag the collections chunk accordingly.
Rule 1: All chunks created in the movies.drama collection will be tagged as "dramas:"

```
mongos> sh.addTagRange("movies.drama", {originality:MinKey}, {originality:MaxKey}, "dramas")
mongos>
```

The rule uses MinKey, which means negative infinity, and MaxKey, which means positive infinity.
Hence the above rule means mark all of the chunks of the collection movies.drama with the tag "dramas."
Similar to this you will make rules for the other two collections.
Rule 2: All chunks created in the movies.action collection will be tagged as "actions."

```
mongos> sh.addTagRange("movies.action", {distribution:MinKey}, {distribution:MaxKey}, "actions")
mongos>
```

Rule 3: All chunks created in the movies.comedy collection will be tagged as "comedies."

```
mongos> sh.addTagRange("movies.comedy", {collection:MinKey}, {collection:MaxKey}, "comedies")
mongos>
```

You need to wait for the cluster to rebalance so that the chunks are distributed based on the tags and rules defined above. As mentioned, the chunk distribution is an automatic process, so after some time the chunks will automatically be redistributed to implement the changes you have made.
Next, issue chunks.find to vet the chunks organization:

```
mongos> use config
switched to db config
mongos> db.chunks.find({ns:"movies.drama"}, {shard:1, _id:0}).sort({shard:1})
{ "shard" : "shard0000" }
{ "shard" : "shard0000" }
{ "shard" : "shard0000" }
{ "shard" : "shard0000" }
{ "shard" : "shard0000" }
{ "shard" : "shard0000" }
{ "shard" : "shard0000" }
{ "shard" : "shard0000" }
{ "shard" : "shard0000" }
{ "shard" : "shard0000" }
mongos> db.chunks.find({ns:"movies.action"}, {shard:1, _id:0}).sort({shard:1})
```

```
{ "shard" : "shard0001" }
{ "shard" : "shard0001" }
{ "shard" : "shard0001" }
{ "shard" : "shard0001" }
{ "shard" : "shard0001" }
{ "shard" : "shard0001" }
{ "shard" : "shard0001" }
{ "shard" : "shard0001" }
{ "shard" : "shard0001" }
{ "shard" : "shard0001" }
{ "shard" : "shard0001" }
{ "shard" : "shard0001" }
{ "shard" : "shard0001" }
mongos> db.chunks.find({ns:"movies.comedy"}, {shard:1, _id:0}).sort({shard:1})
{ "shard" : "shard0002" }
{ "shard" : "shard0002" }
{ "shard" : "shard0002" }
{ "shard" : "shard0002" }
{ "shard" : "shard0002" }
{ "shard" : "shard0002" }
{ "shard" : "shard0002" }
{ "shard" : "shard0002" }
{ "shard" : "shard0002" }
{ "shard" : "shard0002" }
mongos>
```

Thus the collection chunks have been redistributed based on the tags and rules defined (Figure 7-23).

Figure 7-23. *Distribution with tagging*

Scaling with Tagging

Next, you will look at how to scale with tagging. Let's change the scenario. Let's assume the collection movies.action needs two servers for its data. Since you have only three shards, this means the other two collection's data need to be moved to one shard.

In this scenario, you will change the tagging of the shards. You will add the tag "comedies" to Shard0 and remove the tag from Shard2, and further add the tag "actions" to Shard2.

This means that the chunks tagged "comedies" will be moved to Shard0 and chunks tagged "actions" will be spread to Shard2.

You first move the collection movies.comedy chunk to Shard0 and remove the same from Shard2:

```
mongos> sh.addShardTag("shard0000","comedies")
mongos> sh.removeShardTag("shard0002","comedies")
```

Next, you add the tag "actions" to Shard2, so that movies.action chunks are spread across Shard2 also:

```
mongos> sh.addShardTag("shard0002","actions")
```

Re-issuing the find command after some time will show the following results:

```
mongos> db.chunks.find({ns:"movies.drama"}, {shard:1, _id:0}).sort({shard:1})
{ "shard" : "shard0000" }
{ "shard" : "shard0000" }
{ "shard" : "shard0000" }
{ "shard" : "shard0000" }
{ "shard" : "shard0000" }
{ "shard" : "shard0000" }
{ "shard" : "shard0000" }
{ "shard" : "shard0000" }
{ "shard" : "shard0000" }
{ "shard" : "shard0000" }
mongos> db.chunks.find({ns:"movies.action"}, {shard:1, _id:0}).sort({shard:1})
{ "shard" : "shard0001" }
{ "shard" : "shard0001" }
{ "shard" : "shard0001" }
{ "shard" : "shard0001" }
{ "shard" : "shard0001" }
{ "shard" : "shard0001" }
{ "shard" : "shard0001" }
{ "shard" : "shard0002" }
{ "shard" : "shard0002" }
{ "shard" : "shard0002" }
{ "shard" : "shard0002" }
{ "shard" : "shard0002" }
{ "shard" : "shard0002" }
mongos> db.chunks.find({ns:"movies.comedy"}, {shard:1, _id:0}).sort({shard:1})
{ "shard" : "shard0000" }
{ "shard" : "shard0000" }
{ "shard" : "shard0000" }
{ "shard" : "shard0000" }
{ "shard" : "shard0000" }
```

```
{ "shard" : "shard0000" }
{ "shard" : "shard0000" }
{ "shard" : "shard0000" }
{ "shard" : "shard0000" }
{ "shard" : "shard0000" }
mongos>
```

The chunks have been redistributed reflecting the changes made (Figure 7-24).

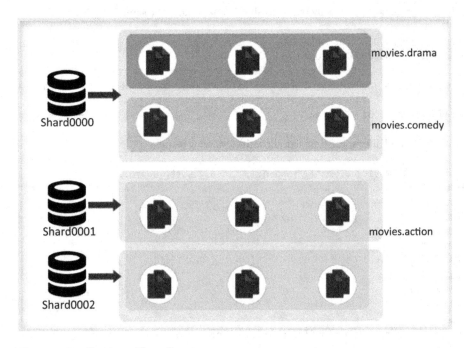

Figure 7-24. *Tagging with scaling*

Multiple Tags

You can have multiple tags associated with the shards. Let's add two different tags to the shards.

Say you want to distribute the writes based on the disk. You have one shard that has a spinning disk and the other has a SSD (solid state drive). You want to redirect 50% of the writes to the shard with SSD and the remaining to the one with the spinning disk.

First, tag the shards based on these properties:

```
mongos> sh.addShardTag("shard0001", "spinning")
mongos> sh.addShardTag("shard0002", "ssd")
mongos>
```

Let's further assume you have a `distribution` field of the `movies.action` collection that you will be using as the shard key. The `distribution` field value is between 0 and 1. Next, you want to say, "If distribution < .5, send this to the spinning disk. If distribution >= .5, send to the SSD." So you define the rules as follows:

```
mongos>sh.addTagRange("movies.action", {distribution:MinKey} ,{distribution:.5} ,"spinning")
mongos>sh.addTagRange("movies.action" ,{distribution:.5} ,{distribution:MaxKey},"ssd")
mongos>
```

Now documents with distribution < .5 will be written to the spinning shard and the others will be written to the SSD disk shard.

With tagging you can control the type of load that each newly added server will get.

Points to Remember When Importing Data in a ShardedEnvironment

Here are some points to keep in mind when importing data.

Pre-Splitting of the Data

Instead of leaving the choice of chunks creation with MongoDB, you can tell MongoDB how to do so using the following command:

```
db.runCommand( { split : "practicalmongodb.mycollection" , middle : { shardkey : value } } );
```

Post this you can also let MongoDB know which chunks goes to which node.

For all this you will need knowledge of the data you will be imported to the database. And this also depends on the use case you are aiming to solve and how the data is being read by your application. When deciding where to place the chunk, keep things like data locality in mind.

Deciding on the Chunk Size

You need to keep the following points in mind when deciding on the chunk size:

1. If the size is too small, the data will be distributed evenly but it will end up having more frequent migrations, which will be an expensive operation at the mongos layer.

2. If the size is large, it will lead to less migration, reducing the expense at the mongos layer, but you will end up with uneven data distribution.

Choosing a Good Shard Key

It's very essential to pick a good shard key for good distribution of data among nodes of the shard cluster.

Monitoring for Sharding

In addition to the normal monitoring and analysis that is done for other MongoDB instances, the sharding cluster requires an additional monitoring to ensure that all its operations are functioning appropriately and the data is distributed effectively among the nodes. In this section, you will see what monitoring you should do for the proper functioning of the sharding cluster.

Monitoring the Config Servers

The config server, as you know by now, stores the metadata of the sharded cluster. The mongos caches the data and routes the request to the respective shards. If the config server goes down but there's a running mongos instance, there's no immediate impact on the shard cluster and it will remain available for a while. However, you won't be able to perform operations like chunk migration or restart a new mongos. In the long run, the unavailability of the config server can severely impact the availability of the cluster. To ensure that the cluster remains balanced and available, you should monitor the config servers.

Monitoring the Shard Status Balancing and Chunk Distribution

For a most effective sharded cluster deployment, it's required that the chunks be distributed evenly among the shards. As you know by now, this is done automatically by MongoDB using a background process. You need to monitor the shard status to ensure that the process is working effectively. For this, you can use the db.printShardingStatus() or sh.status() command in the mongos mongo shell to ensure that the process is working effectively.

Monitoring the Lock Status

In almost all cases the balancer releases its locks automatically after completing its process, but you need to check the lock status of the database in order to ensure there's no long lasting lock because this can block future balancing, which will affect the availability of the cluster. Issue the following from mongos mongo to check the lock status:

```
use config
db.locks.find()
```

Production Cluster Architecture

In this section, you will look at the production cluster architecture. In order to understand it, let's consider a very generic use case of a social networking application where the user can create a circle of friends and can share their comments or pictures across the group. The user can also comment or like her friend's comments or pictures. The users are geographically distributed.

The application requirement is immediate availability across geographies of all the comments; data should be redundant so that the user's comments, posts and pictures are not lost; and it should be highly available. So the application's production cluster should have the following components:

1. At least two mongos instance, but you can have more as per need.

2. Three config servers, each on a separate system.

3. Two or more replica sets serving as shards. The replica sets are distributed across geographies with read concern set to nearest. See Figure 7-25.

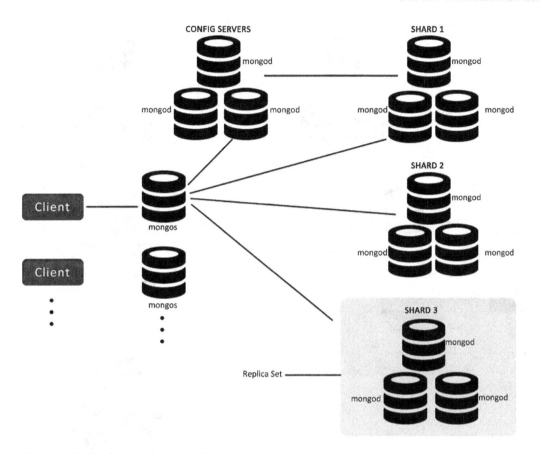

Figure 7-25. *Production cluster architecture*

Now let's look at the possible failure scenarios in MongoDB production deployment and its impact on the environment.

Scenario 1

Mongos become unavailable: The application server where mongos has gone down will not be able to communicate with the cluster but it will not lead to any data loss since the mongos don't maintain any data of its own. The mongos can restart, and while restarting, it can sync up with the config servers to cache the cluster metadata, and the application can normally start its operations (Figure 7-26).

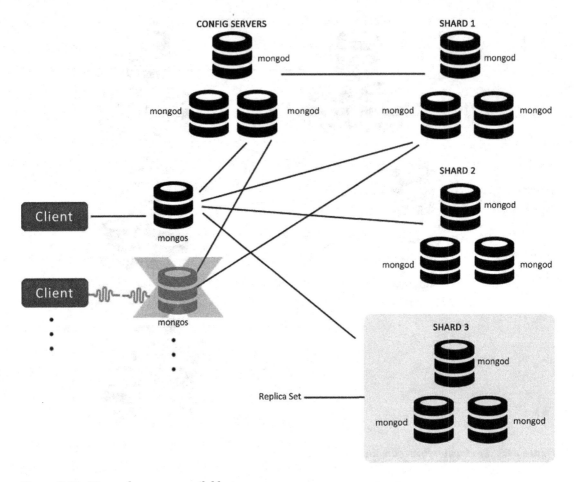

Figure 7-26. *Mongos become unavailable*

Scenario 2

One of the mongod of the replica set becomes unavailable in a shard: Since you used replica sets to provide high availability, there is no data loss. If a primary node is down, a new primary is chosen, whereas if it's a secondary node, then it is disconnected and the functioning continues normally (Figure 7-27).

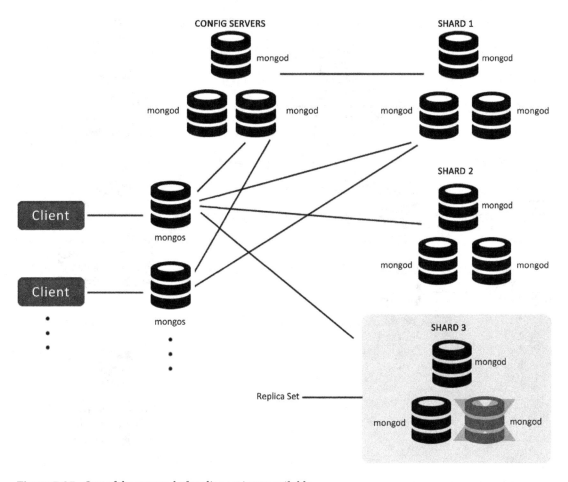

Figure 7-27. *One of the mongod of replica set is unavailable*

The only difference is that the duplication of the data is reduced, making the system little weak, so you should in parallel check if the mongod is recoverable. If it is, it should be recovered and restarted whereas if it's non-recoverable, you need to create a new replica set and replace it as soon as possible.

Scenario 3

If one of the shard becomes unavailable: In this scenario, the data on the shard will be unavailable, but the other shards will be available, so it won't stop the application. The application can continue with its read/write operations; however, the partial results must be dealt with within the application. In parallel, the shard should attempt to recover as soon as possible (Figure 7-28).

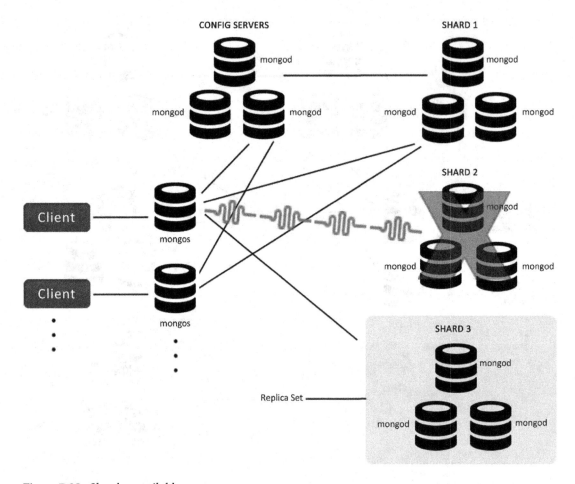

Figure 7-28. *Shard unavailable*

Scenario 4

Only one config server is available out of three: In this scenario, although the cluster will become read-only, it will not serve any operations that might lead to changes in the cluster structure, thereby leading to a change of metadata such as chunk migration or chunk splitting. The config servers should be replaced ASAP because if all config servers become unavailable, this will lead to an inoperable cluster (Figure 7-29).

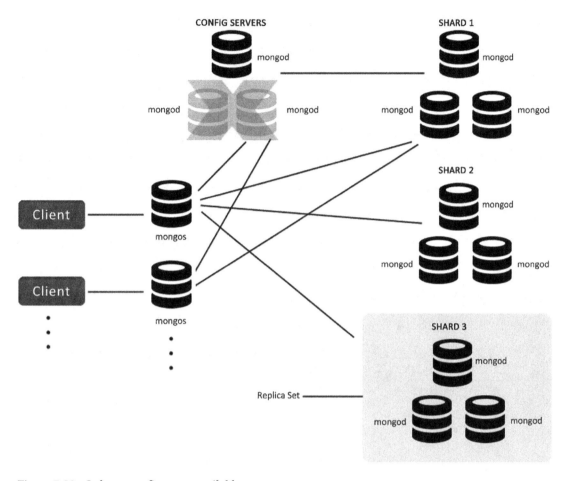

Figure 7-29. *Only one config server available*

Summary

In this chapter you covered the core processes and tools, standalone deployment, sharding concepts, replication concepts, and production deployment. You also looked at how HA can be achieved.

In the following chapter, you will see how data is stored under the hood, how writes happens using journaling, what is GridFS used for, and the different types of indexes available in MongoDB.

CHAPTER 8

MongoDB Explained

"MongoDB explained covers deep-dive concepts of what happens under the hood in MongoDB."

In this chapter, you will learn how data is stored in MongoDB and how writes happen using journaling. Finally, you will learn about GridFS and the different types of indexes available in MongoDB.

Data Storage Engine

In the previous chapter, you looked at the core services that are deployed as part of MongoDB; you also looked at replica sets and sharding. In this section, we will talk about the data storage engine.

MongoDB uses MMAP as its default storage engine. This engine works with memory-mapped files. Memory-mapped files are data files that are placed by the operating system in memory using the mmap() system call. mmap is a feature of OS that maps a file on the disk into virtual memory.

Virtual memory is not equivalent to physical memory. Virtual memory is space on the computer's hard disk that is used in conjunction with physical RAM.

MongoDB uses memory-mapped files for any data interaction or data management activity. As and when the documents are accessed, the data files are memory mapped to the memory. MongoDB allows the OS to control the memory mapping and allocate the maximum amount of RAM. Doing this results in minimal effort and coding at MongoDB level. The caching is done based on LRU behavior wherein the least recently used files are moved out to disk from the working set, making space for the new recently and frequently used pages.

However, this method comes with its own drawbacks. For instance, MongoDB has no control over what data to keep in memory and what to remove. So every server restart will lead to a page fault because every page that is accessed will not be available in the working set, leading to a long data retrieval time.

MongoDB also has no control over prioritizing the content of the memory. Given an evacuation situation, it can mention what content needs to be maintained in the cache and what can be removed. For example, if a read is fired on a large collection that is not indexed, it might result in loading the entire collection to memory, which might lead to evacuation of the RAM contents including removal of indexes of other collections that might be very important. This lack of control might also result in shrinking the cache assigned to MongoDB when any external process outside MongoDB tries to access a large portion of memory; this eventually will lead to slowness in the MongoDB response.

With the release of version 3.0, MongoDB comes along with a pluggable storage engine API wherein it enables you to select between the storage engines based on the workload, application need, and available infrastructure.

The vision behind the pluggable storage engine layer is to have one data model, one querying language, and one set of operational concerns, but under the hood many storage engine options optimized for different use cases, as shown in Figure 8-1.

© Shakuntala Gupta Edward, Navin Sabharwal 2015
S.G. Edward and N. Sabharwal, *Practical MongoDB*, DOI 10.1007/978-1-4842-0647-8_8

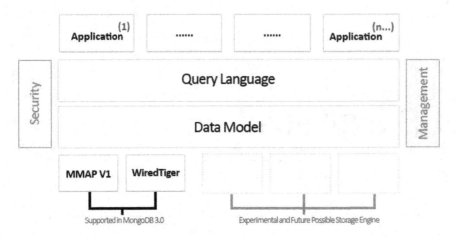

Figure 8-1. *Pluggable storage engine API*

The pluggable storage engine feature also provides flexibility in terms of deployments wherein multiple types of storage engines can coexist in the same deployment.

MongoDB version 3.0 ships with two storage engines.

The default, MMAPv1, is an improved version of the MMAP engine used in the prior versions. The updated MongoDB MMAPv1 storage engine implements collection-level concurrency control. This storage engine excels at workloads with high volume reads, inserts, and in-place updates.

The new WiredTiger storage engine was developed by the architects of Berkeley DB, the most widely deployed embedded data management software in the world. WiredTiger scales on modern multi-CPU architectures. It is designed to take advantage of modern hardware with multi-core CPUs and more RAM.

WIredTiger stores data in compressed fomat on the disk. Compression reduces the data size by up to 70% (disk only) and index size by up to 50% (disk and memory both) depending on the compression algorithm used. In addition to reduced storage space, compression enables much higher I/O scalability as fewer bits are read from disk. It provides significant benefits in the areas of greater hardware utilization, lower storage costs, and more predictable performance.

The following compression algorithms are available to choose from:

- Snappy is the default, which is used for documents and journals. It provides a good compression ratio with little CPU overhead. Depending on data types, the compression ratio is somewhere around 70%.

- zlib provides extremely good compression but at the expense of extra CPU overhead.

- Prefix compression is the default used for indexes, reducing the in-memory footprint of index storage by around 50% (workload dependent) and freeing up more of the working set for frequently accessed documents.

Administrators can modify the default compression settings for all collections and indexes. Compression is also configurable on a per-collection and per-index basis during collection and index creation.

WiredTiger also provides granular document-level concurrency. Writes are no longer blocked by other writes unless they are accessing the same document. Thus it supports concurrent access by readers and writers to the documents in a collection. Clients can read documents while write operations are in progress, and multiple threads can modify different documents in a collection at the same time. Thus it excels for write-intensive workloads (7-10X improvement in write performance).

Higher concurrency also drives infrastructure simplification. Applications can fully utilize available server resources, simplifying the architecture needed to meet performance SLAs. With the more coarse grained database-level locking of previous MongoDB generations, users often had to implement sharding in order to scale workloads stalled by a single write lock to the database, even when sufficient memory, I/O bandwidth, and disk capacity was still available in the host system. Greater system utilization enabled by fine-grained concurrency reduces this overhead, eliminating unnecessary cost and management load.

This storage engine provides control to you per collection per index level to decide on what to compress and what not to compress.

The WiredTiger storage engine is only available with 64-bit MongoDB.

WiredTiger manages data through its cache. The WiredTiger storage engine gives more control of memory by allowing you to configure how much RAM to allocate to the WiredTiger cache, defaulting to either 1GB or 50% of available memory, whichever is larger.

You will next briefly look at how the data is stored on the disk.

Data File (Relevant for MMAPv1)

First, let's examine the data file. As you have seen, under the core services the default data directory used by mongod is /data/db/.

Under this directory there are separate files for every database. Each database has a single .ns file and multiple data files with monotonically increasing numeric extensions.

For example, if you create a database called mydbpoc, it will be stored in the following files: mydb.ns, mydb.1, mydb.2, and so on, as shown in Figure 8-2.

Name ▲	Date modified	Type	Size
_tmp	7/10/2015 12:41 AM	File folder	
journal	7/12/2015 11:39 PM	File folder	
admin.0	7/2/2015 11:55 PM	0 File	65,536 KB
admin.ns	7/2/2015 11:55 PM	NS File	16,384 KB
local.0	7/2/2015 11:54 PM	0 File	65,536 KB
local.ns	7/2/2015 11:54 PM	NS File	16,384 KB
mongod.lock	7/12/2015 11:39 PM	LOCK File	0 KB
mydb.0	7/5/2015 10:41 PM	0 File	65,536 KB
mydb.1	7/5/2015 11:35 PM	1 File	131,072 KB
mydb.2	7/5/2015 11:42 PM	2 File	262,144 KB
mydb.ns	7/5/2015 10:41 PM	NS File	16,384 KB
storage.bson	7/2/2015 11:54 PM	BSON File	1 KB
test.0	7/10/2015 12:41 AM	0 File	65,536 KB
test.ns	7/10/2015 12:41 AM	NS File	16,384 KB

Figure 8-2. *Data files*

For each new numeric data file for a database, the size will be double the size of the previous number data file. The limit of the file size is 2GB. If the file size has reached 2GB, all subsequent numbered files will remain 2GB in size. This behavior is by design. *This behavior ensures that small databases do not waste too much space on disk, and large databases are mostly kept in contiguous regions on the disk.*

Note that in order to ensure consistent performance, MongoDB preallocates data files. The preallocation happens in the background and is initiated every time a data file is filled. This means that the MongoDB server always attempts to keep an extra, empty data file for every database in order to avoid blocking on file allocation.

If multiple small databases exist on disk, using the `storage.mmapv1.smallFiles` option will reduce the size of these files.

Next, you will see how the data is actually stored under the hood. Doubly linked lists are the key data structure used for storing the data.

Namespace (.ns File)

Within the data files you have data space divided into namespaces, where the namespace can correspond to either a collection or an index.

The metadata of these namespaces are stored in the `.ns` file. If you check your data directory, you will find a file named `[dbname].ns`.

The size of the `.ns` file that is used for storing the metadata is 16MB. This file can be thought of as a big hash table that is partitioned into small buckets, which are approximately 1KB in size.

Each bucket stores metadata specific to a namespace (Figure 8-3).

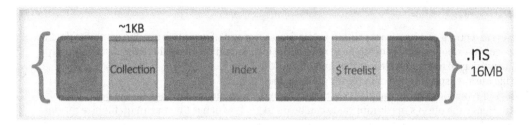

Figure 8-3. *Namespace data structure*

Collection Namespace

As shown in Figure 8-4, the collection namespace bucket contains metadata such as

- Name of the collection
- A few statistics on the collection such as count, size, etc. (This is why whenever a count is issued against the collection it returns quick response.)
- Index details, so it can maintain links to each index created
- A deleted list
- A doubly linked list storing the extent details (it stores pointer to the first and the last extent)

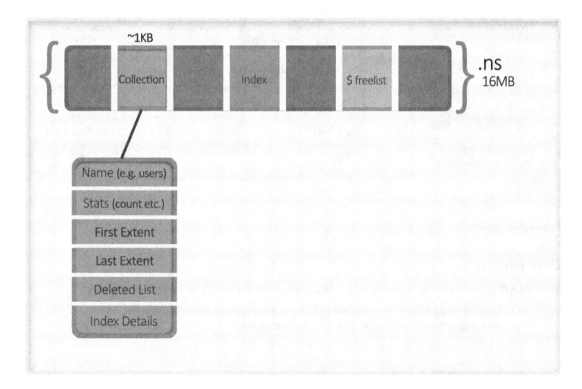

Figure 8-4. *Collection namespace details*

Extent

Extent refers to a group of data records within a data file, so a group of extents forms the complete data for a namespace. An extent uses disk locations to refer to the location on the disk where the data is actually residing. It consists of two parts: file number and offset.

The file number specifies the data file it's pointing to (0, 1, etc.).

Offset is the position within the file (how deep within the file you need to look for the data). The offset size is 4KB. Hence the offset's maximum value can be up to 2^{31}-1, which is the maximum file size the data files can grow to (2048MB or 2 GB).

As shown in Figure 8-5, an extent data structure consists of the following things:

- Location on the disk, which is the file number it is pointing to.

- Since an extent is stored as a doubly linked list element, it has a pointer to the next and the previous extent.

- Once it has the file number it's referring to, the group of the data records within the file it's pointing to are further stored as doubly linked list. Hence it maintains a pointer to the first data record and the last data record of the data block it's pointing to, which are nothing but the offsets within the file (how deep within the file the data is stored).

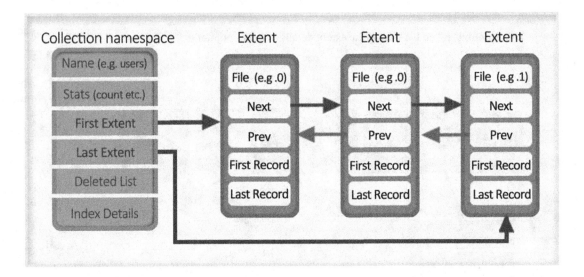

Figure 8-5. *Extent*

Data Record

Next you will look at the data record structure. The data structure consists of the following details:

- Since the data record structure is an element of the extent's doubly linked list, it stores information of the previous and the next record.

- It has length with headers.

- The data block.

The data block can have either a BTree Bucket (in case of an index namespace) or a BSON object. You will be looking into the BTree structure in a while.

The BSON object corresponds to the actual data for the collection. The size of the BSON object need not be same as the data block. Power of 2-sized allocation is used by default so that every document is stored in a space that contains the document plus extra space or padding. This design decision is useful to avoid movement of an object from one block to another whenever an update leads to a change in the object size.

MongoDB supports multiple allocation strategies, which determine how to add padding to a document (Figure 8-6). As in-place updates are more efficient than relocations, all padding strategies trade extra space for increased efficiency and decreased fragmentation. Different workloads are supported by different strategies. For instance, exact fit allocation is ideal for collections with insert-only workloads where the size is fixed and never varies, whereas power of 2 allocations are efficient for insert/update/delete workloads.

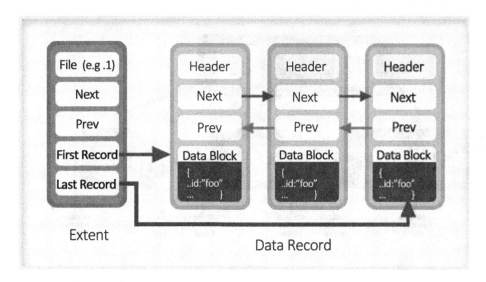

Figure 8-6. *Record data structure*

Deleted List

The deleted list stores details of the extent whose data has been deleted or moved (movement whenever an update has caused change in size, leading to non-fitment of data in the allocated space).

The size of the record determines the bucket in which the free extent needs to be placed. Basically these are bucketed single linked lists. When a new extent is required for fitting the data for the namespace, it will first search the free list to check whether any appropriate size extent is available.

In Summary

Hence you can assume the data files (files with numeric extensions) to be divided across different collection namespaces where extents of the namespace specify the range of data from the data file belonging to that respective collection.

Having understood how the data is stored, now let's see how db.users.find() works.

It will first check the mydbpoc.ns file to reach the users' namespace and find out the first extent it's pointing to. It'll follow the first extent link to the first record, and following the next record pointer, it will read the data records of the first extent until the last record is reached. Then it will follow the next extent pointer to read its data records in a similar fashion. This pattern is followed until the last extent data records are read.

$freelist

The .ns file has a special namespace called $freelist for extents. $freelist keeps track of the extents that are no longer used, such as extents of a dropped index or collection.

Indexes BTree

Now let's look at how the indexes are stored. The BTree structure is used for storing the indexes. A BTree is shown in Figure 8-7.

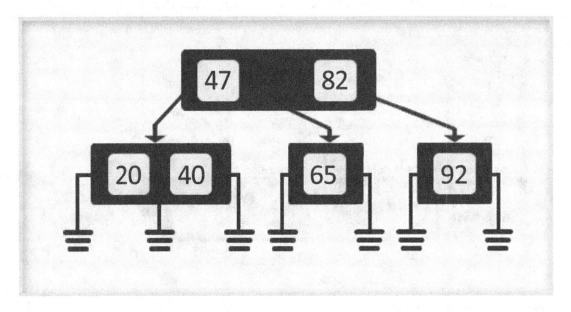

Figure 8-7. *BTree*

In a standard implementation of BTree, whenever a new key is inserted in a BTree, the default behavior is as shown in Figure 8-8.

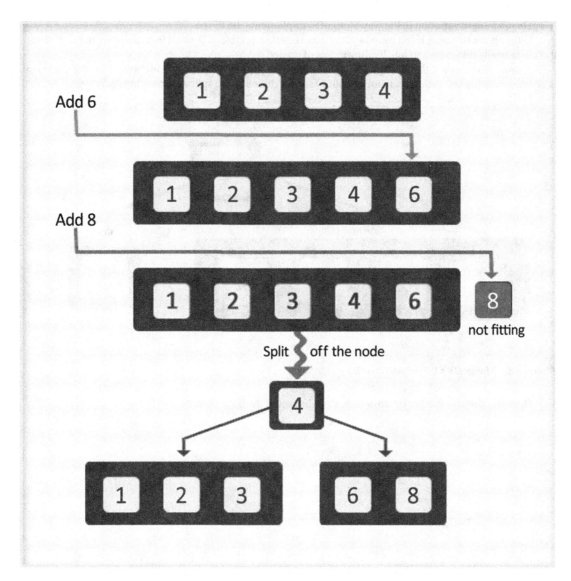

Figure 8-8. *B-Tree standard implementation*

There's a slight variation in the way MongoDB implements the BTree.

In the above scenario, if you have keys such as Timestamp, ObjectID, or an incrementing number, then the buckets will always be half full, leading to lots of wasted space.

In order to overcome this, MongoDB has modified this slightly. Whenever it identifies that the index key is an incrementing key, rather than doing a 50/50 split, it does a 90/10 split as shown in Figure 8-9.

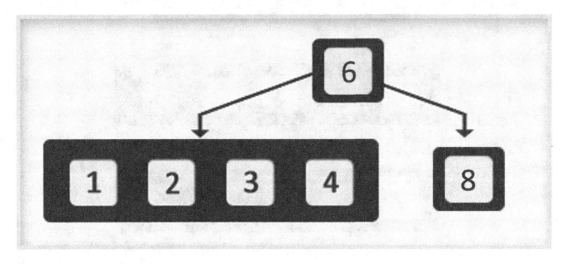

Figure 8-9. *MongoDB's B-Tree 90/10 split*

Figure 8-10 shows the bucket structure. Each bucket of the BTree is of 8KB.

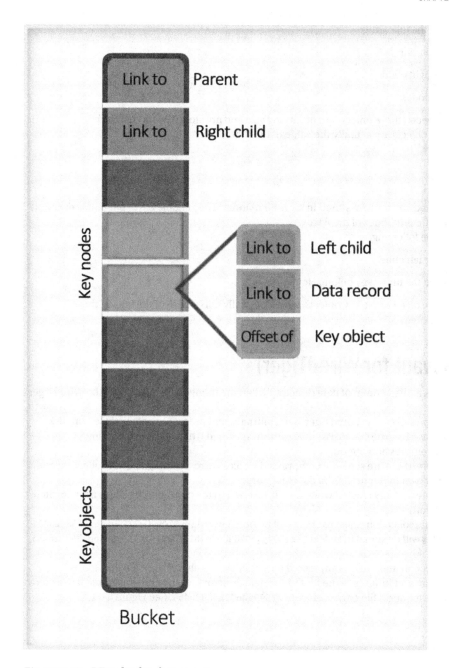

Figure 8-10. *BTree bucket data structure*

The bucket consists of the following:

- Pointer to the parent

- Pointer to the right child

- Pointer to key nodes

- A list of key objects (these objects are of varying size and are stored in an unsorted manner; these objects are actually the value of the index keys)

Key Nodes

Key nodes are nodes of a fixed size and are stored in a sorted manner. They enable easy split and movement of the elements between different nodes of the BTree.

A key node contains the following:

- A pointer to the left child

- The data record the index key belongs to

- A key offset (the offset of the key objects, which basically tells where in the bucket the key's value is stored)

Data File (Relevant for WiredTiger)

In this section, you will look at the content of data directory when the mongod is started with the WiredTiger storage engine.

When the storage option selected is WiredTiger, data, journals, and indexes are compressed on disk. The compression is done based on the compression algorithm specified when starting the mongod.

Snappy is the default compression option.

Under the data directory, there are separate compressed wt files corresponding to each collection and indexes. Journals have their own folder under the data directory.

The compressed files are actually created when data is inserted in the collection (the files are allocated at write time, no preallocation).

For example, if you create collection called users, it will be stored in `collection-0-2259994602858926461` files and the associated index will be stored in `index-1-2259994602858926461`, `index-2-2259994602858926461`, and so on.

In addition to the collection and index compressed files, there is a `_mdb_catalog` file that stores metadata mapping collection and indexes to the files in the data directory. In the above example it will store mapping of collection users to the wt file `collection-0-2259994602858926461`. See Figure 8-11.

Name ^	Date modified	Type	Size
journal	7/19/2015 10:12 PM	File folder	
_mdb_catalog	7/19/2015 10:46 PM	WT File	36 KB
collection-0--2259994602858926461	7/19/2015 10:13 PM	WT File	16 KB
collection-2--2259994602858926461	7/19/2015 10:13 PM	WT File	16 KB
collection-4--2259994602858926461	7/19/2015 10:24 PM	WT File	16 KB
collection-6--2259994602858926461	7/19/2015 10:24 PM	WT File	16 KB
collection-8--2259994602858926461	7/19/2015 10:26 PM	WT File	16 KB
collection-10--2259994602858926461	7/19/2015 10:27 PM	WT File	16 KB
collection-18--2259994602858926461	7/19/2015 10:39 PM	WT File	492 KB
index-1--2259994602858926461	7/19/2015 10:13 PM	WT File	16 KB
index-3--2259994602858926461	7/19/2015 10:13 PM	WT File	16 KB
index-5--2259994602858926461	7/19/2015 10:24 PM	WT File	16 KB
index-7--2259994602858926461	7/19/2015 10:24 PM	WT File	16 KB
index-9--2259994602858926461	7/19/2015 10:26 PM	WT File	16 KB
index-11--2259994602858926461	7/19/2015 10:27 PM	WT File	16 KB
index-19--2259994602858926461	7/19/2015 10:39 PM	WT File	172 KB
index-20--2259994602858926461	7/19/2015 10:43 PM	WT File	92 KB
mongod.lock	7/19/2015 10:12 PM	LOCK File	1 KB
sizeStorer	7/19/2015 10:47 PM	WT File	36 KB
storage	7/19/2015 10:12 PM	BSON File	1 KB
WiredTiger	7/19/2015 10:12 PM	File	1 KB
WiredTiger	7/19/2015 10:12 PM	BASECFG File	1 KB
WiredTiger.lock	7/19/2015 10:12 PM	LOCK File	1 KB
WiredTiger.turtle	7/19/2015 10:48 PM	TURTLE File	1 KB
WiredTiger	7/19/2015 10:48 PM	WT File	68 KB

Figure 8-11. *WiredTiger Data folder*

Separate volumes can be specified for storing indexes.

When specifying the DBPath you need to ensure that the directory corresponds to the storage engine, which is specified using the –storageEngine option when starting the mongod. The mongod will fail to start if the dbpath contains files created by a storage engine other than the one specified using the –storageEngine option. So if MMAPv1 files are found in DBPath, then WT will fail to start.

Internally, WiredTiger uses the traditional B+ tree structure for storing and managing data but that's where the similarity ends. Unlike B+ tree, it doesn't support in-place updates.

WiredTiger cache is used for any read/write operations on the data. The trees in cache are optimized for in-memory access.

Reads and Writes

You will briefly look at how the reads and writes happen. As mentioned, when MongoDB updates and reads from the DB, it is actually reading and writing to memory.

If a modification operation in the MongoDB MMAPv1 storage engine increases the record size bigger then the space allocated for it, then the entire record will be moved to a much bigger space with extra padding bytes. By default, MongoDB uses power of 2-sized allocations so that every document in MongoDB is stored in a record that contains the document itself and extra space (padding). Padding allows the document to grow as the result of updates while minimizing the likelihood of reallocations. Once the record is moved, the space that was originally occupied is freed up and will be tracked as free lists of different size. As mentioned, it's the $freelist namespace in the .ns file.

In the MMAPv1 storage engine, as objects are deleted, modified, or created, fragmentation will occur over time, which will affect the performance. The compact command should be executed to move the fragmented data into contiguous spaces.

Every 60 seconds the files in RAM are flushed to disk. To prevent data loss in the event of a power failure, the default is to run with journaling switched on. The behavior of journal is dependent on the configured storage engine.

The MMAPv1 journal file is flushed to disk every 100ms, and if there is power loss, it is used to bring the database back to a consistent state.

In WiredTiger, the data in the cache is stored in a B+ tree structure which is optimized for in-memory. The cache maintains an on-disk page image in association with an index, which is used to identify where the data being asked for actually resides within the page (see Figure 8-12).

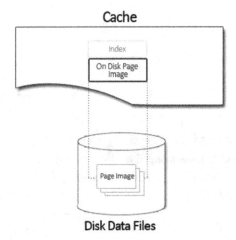

Figure 8-12. *WiredTiger cache*

The write operation in WiredTiger never updates in-place.

Whenever an operation is issued to WiredTiger, internally it's broken into multiple transactions wherein each transaction works within the context of an in-memory snapshot. The snapshot is of the committed version before the transactions started. Writers can create new versions concurrent with the readers.

The write operations do not change the page; instead the updates are layered on top of the page. A skipList data structure is used to maintain all the updates, where the most recent update is on the top. Thus, whenever a user reads/writes the data, the index checks whether a skiplist exists. If a skiplist is not there, it returns data from the on-disk page image. If skiplist exists, the data at the head of the list is returned to the threads, which then update the data. Once a commit is performed, the updated data is added to the head of the list and the pointers are adjusted accordingly. This way multiple users can access data concurrently without any conflict. The conflict occurs only when multiple threads are trying to update the same record. In that case, one update wins and the other concurrent update needs to retry.

Any changes to the tree structure due to the update, such as splitting the data if the page sizes increase, relocation, etc., are later reconciled by a background process. This accounts for the fast write operations of the WiredTiger engine; the task of data arrangement is left to the background process. See Figure 8-13.

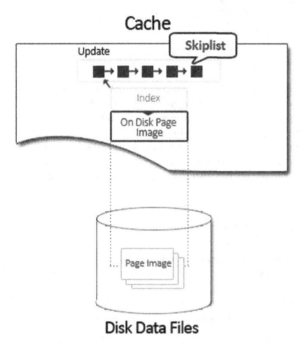

Figure 8-13. *SkipList*

WiredTiger uses the MVCC approach to ensure concurrency control wherein multiple versions of the data are maintained. It also ensures that every thread that is trying to access the data sees the most consistent version of the data. As you have seen, the writes are not in place; instead they are appended on top of the data in a skipList data structure with the most recent update on the top. Threads accessing the data get the latest copy, and they continue to work with that copy uninterrupted until the time they commit. Once they commit, the update is appended at the top of the list and thereafter any thread accessing the data will see that latest update.

This enables multiple threads to access the same data concurrently without any locking or contention. This also enables the writers to create new versions concurrently with the readers. The conflict occurs only when multiple threads are trying to update the same record. In that case, one update wins and the other concurrent update needs to retry.

Figure 8-14 depicts the MVCC in action.

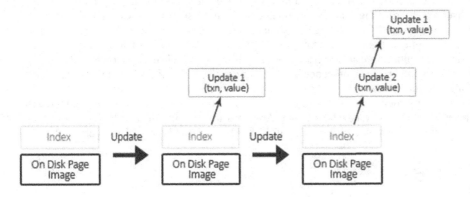

Figure 8-14. *Update in action*

The WiredTiger journal ensures that writes are persisted to disk between checkpoints. WiredTiger uses checkpoints to flush data to disk by default every 60 seconds or after 2GB of data has been written. Thus, by default, WiredTiger can lose up to 60 seconds of writes if running without journaling, although the risk of this loss will typically be much less if using replication for durability. The WiredTiger transaction log is not necessary to keep the data files in a consistent state in the event of an unclean shutdown, and so it is safe to run without journaling enabled, although to ensure durability the "replica safe" write concern should be configured. Another feature of the WiredTiger storage engine is the ability to compress the journal on disk, thereby reducing storage space.

How Data Is Written Using Journaling

In this section you will briefly look at how write operations are performed using journaling.

MongoDB disk writes are lazy, which means if there are 1,000 increments in one second, it will only be written once. The physical writes occurs a few seconds after the operation.

You will now see how an update actually happens in mongod.

As you know, in the MongoDB system, mongod is the primary daemon process. So the disk has the data files and the journal files. See Figure 8-15.

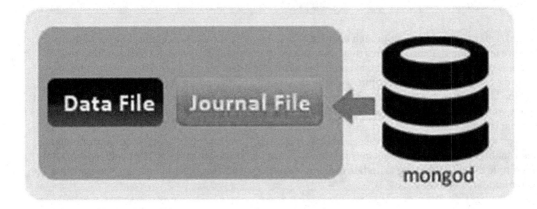

Figure 8-15. *mongod*

When the mongod is started, the data files are mapped to a shared view. In other words, the data file is mapped to a virtual address space. See Figure 8-16.

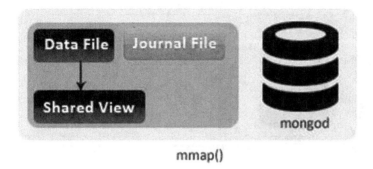

Figure 8-16. *maps to shared view*

Basically, the OS recognizes that your data file is 2000 bytes on disk, so it maps this to memory address 1,000,000 – 1,002,000. Note that the data will not be actually loaded until accessed; the OS just maps it and keeps it.

Until now you still had files backing up the memory. Thus any change in memory will be flushed to the underlying files by the OS.

This is how the mongod works when journaling is not enabled. Every 60 seconds the in-memory changes are flushed by the OS.

In this scenario, let's look at writes with journaling enabled. When journaling is enabled, a second mapping is made to a private view by the mongod.

That's why the virtual memory amount used by mongod doubles when the journaling is enabled. See Figure 8-17.

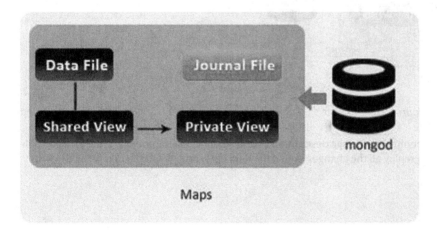

Figure 8-17. *maps to private view*

You can see in Figure 8-17 how the data file is not directly connected to the private view, so the changes will not be flushed from the private view to the disk by the OS.

Let's see what sequence of events happens when a write operation is initiated. When a write operation is initiated it, first it writes to the private view (Figure 8-18).

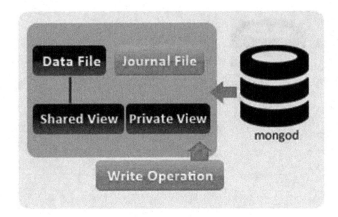

Figure 8-18. *Initiated write operation*

Next, the changes are written to the journal file, appending a brief description of what's changed in the files (Figure 8-19).

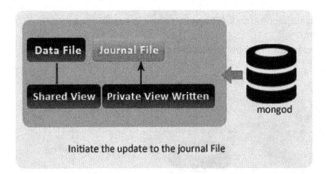

Figure 8-19. *Updating the journal file*

The journal keeps appending the change description as and when it gets the change. If the mongod fails at this point, the journal can replay all the changes even if the data file is not yet modified, making the write safe at this point.

The journal will now replay the logged changes on the shared view (Figure 8-20).

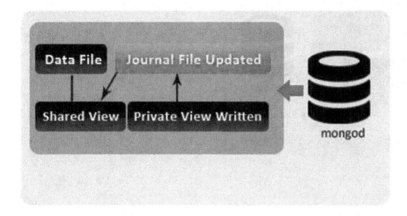

Figure 8-20. *Updating the shared view*

Finally, with a very fast speed the changes are written to the disk. By default, the OS is requested to do this every 60 seconds by the mongod (Figure 8-21).

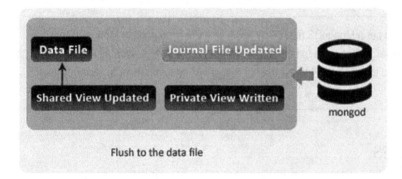

Figure 8-21. *Updating the data file*

In the last step, the shared view is remapped to the private view by the mongod. This is done to prevent the private view from getting too dirty (Figure 8-22).

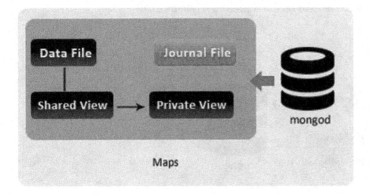

Figure 8-22. *Remapping*

GridFS – The MongoDB File System

You looked at what happens under the hood. You saw that MongoDB stores data in BSON documents. BSON documents have a document size limit of 16MB.

GridFS is MongoDB's specification for handling large files that exceed BSON's document size limit. This section will briefly cover GridFS.

Here "specification" means that it is not a MongoDB feature by itself, so there is no code in MongoDB that implements it. It just specifies how large files need to be handled. The language drivers such as PHP, Python, etc. implement this specification and expose an API to the user of that driver, enabling them to store/retrieve large files in MongoDB.

The Rationale of GridFS

By design, a MongoDB document (i.e. a BSON object) cannot be larger than 16MB. This is to keep performance at an optimum level, and the size is well suited for our needs. For example, 4MB of space might be sufficient for storing a sound clip or a profile picture. However, if the requirement is to store high quality audio or movie clips, or even files that are more than several hundred megabytes in size, MongoDB has you covered by using GridFS.

GridFS specifies a mechanism for dividing a large file among multiple documents. The language driver that implements it, for example, the PHP driver, takes care of the splitting of the stored files (or merging the split chunks when files are to be retrieved) under the hood. The developer using the driver does not need to know of such internal details. This way GridFS allows the developer to store and manipulate files in a transparent and efficient way.

GridFS uses two collections for storing the file. One collection maintains the metadata of the file and the other collection stores the file's data by breaking it into small pieces called chunks. This means the file is divided into smaller chunks and each chunk is stored as a separate document. By default the chunk size is limited to 255KB.

This approach not only makes the storing of data scalable and easy but also makes the range queries easier to use when a specific part of files are retrieved.

Whenver a file is queried in GridFS, the chunks are reassembled as required by the client. This also provides the user with the capability to access arbitrary sections of the files. For example, the user can directly move to the middle of a video file.

The GridFS specification is useful in cases where the file size exceeds the default 16MB limitation of MongoDB BSON document. It's also used for storing files that you need to access without loading the entire file in memory.

GridFSunder the Hood

GridFS is a lightweight specification used for storing files.

There's no "special case" handling done at the MongoDB server for the GridFS requests. All the work is done at the client side.

GridFS enables you to store large files by splitting them up into smaller chunks and storing each of the chunks as separate documents. In addition to these chunks, there's one more document that contains the metadata about the file. Using this metadata information, the chunks are grouped together, forming the complete file.

The storage overhead for the chunks can be kept to a minimum, as MongoDB supports storing binary data in documents.

The two collections that are used by GridFS for storing of large files are by default named as fs.files and fs.chunks, although a different bucket name can be chosen than fs.

The chunks are stored by default in the fs.chunks collection. If required, this can be overridden. Hence all of the data is contained in the fs.chunks collection.

The structure of the individual documents in the chunks collection is pretty simple:

```
{
"_id" : ObjectId("..."),"n" : 0,"data" : BinData("..."),
"files_id" : ObjectId("...")
}
```

The chunk document has the following important keys.

- "_id": This is the unique identifier.

- "files_id": This is unique identifier of the document that contains the metadata related to the chunk.

- "n": This is basically depicting the position of the chunk in the original file.

- "data": This is the actual binary data that constitutes this chunk.

The fs.files collection stores the metadata for each file. Each document within this collection represents a single file in GridFS. In addition to the general metadata information, each document of the collection can contain custom metadata specific to the file it's representing.

The following are the keys that are mandated by the GridFS specification:

- _id: This is the unique identifier of the file.

- Length: This depicts the total bytes that make up the complete content of the file.

- chunkSize: This is the file's chunk size, in bytes. By default it's 255KB, but if needed this can be adjusted.

- uploadDate: This is the timestamp when the file was stored in GridFS.

- md5: This is generated on the server side and is the md5 checksum of the files contents. MongoDB server generates its value by using the filemd5 command, which computes the md5 checksum of the uploaded chunks. This implies that the user can check this value to ensure that the file is uploaded correctly.

A typical fs.files document looks as follows (see also Figure 8-23):

```
{
  "_id" : ObjectId("..."),  "length" : data_number,
  "chunkSize" : data_number,
  "uploadDate" : data_date,
  "md5" : data_string
}
```

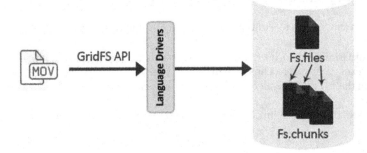

Figure 8-23. *GridFS*

Using GridFS

In this section, you will be using the PyMongo driver to see how you can start using GridFS.

Add Reference to the Filesystem

The first thing that is needed is a reference to the GridFS filesystem:

```
>>> import pymongo
>>> import gridfs
>>>myconn=pymongo.Connection()
>>>mydb=myconn.gridfstest
>>>myfs=gridfs.GridFS(db)
```

write( )

Next you will execute a basic write:

```
>>> with myfs.new_file() as myfp:
        myfp.write('This is my new sample file. It is just grand!')
```

find( )

Using the mongo shell let's see what the underlying collections holds:

```
>>> list(mydb.myfs.files.find())
[{u'length': 38, u'_id': ObjectId('52fdd6189cd2fd08288d5f5c'), u'uploadDate': datetime.
datetime(2014, 11, 04, 4, 20, 41, 800000), u'md5': u'332de5ca08b73218a8777da69293576a',
u'chunkSize': 262144}]
>>> list(mydb.myfs.chunks.find())
[{u'files_id': ObjectId('52fdd6189cd2fd08288d5f5c'), u'_id': ObjectId('52fdd6189cd2fd08288d5
f5d'), u'data': Binary('This is my new sample file. It is just grand!', 0), u'n': 0}]
```

Force Split the File

Let's force split the file. This is done by specifying a small chunkSize while file creation, like so:

```
>>> with myfs.new_file(chunkSize=10) as myfp:
myfp.write('This is second file. I am assuming it will be split into various chunks')
>>>
>>>myfp
<gridfs.grid_file.GridIn object at 0x0000000002AC79B0>
>>>myfp._id
ObjectId('52fdd76e9cd2fd08288d5f5e')
>>> list(mydb.myfs.chunks.find(dict(files_id=myfp._id)))
................
ObjectId('52fdd76e9cd2fd08288d5f65'), u'data': Binary('s', 0), u'n': 6}]
```

read( )

You now know how the file is actually stored in the database. Next, using the client driver, you will now read the file:

```
>>> with myfs.get(myfp._id) as myfp_read:
        print myfp_read.read()
```

"This is second file. I am assuming it will be split into various chunks."

The user need not be aware of the chunks at all. You need to use the APIs exposed by the client to read and write files from GridFS.

Treating GridFS More Like a File System

new_file( ) - Create a new file in GridFS

You can pass any number of keywords as arguments to the new_file(). This will be added in the fs.files document:

```
>>> with myfs.new_file(
        filename='practicalfile.txt',
        content_type='text/plain',
        my_other_attribute=42) as myfp:
                myfp.write('My New file')
>>>myfp
<gridfs.grid_file.GridIn object at 0x0000000002AC7AC8>
>>> db.myfs.files.find_one(dict(_id=myfp._id))
{u'contentType': u'text/plain', u'chunkSize': 262144, u'my_other_attribute': 42,
u'filename': u'practicalfile.txt', u'length': 8, u'uploadDate': datetime.datetime(2014, 11,
04, 9, 01, 32, 800000), u'_id': ObjectId('52fdd8db9cd2fd08288d5f66'), u'md5':
u'681e10aecbafd7dd385fa51798ca0fd6'}
>>>
```

A file can be overwritten using filenames. Since _id is used for indexing files in GridFS, the old file is not removed. Just a file version is maintained.

```
>>> with myfs.new_file(filename='practicalfile.txt', content_type='text/plain') as myfp:
        myfp.write('Overwriting the "My New file"')
```

get_version( )/get_last_version( )

In the above case, get_version or get_last_version can be used to retrieve the file with the filename.

```
>>>myfs.get_last_version('practicalfile.txt').read()
'Overwriting the "My New file"'
>>>myfs.get_version('practicalfile.txt',0).read()
'My New file'
```

You can also list the files in GridFS:

```
>>>myfs.list()
 [u'practicalfile.txt', u'practicalfile2.txt']
```

delete( )

Files can also be removed:

```
>>>myfp=myfs.get_last_version('practicalfile.txt')
>>>myfs.delete(myfp._id)
>>>myfs.list()
[u'practicalfile.txt', u'practicalfile2.txt']
>>>myfs.get_last_version('practicalfile.txt').read()
'My New file'
>>>
```

Note that only one version of practicalfile.txt was removed. You still have a file named practicalfile.txt in the filesystem.

exists( ) and put( )

Next, you will use exists() to check if a file exists and put() to quickly write a short file into GridFS:

```
>>>myfs.exists(myfp._id)
False
>>>myfs.exists(filename='practicalfile.txt')
True
>>>myfs.exists({'filename':'practicalfile.txt'}) # equivalent to above
True
>>>myfs.put('The red fish', filename='typingtest.txt')
ObjectId('52fddbc69cd2fd08288d5f6a')
>>>myfs.get_last_version('typingtest.txt').read()
'The red fish'
>>>
```

Indexing

In this part of the book, you will briefly examine what an index is in the MongoDB context. Following that, we will highlight the various types of indexes available in MongoDB, concluding the section by highlighting the behavior and limitations.

An index is a data structure that speeds up the read operations. In layman terms, it is comparable to a book index where you can reach any chapter by looking in the index for the chapter and jumping directly to the page number rather than scanning the entire book to reach to the chapter, which would be the case if no index existed.

Similarly, an index is defined on fields, which can help in searching for information in a better and efficient manner.

As in other databases, in MongoDB also it's perceived in a similar fashion (it's used for speeding up the find () operation). The type of queries you run help to create efficient indexes for the databases. For example, if most of the queries use a Date field, it would be beneficial to create an index on the Date field. It can be tricky to figure out which index is optimal for your query, but it's worth a try because the queries that otherwise take minutes will return results instantaneously if a proper index is in place.

In MongoDB, an index can be created on any field or sub-field of a document. Before you look at the various types of indexes that can be created in MongoDB, let's list a few core features of the indexes:

- The indexes are defined at the per-collection level. For each collection, there are different sets of indexes.

- Like SQL indexes, a MongoDB index can also be created either on a single field or set of fields.

- In SQL, although indexes enhance the query performance, you incur overhead for every write operation. So before creating any index, consider the type of queries, frequency, the size of the workload, and the insert load along with application requirements.

- A BTree data structure is used by all MongoDB indexes.

- Every query using the update operations uses only one index, which is decided by the query optimizer. This can be overridden by using a hint.

- A query is said to be covered by an index if all fields are part of the index, irrespective of whether it's used for querying or for projecting.

- A covering index maximizes the MongoDB performance and throughput because the query can be satiated using an index only, without loading the full documents in memory.

- An index will only be updated when the fields on which the index has been created are changed. Not all update operations on a document cause the index to be changed. It will only be changed if the associated fields are impacted.

Types of Indexes

In this section, you will look at the different types of indexes that are available in MongoDB.

_id index

This is the default index that is created on the _id field. This index cannot be deleted.

Secondary Indexes

All indexes that are user created using ensureIndex() in MongoDB are termed as secondary indexes.

1. These indexes can be created on any field in the document or the sub document. Let's consider the following document:

    ```
    {"_id": ObjectId(...),  "name": "Practical User", "address":
    {"zipcode": 201301, "state": "UP"}}
    ```

    In this document, an index can be created on the name field as well as the state field.

2. These indexes can be created on a field that is holding a sub-document.

    If you consider the above document where address is holding a sub-document, in that case an index can be created on the address field as well.

3. These indexes can either be created on a single field or a set of fields. When created with set of fields, it's also termed a **compound index**.

    To explain it a bit further, let's consider a products collection that holds documents of the following format:

    ```
    { "_id": ObjectId(...),"category": ["food", "grocery"], "item": "Apple",
    "location": "16th Floor Store",  "arrival": Date(...)}
    ```

    If the maximum of the queries use the fields Item and Location, then the following compound index can be created:

    ```
    db.products.ensureIndex ({"item": 1, "location": 1})
    ```

    In addition to the query that is referring to all the fields of the compound index, the above compound index can also support queries that are using any of the index prefixes (i.e. it can also support queries that are using only the item field).

4. If the index is created on a field that holds an array as its value, then a multikey index is used for indexing each value of the array separately.

    Consider the following document:

    ```
    { "_id" : ObjectId("..."),"tags" : [ "food", "hot", "pizza", "may" ] }
    ```

    An index on tags is a multikey index, and it will have the following entries:

    ```
    { tags: "food" }
    { tags: "hot" }
    { tags: "pizza" }
    { tags: "may" }
    ```

5. Multikey compound indexes can also be created. However, at any point, only one field of the compound index can be of the array type.

    If you create a compound index of {a1: 1, b1: 1}, the permissible documents are as follows:

    ```
    {a1: [1, 2], b1: 1}
    {a1: 1, b1: [1, 2]}
    ```

    The following document is not permissible; in fact, MongoDB won't be even able to insert this document:

    ```
    {a1: [21, 22], b1: [11, 12]}
    ```

    If an attempt is made to insert such a document, the insertion will be rejected and the following error results will be produced: "cannot index parallel arrays".

You will next look at the various options/properties that might be useful while creating indexes.

Indexes with Keys Ordering

MongoDB indexes maintain references to the fields. The refernces are maintained in either an ascending order or descending order. This is done by specifying a number with the key when creating an index. This number indicates the index direction. Possible options are 1 and -1, where 1 stands for ascending and -1 stands for descending.

In a single key index, it might not be too important; however, the direction is very important in compound indexes.

Consider an Events collection that includes both username and timestamp. Your query is to return events ordered by username first and then with the most recent event first. The following index will be used:

```
db.events.ensureIndex({ "username" : 1, "timestamp" : -1 })
```

This index contains references to the documents that are sorted in the following manner:

1. First by the username field in ascending order.

2. Then for each username sorted by the timestamp field in the descending order.

Unique Indexes

When you create an index, you need to ensure uniqueness of the values being stored in the indexed field. In such cases, you can create indexes with the Unique property set to true (by default it's false).

Say you want a unique_index on the field userid. The following command can be run to create the unique index:

```
db.payroll.ensureIndex( { "userid": 1 }, { unique: true } )
```

This command ensures that you have unique values in the user_id field. A few points that you need to note for the uniqueness constraint are

- If the unique constraint is used on a compound index in that scenario, uniqueness is enforced on the combination of values.

- A null value is stored in case there's no value specified for the field of a unique index.

- At any point only one document is permitted without a unique value.

dropDups

If you are creating a unique index on a collection that already has documents, the creation might fail because you may have some documents that contain duplicate values in the indexed field. In such scenarios, the dropDups options can be used for force creation of the unique index. This works by keeping the first occurrence of the key value and deleting all the subsequent values. By default dropDups is false.

Sparse Indexes

A sparse index is an index that holds entries of the documents within a collection that has the fields on which the index is created. If you want to create a sparse index on the LastName field of the User collection, the following command can be issued:

```
db.User.ensureIndex( { "LastName": 1 }, { sparse: true } )
```

This index will contain documents such as

```
{FirstName: Test, LastName: User}
or
{FirstName: Test2, LastName: }
```

However, the following document will not be part of the sparse index:

```
{FirstName: Test1}
```

The index is said to be sparse because this only contains documents with the indexes field and miss the documents when the fields are missing. Due to this nature, sparse indexes provide a significant space saving.

In contrast, the non-sparse index includes all documents irrespective of whether the indexed field is available in the document or not. Null value is stored in case the fields are missing.

TTL Indexes (Time To Live)

A new index property was introduced in version 2.2 that enables you to remove documents from the collection automatically after the specified time period is elapsed. This property is ideal for scenarios such as logs, session information, and machine-generated event data, where the data needs to be persistent only for a limited period.

If you want to set the TTL of one hour on collection logs, the following command can be used:

```
db.Logs.ensureIndex( { "Sample_Time": 1 }, { expireAfterSeconds: 3600} )
```

However, you need to note the following limitations:

- The field on which the index is created must be of the date type only. In the above example, the field sample_time must hold date values.

- It does not support compound indexes.

- If the field that is indexed contains an array with multiple dates, the document expires when the smallest date in the array matches the expiration threshold.

- It cannot be created on the field which already has an index created.

- This index cannot be created on capped collections.

- TTL indexes expire data using a background task, which is run every minute, to remove the expired documents. So you cannot guarantee that the expired document no longer exists in the collection.

Geospatial Indexes

With the rise of the smartphone, it's becoming very common to query for things near a current location. In order to support such location-based queries, MongoDB provides geospatial indexes.

To create a geospatial index, a coordinate pair in the following forms must exist in the documents:

- Either an array with two elements

- Or an embedded document with two keys (the key names can be anything).

The following are valid examples:

```
{ "userloc" : [ 0, 90 ] }
{ "loc" : { "x" : 30, "y" : -30 } }
{ "loc" : { "latitude" : -30, "longitude" : 180 } }
{"loc" : {"a1" : 0, "b1" : 1}}.
```

The following can be used to create a geospatial index on the userloc field:

```
db.userplaces.ensureIndex( { userloc : "2d" } )
```

A geospatial index assumes that the values will range from -180 to 180 by default. If this needs to be changed, it can be specified along with ensureIndex as follows:

```
db.userplaces.ensureIndex({"userloc" : "2d"}, {"min" : -1000, "max" : 1000})
```

Any documents with values beyond the maximum and the minimum values will be rejected. You can also create compound geospatial indexes.

Let's understand with an example how this index works. Say you have documents that are of the following type:

```
{"loc":[0,100], "desc":"coffeeshop"}
{"loc":[0,1], "desc":"pizzashop"}
```

If the query of a user is to find all coffee shops near her location, the following compound index can help:

```
db.ensureIndex({"userloc" : "2d", "desc" : 1})
```

Geohaystack Indexes

Geohaystack indexes are bucket-based geospatial indexes (also called **geospatial haystack indexes**). They are useful for queries that need to find out locations in a small area and also need to be filtered along another dimension, such as finding documents with coordinates within 10 miles and a type field value as restaurant.

While defining the index, it's mandatory to specify the bucketSize parameter as it determines the haystack index granularity. For example,

```
db.userplaces.ensureIndex({ userpos : "geoHaystack", type : 1 }, { bucketSize : 1 })
```

This example creates an index wherein keys within 1 unit of latitude or longitude are stored together in the same bucket. You can also include an additional category in the index, which means that information will be looked up at the same time as finding the location details.

If your use case typically searches for "nearby" locations (i.e. "restaurants within 25 miles"), a haystack index can be more efficient.

The matches for the additional indexed field (e.g. category) can be found and counted within each bucket.

If, instead, you are searching for "nearest restaurant" and would like to return results regardless of distance, a normal 2d index will be more efficient.

There are currently (as of MongoDB 2.2.0) a few limitations on haystack indexes:

- Only one additional field can be included in the haystack index.

- The additional index field has to be a single value, not an array.

- Null long/lat values are not supported.

In addition to the above mentioned types, there is a new type of index introduced in version 2.4 that supports text search on a collection.

Previously in beta, in the 2.6 release, text search is a built-in feature. It includes options such as searching in 15 languages and an aggregation option that can be used to set up faceted navigation by product or color, for example, on an e-commerce website.

Index Intersection

Index intersection is introduced in version 2.6 wherein multiple indexes can be intersected to satiate a query. To explain it a bit further, let's consider a products collection that holds documents of the following format

```
{ "_id": ObjectId(...),"category": ["food", "grocery"], "item": "Apple", "location": "16th
Floor Store", "arrival": Date(...)}.
```

Let's further assume that this collection has the following two indexes:

```
{ "item": 1 }.
{ "location": 1 }.
```

Intersection of the above two indexes can be used for the following query:

```
db.products.find ({"item": "xyz", "location": "abc"})
```

You can run explain() to determine if index intersection is used for the above query. The explain output will include either of the following stages: AND_SORTED or AND_HASH. When doing index intersection, either the entire index or only the index prefix can be used.

You next need to understand how this index intersection feature impacts the compound index creation.

While creating a compound index, both the order in which the keys are listed in the index and the sort order (ascending and descending) matters. Thus a compound index may not support a query that does not have the index prefix or has keys with different sort order.

To explain it a bit further, let's consider a products collection that has the following compound index:

```
db.products.ensureIndex ({"item": 1, "location": 1})
```

In addition to the query, which is referring to all the fields of the compound index, the above compound index can also support queries that are using any of the index prefix (it can also support queries that are using only the item field). But it won't be able to support queries that are using either only the location field or are using the item key with a different sort order.

Instead, if you create two separate indexes, one on the item and the other on the location, these two indexes can either individually or though intersections support the four queries mentioned above. Thus, the choice between whether to create a compound index or to rely on intersection of indexes depends on the system's needs.

Note that index intersection will not apply when the sort() operation needs an index that is completely separate from the query predicate.

For example, let's assume for the products collection you have the following indexes:

```
{ "item": 1 }.
{ "location": 1 }.
{ "location": 1, "arrival_date":-1 }.
{ "arrival_date": -1 }.
```

Index intersection will not be used for the following query:

```
db.products.find( { item: "xyz"} ).sort( { location: 1 } )
```

That is, MongoDBwill not use the { item: 1 } index for the query, and the separate { location: 1 } or the { location: 1, arrival_date: -1 } index for the sort.

However, index intersection can be used for the following query since the index {location: 1, arrival_date: -1 } can fulfil part of the query predicate:

```
db.products.find( { item: { "xyz"} , location: "A" } ).sort( { arrival_date: -1 } )
```

Behaviors and Limitations

Finally, the following are a few behaviors and limitations that you need to be aware of:

- More than 64 indexes may not be allowed in a collection.

- Index keys cannot be larger than 1024 bytes.

- A document cannot be indexed if its fields' values are greater than this size.

- The following command can be used to query documents that are too large to index:

  ```
  db.practicalCollection.find({<key>: <too large to index>}).hint({$natural: 1})
  ```

- An index name (including the namespace) must be less than 128 characters.

- The insert/update speeds are impacted to some extent by an index.

- Do not maintain indexes that are not used or will not be used.

- Since each clause of an $or query executes in parallel, each can use a different index.

- The queries that use the sort() method and the $or operator will not be able to use the indexes on the $or fields.

- Queries that use the $or operator are not supported by the second geospatial query.

Summary

In this chapter, you covered how data is stored under the hood and how writes happen using journaling. You also looked at GridFS and the different types of indexes available in MongoDB.

In the following chapter, you will look at MongoDB from administration perspective.

CHAPTER 9

Administering MongoDB

"Administering MongoDB is not like administering traditional RDBMS databases. Although most of the administrative tasks are not required or are done automatically by the system, still there are few tasks that need manual intervention."

In this chapter, you will go over the process of basic administrative operations for backups and restoration, importing and exporting data, managing the server, and monitoring the database instances.

Administration Tools

Before you dive into the administration tasks, here's a quick overview of the tools. Since MongoDB does not have a GUI-style administrative interface, most of the administrative tasks are done using the command line mongo shell. However, some UIs are available as separate community projects.

mongo

The mongo shell is part of the MongoDB distribution. It's an interactive JavaScript shell for the MongoDB database. It provides a powerful interface for administrators as well as developers to test queries and operations directly with the database.

In previous chapters, you covered development using the shell. In this chapter, you will go through the system administration tasks using the shell.

Third-Party Administration Tools

A number of third party tools are available for MongoDB. Most of the tools are web-based.

A list of all of the third party administration tools that support MongoDB is maintained by 10gen on the MongoDB web site at `https://docs.mongodb.org/ecosystem/tools/administration-interfaces/`.

© Shakuntala Gupta Edward, Navin Sabharwal 2015
S.G. Edward and N. Sabharwal, *Practical MongoDB*, DOI 10.1007/978-1-4842-0647-8_9

Backup and Recovery

Backup is one of the most important administrative tasks. It ensures that the data is safe and in case of any emergency can be restored back.

If the data cannot be restored back, the backup is useless. So, after taking a backup, the administrator needs to ensure that it's in a usable format and has captured the data in a consistent state.

The first skill an administrator needs to learn is how to take backups and restore it back.

Data File Backup

The easiest way to back up the database is to copy the data into the data directory folder.

All of the MongoDB data is stored in a data directory, which by default is `C:\data\db` (in Windows) or `/data/db` (in LINUX). The default path can be changed to a different directory using the `-dbpath` option when starting the mongod.

The data directory content is a complete picture of the data that is stored in the MongoDB database. Hence taking a MongoDB backup is simply copying the entire contents of the data directory folder.

Generally, it is not safe to copy the data directory content when MongoDB is running. One option is to shut down the MongoDB server before copying the data directory content.

If the server is shut down properly, the content of the data directory represents a safe snapshot of the MongoDB data, so it can be copied before the server is restarted again.

Although this is a safe and effective way of taking backups, it's not an ideal way, because it requires downtime.

Next, you will discuss techniques of taking backups that do not require downtime.

mongodump and mongorestore

mongodump is the MongoDB backup utility that is supplied as part of the MongoDB distribution. It works as a regular client by querying a MongoDB instance and writing all the read documents to the disk.

Let's perform a backup and then restore it to validate that the backup is in usable and consistent format.

The following code snippets are from running the utilities on a Windows platform. The MongoDB server is running on the localhost instance.

Open a terminal window and enter the following command:

```
C:\>cd c:\practicalmongodb\bin
c:\practicalmongodb\bin>mongod --rest
2015-07-15T22:26:47.288-0700 I CONTROL  [initandlisten] MongoDB starting : pid=3820
port=27017 dbpath=c:\data\db\ 64-bit host=ANOC9
.................................................................................

2015-07-15T22:28:23.563-0700 I NETWORK  [websvr] admin web console waiting for connections
on port 28017
```

In order to run mongodump, execute the following in a new terminal window:

```
C:\>cd c:\practicalmongodb\bin
c:\practicalmongodb\bin>mongodump
2015-07-15T22:29:41.538-0700 writing admin.system.indexes to dump\admin\system.indexes.bson
..............................
2015-07-14T22:29:46.720-0700    writing mydbproc.users to dump\mydbproc\users.bson
c:\practicalmongodb\bin>
```

This dumps the entire database under the dump folder in the bin folder directory itself, as shown in Figure 9-1.

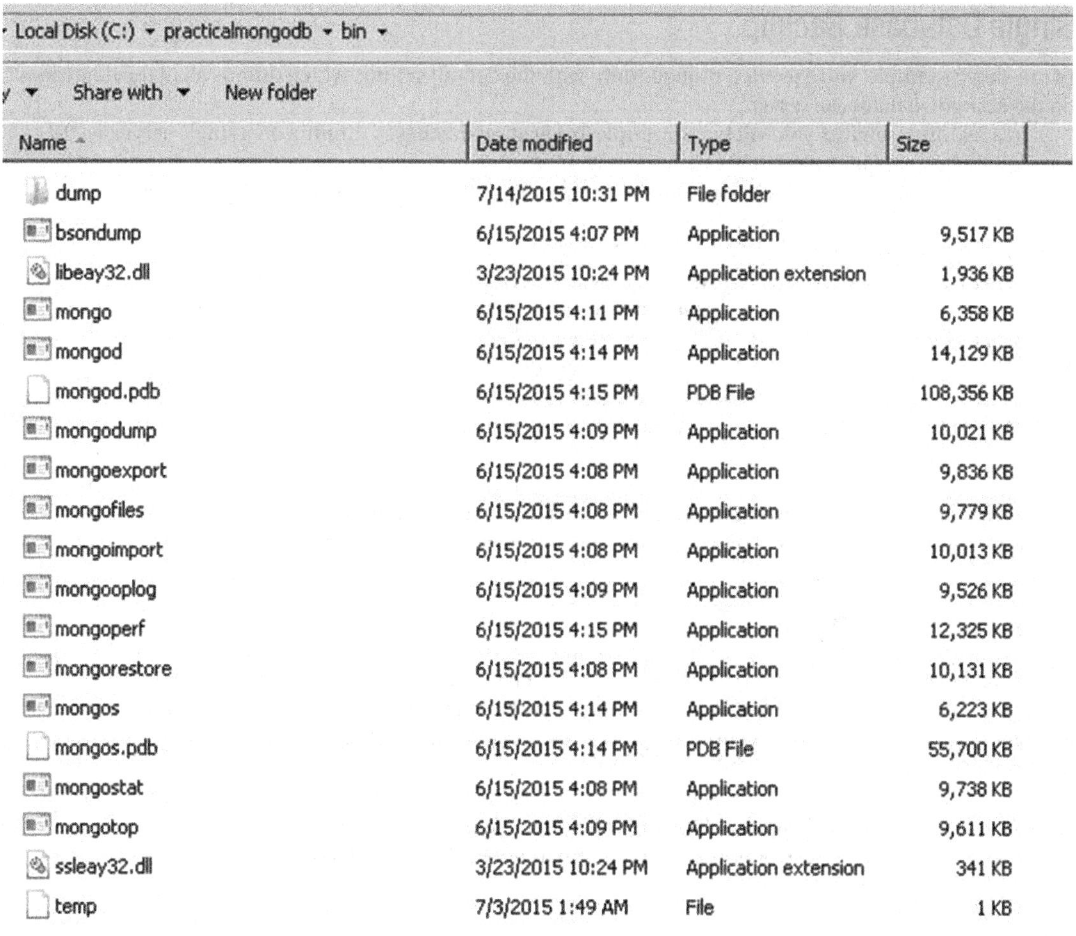
Local Disk (C:) ▸ practicalmongodb ▸ bin ▸
Share with ▼
New folder
Name
Date modified
Type
Size
dump 7/14/2015 10:31 PM File folder
bsondump 6/15/2015 4:07 PM Application 9,517 KB
libeay32.dll 3/23/2015 10:24 PM Application extension 1,936 KB
mongo 6/15/2015 4:11 PM Application 6,358 KB
mongod 6/15/2015 4:14 PM Application 14,129 KB
mongod.pdb 6/15/2015 4:15 PM PDB File 108,356 KB
mongodump 6/15/2015 4:09 PM Application 10,021 KB
mongoexport 6/15/2015 4:08 PM Application 9,836 KB
mongofiles 6/15/2015 4:08 PM Application 9,779 KB
mongoimport 6/15/2015 4:08 PM Application 10,013 KB
mongooplog 6/15/2015 4:09 PM Application 9,526 KB
mongoperf 6/15/2015 4:15 PM Application 12,325 KB
mongorestore 6/15/2015 4:08 PM Application 10,131 KB
mongos 6/15/2015 4:14 PM Application 6,223 KB
mongos.pdb 6/15/2015 4:14 PM PDB File 55,700 KB
mongostat 6/15/2015 4:08 PM Application 9,738 KB
mongotop 6/15/2015 4:09 PM Application 9,611 KB
ssleay32.dll 3/23/2015 10:24 PM Application extension 341 KB
temp 7/3/2015 1:49 AM File 1 KB

Figure 9-1. *The dump folder*

The mongodump utility by default connects to the localhost interface of the database on the default port.

Next, it pulls and stores each database and collection's associated data files into a predefined folder structure, which defaults to ./dump/[databasename]/[collectionname].bson.

The data is saved in .bson format, which is similar to the format used by MongoDB for storing its data internally.

If content is already in the directory, it will remain untouched unless the dump contains same file. For example, if the dump contains the files c1.bson and c2.bson, and the output directory has files c3.bson and c1.bson, then mongodump will replace the c1.bson file of the folder with its c1.bson file, and will copy the c2.bson file, but it won't remove or change the c3.bson file.

You should make sure that the directory is empty before using it for mongodump unless you have a requirement of overlaying the data in your backups.

Single Database Backup

In the above example, you executed mongodump with the default setting, which dumps all of the databases on the MongoDB database server.

In a real-life scenario, you will have multiple application databases running on a single server, each having a different requirement of backup strategies.

Specifying the -d parameter in the mongodump utility will let you take the backup's database wise.

```
c:\practicalmongodb\bin>mongodump -d mydbpoc
2015-07-14T22:37:49.088-0700     writing mydbproc.mapreducecount1 to dump\mydbproc\
                                 mapreducecount1.bson
.....................
2015-07-14T22:37:54.217-0700     writing mydbproc.users metadata to dump\mydbproc\
                                 users.metadata.json
2015-07-14T22:37:54.218-0700     done dumping mydbproc.users
c:\practicalmongodb\bin>
```

As of MongoDB-2.6, database administrator must have access to admin database in order to backup users and user-defined roles for given database as MongoDB stores these information in admin database only.

Collection Level Backup

There are two types of data in every database: data that changes rarely, such as configuration data where you maintain the users, their roles, and any application-related configurations, and then you have data that changes frequently such as the events data (in case of a monitoring application), posts data (in case of blog application), and so on.

As a result, the backup requirements are different. For instance, the complete database can be backed up once a week whereas the rapidly changing collection needs to be backed up every hour.

Specifying the -c parameter in the mongodump utility enables the user to implement backups for a specified collection individually.

```
c:\practicalmongodb\bin>mongodump -d mydbpoc -c users
2015-07-14T22:41:19.850-0700     writing mydbproc.users to dump\mydbproc\users.bson
2015-07-14T22:41:30.710-0700     writing mydbproc.users metadata to dump\mydbproc\
                                 users.metadata.json
..........................................................
2015-07-14T22:41:30.712-0700     done dumping mydbproc.users
c:\practicalmongodb\bin>
```

If the folder where the data needs to be dumped is not specified, by default it dumps the data in a directory named dump in the current working directory, which in this case is c:\practicalmongodb\bin.

mongodump –Help

You have covered the basics of executing mongodump. Apart from the options mentioned above, mongodump provides other options that let you tailor the backups as per requirements. As with all other utilities, executing the utility with the -help option will provide the list of all available options.

mongorestore

As mentioned, it is mandatory for the administrators to ensure that the backups are happening in a consistent and usable format. So the next step is to restore the data dump back using mongorestore.

This utility will restore the database back to the state when the dump was taken. Prior to version 3.0, it was allowed to run the command without even starting the mongod/mongos. Starting from version 3.0, if the command is executed before starting the mongod/mongos the following error(s) will show:

```
c:\>cd c:\practicalmongodb\bin
c:\ practicalmongodb\bin>mongorestore

2015-07-15T22:43:07.365-0700    using default 'dump' directory
2015-07-15T22:43:17.545-0700    Failed: error connecting to db server: no reachable servers
```

You must run the mongod/mongos instance prior to running the mongorestore command.

```
c:\>cd c:\practicalmongodb\bin
c:\ practicalmongodb\bin>mongod --rest
2015-07-15T22:43:25.765-0700 I CONTROL  [initandlisten] MongoDB starting : pid=3820
                                        port=27017 dbpath=c:\data\db\ 64-bit host=ANOC9
.........................................................................
2015-07-15T22:43:25.865-0700 I NETWORK  [websvr] admin web console waiting for connections
                                        on port 28017
c:\ practicalmongodb\bin>mongorestore
2015-07-15T22:44:09.786-0700    using default 'dump' directory
2015-07-15T22:44:09.792-0700    building a list of dbs and collections to restore from dump dir
.................................
2015-07-15T22:44:09.732-0700    restoring indexes for collection mydbproc.users from metadata
2015-07-15T22:44:09.864-0700    finished restoring mydbproc.users
c:\practicalmongodb\bin>
```

This force appends the data to the back of the existing data.

To override the default behavior, -drop should be used in the above snippet.

The -drop command indicates to the mongorestore utility that it needs to delete all the collections and data within the aforementioned database and then restore the dump data back to the database.

If -drop is not used, the command appends the data to the end of the existing data.

Note that starting from version 3.0, the mongorestore command can also accept input from standard input.

Restoring a Single Database

As you saw in the backup section, the backup strategies can be specified at individual database level. You can run mongodump to take a backup of a single database by using the –d option.

Similarly, you can specify the –d option to mongorestore to restore individual databases.

```
c:\ practicalmongodb\bin>mongorestore  -d mydbpocc:\practicalmongodb\bin\dump\mydbproc  -drop
2015-07-14T22:47:01.155-0700    building a list of collections to restore from
C :\practicalmongodb\bin\dump\mydbproc dir
2015-07-14T22:47:01.156-0700 reading metadata file from
C :\practicalmongodb\bin\dump\mydbproc \users.metadata.json
........................................................................
2015-07-14T22:50:09.732-0700    restoring indexes for collection mydbproc.users from metadata
2015-07-14T22:50:09.864-0700    finished restoring mydbproc.users
c:\practicalmongodb\bin>
```

Restoring a Single Collection

As with mongodump where you can use –c option to specify collection-level backups, you can also restore individual collections by using the –c option with the mongorestore utility.

```
c:\ practicalmongodb\bin>mongorestore -d mydbpoc -c users
C:\ practicalmongodb\bin\dum\mydb\user.bson -drop

2015-07-14T22:52:14.732-0700    restoring indexes for collection mydbproc.users from metadata
2015-07-14T22:52:14.864-0700    finished restoring mydbproc.users
c:\practicalmongodb\bin>
```

Mongorestore –Help

The mongorestore also has multiple options, which can be viewed using the –help option. Consult the following web site also: http://docs.mongodb.org/manual/core/backups/.

fsync and Lock

Although the above two methods (mongodump and mongorestore) enable you take a database backup without any downtime, they don't provide the ability to get a point-in-time data view.

You saw how to copy the data files to take the backups, but this requires shutting down the server before copying the data, which is not feasible in a production environment.

MongoDB's fsync command lets you copy content of the data directory by running MongoDB without changing any data.

The fsync command forces all pending writes to be flushed to the disk. Optionally, it holds a lock in order to prevent further writes until the server is unlocked. This lock only makes the fsync command usable for backups.

To run the command from the shell, connect to the mongo console in a new terminal window.

```
c:\practicalmongodb\bin>mongo
MongoDB shell version: 3.0.4
connecting to: test
>
```

Next, switch to admin and issue the runCommand to fsync:

```
>use admin
switched to db admin
>db.runCommand({"fsync":1, "lock":1})
{
        "info" : "now locked against writes, use db.fsyncUnlock() to unlock",
        "seeAlso" : "http://dochub.mongodb.org/core/fsynccommand",
        "ok" : 1
}
>
```

At this point, the server is locked for any writes, ensuring that the data directory is representing a consistent, point-in-time snapshot of the data. The data directory contents can be safely copied to be used as the database backup.

You must unlock the database post the completion of the backup activity. In order to do so, issue the following command:

```
>db.$cmd.sys.unlock.findOne()
{ "ok" : 1, "info" : "unlock completed" }
>
```

The currentOp command can be used to check whether the database lock has been released or not.

```
>db.currentOp()
{ "inprog" : [ ] }
 (It may take a moment after the unlock is first requested.)
```

The fsync command lets you take a backup without downtime and without sacrificing the backup's point-in-time nature. However, there is a momentary blocking of the writes (also called a momentary write downtime).

Starting from version 3.0, when using WiredTiger, fsync cannot guarantee that the data files will not change. So it cannot be used to ensure consistency for creating backups.

Next, you'll learn about slave backup. This is the only backup technique that enables taking a point-in-time snapshot without any kind of downtime.

Slave Backups

Slave backups are the recommended way for data backups in MongoDB. The slave always stores a data copy that is nearly in sync with the master, and the slave availability or performance is not much of an issue. You can apply any of the techniques discussed earlier on the slave rather than the master: shutting down, fsync with lock, or dump and restore.

Importing and Exporting

When you are trying to migrate your application from one environment to another, you often need to import data or export data.

mongoimport

MongoDB provides the mongoimport utility that lets you bulk load data directly into a collection of the database. It reads from a file and bulk loads the data into a collection.

These methods are not suitable for production environment.

The following three file formats are supported by mongoimport:

- JSON: In this format you have JSON blocks per line, which represent a document.

- CSV: This is a comma-separated file.

- TSV: TSV files are same as CSV files; the only difference is it uses a tab as the separator.

Using -help with mongoimport will provide all the options available with the utility. mongoimport is very simple. Most of the time you will end up using the following options:

- -h or -host: This specifies the mongod hostname where the data need to be restored. If the option is not specified, the command will connect to the mongod running on localhost at port 27017 by default. Optionally, a port number can be specified to connect to mongod running on a different port.

- -d or -db: Specifies the database where the data needs to be imported.

- -c or -collection: Specifies the collection where data need to be uploaded.

- --type: This is the file type (i.e. CSV, TSV or JSON).

- --file: This is the file path from where the data need to be imported.

- --drop: If this option is set, it will drop the collection and recreate the collection from the imported data. Otherwise, the data is appended at the end of the collection.

- --headerLine: This is used for CSV or TSV files only, and is used to indicate that the first line is a header line.

The following command imports the data from a CSV file to the testimport collection on the localhost:

```
c:\practicalmongodb\bin>mongoimport --host localhost --db mydbpoc --collection testimport
--type csv -file c:\exporteg.csv --headerline
2015-07-14T22:54:08.407-0700    connected to: localhost
2015-07-14T22:54:08.483-0700    imported 15 documents
c:\ practicalmongodb\bin>
```

mongoexport

Similar to the mongoimport utility, MongoDB provides a mongoexport utility that lets you export data from the MongoDB database. As the name suggests, this utility exports files from the existing MongoDB collections.

Using –help shows available options with the mongoexport utility. The following options are the ones you will end up using most:

- -q: This is used to specify the query that will return as output the records that need to be exported. This is similar to what you specify in the db.CollectionName.find() function when you have to retrieve records matching the selection criteria. If no query is specified, all the documents are exported.

- -f: This is used to specify the fields that you need to export from the selected documents.

The following command exports the data from Users collection to a CSV file:

```
c:\practicalmongodb\bin>mongoexport -d mydbpoc -c myusers -f _id,Age –type=csv > myusers.csv
2015-07-14T22:54:48.604-0700 connected to: 127.0.0.1
2015-07-14T22:54:48.604-0700 exported 22 records
c:\practicalmongodb\bin>
```

Managing the Server

In this section, you will look at the various options that you need to be aware of as an administrator of the system.

Starting a Server

This section covers how to start the server. Previously, you used the mongo shell to start the server by running mongod.exe.

The MongoDB server can be started manually by opening a command prompt (run as administrator) in Windows or a terminal window on Linux systems and typing the following command:

```
C:\>cd c:\practicalmongodb\bin
c:\ practicalmongodb\bin>mongod
mongod --help for help and startup options
.......................................
```

This window will display all the connections that are being made to the mongod. It also displays information that can be used to monitor the server.

If no configuration is specified, MongoDB starts up with the default database path of C:\data\db on Windows and /data/db on Linux and binds to the localhost using default ports 27017 and 27018.

Typing ^C will shut down the server cleanly.

MongoDB provides two methods for specifying configuration parameters for starting up the server.

The first is to specify using command-line options (refer to Chapter tk).

The second method is to load a configuration file. The server configuration can be changed by editing the file and then restarting the server.

Stopping a Server

The server can be shut down pressing CTRL+C in the mongod console itself. Otherwise, you can use the shutdownServer command from the mongo console.

Open a terminal window, and connect to the mongo console.

```
C:\>cd c:\practicalmongodb\bin
c:\practicalmongodb\bin>mongo
MongoDB shell version: 3.0.4
connecting to: test
>
```

Switch to admin db and issue the shutdownServer command:

```
>use admin
switched to db admin
>db.shutdownServer()
2015-07-14T22:57:20.413-0700 I NETWORK DBClientCursor::init call() failed server should be down...
2015-07-14T22:57:20.418-0700 I NETWORK trying reconnect to 127.0.0.1:27017
2015-07-14T22:57:21.413-0700 I NETWORK 127.0.0.1:27017 failed couldn't connect to server 127.0.0.1:27017
>
```

If you check the mongod console where you started the server in the previous step, you will see that the server has been shut down successfully.

```
......................
2015-07-14T22:57:30.259-0700 I COMMAND  [conn1] terminating, shutdown command received
2015-07-14T22:57:30.260-0700 I CONTROL  [conn1] now exiting
...................................................
2015-07-14T22:57:30.380-0700 I STORAGE  [conn1] shutdown: removing fs lock...
2015-07-14T22:57:30.380-0700 I CONTROL  [conn1] dbexit:  rc: 0
```

Viewing Log Files

By default the entire log output of MongoDB is written to stdout but this can be changed by specifying the logpath option in the configuration when starting the server to redirect the output to a file.

The log file contents can be used to identify problems such as exceptions, which may indicate some data problem or connection issues.

Server Status

db.ServerStatus() is a simple method provided by MongoDB for checking the server status, such as number of connections, uptime, and so on. The output of the server status command depends upon the operating system platform, MongoDB version, storage engine used, and type of configuration (like standalone, replica set, and sharded cluster).

Starting from version 3.0, the following sections are removed from the output: workingSet, indexCounters, and recordStats.

In order to check the status of a server using the MMAPv1 storage engine, connect to the mongo console, switch to admin db, and issue the db.serverStatus() command.

```
c:\practicalmongodb\bin>mongo
MongoDB shell version: 3.0.4
connecting to: test
>use admin
switched to db admin
>db.serverStatus()
host" : "ANOC9",
 "version" : "3.0.4",
 "process" : "mongod",
 "pid" : NumberLong(1748),
 "uptime" : 14,
 "uptimeMillis" : NumberLong(14395),
"uptimeEstimate" : 13,
 "localTime" : ISODate("2015-07-14T22:58:44.532Z"),
"asserts" : {
"regular" : 0,
        "warning" : 0,
        "msg" : 0,
        "user" : 1,
        "rollovers" : 0
},
.......................................................
```

The above serverStatus output will also have a "backgroundflushing" section, which displays reports corresponding to the process used by MongoDB to flush data to disk using MMAPv1 as the storage engine.

The "opcounters" and "asserts" sections provide useful information that can be analyzed to classify any problem.

The "opcounters" section shows the number of operations of each type. In order to find out if there's any problem, you should have a baseline of these operations. If the counters start deviating from the baseline, this indicates a problem and will require taking action to bring it back to the normal state.

The "asserts" section depicts the number of client and server warnings or exceptions that have occurred. If you find a rise in such exceptions and warnings, you need to take a good look at the logfiles to identify if a problem is developing. A rise in the number of asserts may also indicate a problem with the data, and in such scenarios MongoDB validate functions should be used to check that the data is undamaged.

Next, let's start the server using the WiredTiger storage engine and see the serverStatus output.

```
c:\practicalmongodb\bin>mongod -storageEngine wiredTiger
2015-07-14T22:51:05.965-0700 I CONTROL  Hotfix KB2731284 or later update is installed, no
need to zero-out data files
2015-07-29T22:51:05.965-0700 I STORAGE  [initandlisten] wiredtiger_open config:
create,cache_size=1G,session_max=20000,eviction=(threads_max=4),statistics=(fast),log=(enabl
ed=true,archive=true,path=journal,compressor=snappy),file_manager=(close_idle_time=100000),
checkpoint=(wait=60,log_size=2GB),statistics_log=(wait=0)
.......................................................
```

In order to check the server status, connect to the mongo console, switch to admin db, and issue the db.serverStatus() command.

```
c:\practicalmongodb\bin>mongo
MongoDB shell version: 3.0.4
connecting to: test
>use admin
switched to db admin
>db.serverStatus()

"wiredTiger" : {
"uri" : "statistics:",
"LSM" : {
"......................................................,
"tree maintenance operations scheduled":0,
......................................................,
},
"async" : {
        "number of allocation state races":0,
        "number of operation slots viewed for allocation":0,
        "current work queue length" : 0,
        "number of flush calls" : 0,
        "number of times operation allocation failed":0,
        "maximum work queue length" : 0,
......................................................,
},
"block-manager" : {
        "mapped bytes read" : 0,
        "bytes read" : 966656,
        "bytes written" : 253952,
        ..............................,
        "blocks written" : 45
},
......................................................,
```

As you can see, the server status output has a new section known as wiredTiger statistics when started with storage engine WiredTiger.

Identifying and Repairing MongoDB

In this section, you will look at how you can repair a corrupt database.

If you are getting errors like

- Database server refuses to start, stating data files are corrupt

- Asserts are seen in the log files or db.serverStatus() command

- Strange or unexpected queries results

this means the database is corrupt and a repair must be run in order to recover the database.

The first thing you need to do before you can start the repair is to take the server offline if it's not already. You can use either option mentioned above. In this example, type ^C in the mongod console. This will shut down the server.

Next, start the mongod using the –repair option, as shown:

```
c:\practicalmongodb\bin>mongod --repair
2015-07-14T22:58:31.171-0700 I CONTROL    Hotfix KB2731284 or later update is installed,
                                           no need to zero-out data files
2015-07-14T22:58:31.173-0700 I CONTROL    [initandlisten] MongoDB starting : pid=3996
                                           port=27017 dbpath=c:\data\db\ 64-bit host=ANOC9
2015-07-14T22:58:31.174-0700 I CONTROL    [initandlisten] db version v3.0.4
..................................
2015-07-14T22:58:31.447-0700 I STORAGE    [initandlisten] shutdown: removing fs lock...
2015-07-14T22:58:31.449-0700 I CONTROL    [initandlisten] dbexit:  rc: 0
c:\ practicalmongodb\bin>
```

This will repair mongod. If you look at the output, you'll find various discrepancies that the utility is repairing. Once the repair process is over, it exits.

After completion of the repair process, the server can be started as normal and then the latest database backups can be used to restore missing data.

At times, you may notice that the drive is running out of disk space when a large database is under repair. This is due to the fact that the MongoDB needs to create a temporary copy of the files on the same drive as the data files. To overcome this issue, while repairing a database you should use the –repairpath parameter to specify the drive where the temporary files can be created during the repair process.

Identifying and Repairing Collection Level Data

Sometimes you might want to validate that the collection holds valid data and had valid indexes. For such cases, MongoDB provides a validate() method that validates the content of the specified collection.

The following example validates the data of the Users collection:

```
c:\practicalmongodb\bin>mongo
MongoDB shell version: 3.0.4
connecting to: test
>use mydbpoc
switched to db mydbpoc
>db.myusers.validate()
{
        "ns" : "mydbpoc.myusers",
        "firstExtent" : "1:4322000 ns:mydbpoc.myusers",
        "lastExtent" : "1:4322000 ns:mydbpoc.myusers",
        "..............
        "valid" : true,
        "errors" : [ ],
        "warning" : "Some checks omitted for speed. use {full:true} option to do
 more thorough scan.",
        "ok" : 1
}
```

Both the data files and the associated indexes are checked by default by the validate() option. The collection statistics are provided to help in identifying if there's any problem with the data files or the indexes.

If running validate() indicates that the indexes are damaged, in that case reIndex can be used to re-index the indexes of the collection. This drops and rebuilds all the indexes of the collection.

The following command reindexes the Users collection's indexes:

```
>use mydbpoc
switched to db mydbpoc
>db.myusers.reIndex()
{
        "nIndexesWas" : 1,
        "msg" : "indexes dropped for collection",
        "nIndexes" : 1,
        "indexes" : [
                {
                        "key" : {
                                "_id" : 1
                        },
                        "ns" : "mydbpoc.myusers",
                        "name" : "_id_"
                }
        ],
        "ok" : 1
}
>
```

If the collection's data files are corrupt, then running the -repair option is the best way to repair all of the data files.

Monitoring MongoDB

As a MongoDB server administrator, it's important to monitor the system's performance and health. In this section, you will learn ways of monitoring the system.

mongostat

mongostat comes as part of the MongoDB distribution. This tool provides simple stats on the server; although it's not extensive, it provides a good overview. The following shows the statistics of the localhost. Open a terminal window and execute the following:

```
c:\>cd c:\practicalmongodb\bin
c:\practicalmongodb\bin>mongostat
```

The first six columns show the rate at which various operations are handled by the mongod server. Apart from these columns, the following column is also worth mentioning and can be of use when diagnosing problems:

> Conn: This is an indicator of the number of connections to the mongod instance. A high value here can indicate a possibility that the connections are not getting released or closed from the application, which means that although the application is issuing an open connection, it's not closing the connection after completion of the operation.

Starting from version 3.0, mongostat can also return its response in json format using option -json.

```
c:\>cd c:\practicalmongodb\bin
c:\practicalmongodb\bin>mongostat -json
```

{"ANOC9":{"ar|aw":"0|0","command":"1|0","conn":"1","delete":"*0","faults":"1","flushes":"0",
"getmore":"0","host":"ANOC9","insert":"*0","locked":"" ,"mapped":"560.0M","netIn":"79b",
"netOut":"10k","non mapped":"","qr|qw":"0|0","query":"*0","res":"153.0M","time":"05:16:17",
"update":"*0","vsize":"1.2G"}}

mongod Web Interface

Whenever a mongod is started up, it creates a web port by default, which is 1000 higher than the port number mongod uses to listen for a connection. By default the HTTP port is 28017.

This mongod web interface is accessed via your web browser, and it displays most of the statistical information. If the mongod is running on localhost and is listening for the connections on port 27017, then the HTTP status page can be accessed using the following URL: http://localhost:28017. The page looks like Figure 9-2.

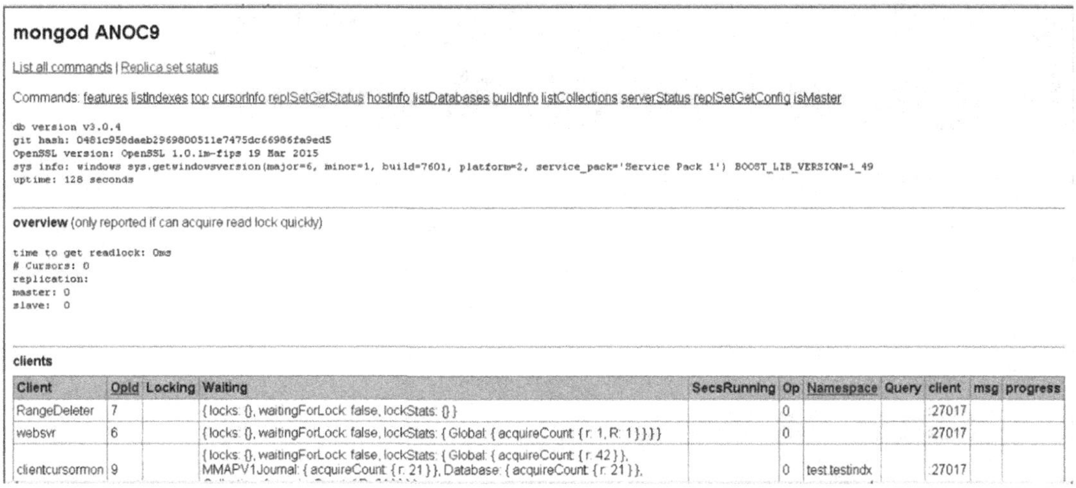

Figure 9-2. Web interface

Third-Party Plug-Ins

In addition to this tool, there are various third-party adapters available for MongoDB which let you use common open source or commercial monitoring systems such as cacti, Ganglia, etc. On its website, 10gen maintains a page that shares the latest information about available MongoDB monitoring interfaces.

To get an up-to-date list of third-party plug-ins, go to www.mongodb.org/display/DOCS/Monitoring+and+ Diagnostics.

MongoDB Cloud Manager

In addition to the tools and techniques discussed above for monitoring and backup purposes, there is the MongoDB Cloud Manager (formerly known as MMS – MongoDB Monitoring Services). It's developed by the team who developed MongoDB and is free to use (30-day trial license). In contrast to the techniques discussed above, MongoDB Cloud Manager provides user interface as well as logs and performance details in the form of graphs and charts.

MongoDB Cloud Manager charts are interactive, enabling the user to set a custom date range, as depicted in Figure 9-3.

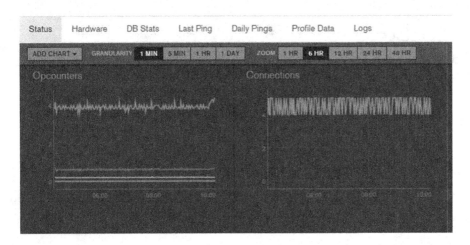

Figure 9-3. *Setting a custom date range*

Another neat feature of the Cloud Manager is the ability to use email and text alerts in case of different events. This is depicted in Figure 9-4.

Figure 9-4. *Email and text alerts*

Not only does Cloud Manager provides graphs and alerts, it also lets you view the slower queries ordered by response time. You can easily see how your queries are performing all at one place. Figure 9-5 shows the graph that charts query performance.

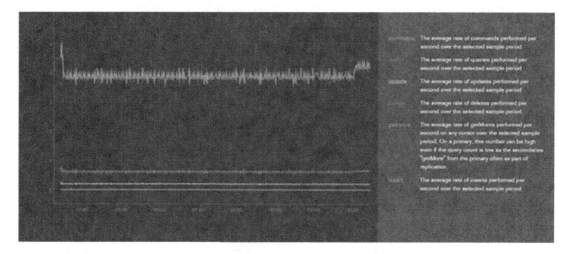

Figure 9-5. *Query response time*

Cloud Manager lets you do the following:

- Automate your MongoDB deployment (the configuration of MongoDB nodes, clusters, and upgrading of the existing deployment)

- Protect your data with continuous backup

- Provide any topology with AWS integration

- Monitor the performance in your dashboard

- Perform operational tasks such as adding capacity

For AWS users, it offers direct integration so the MongoDB can be launched on AWS without ever leaving Cloud Manager. You saw how to provision with AWS in Chapter tk.

Cloud Manager also helps you discover inefficiencies in your system and make corrections for smooth operation.

It collects and reports metrics using the agent you install. Cloud Manager provides a quick glance of the MongoDB system health and helps you identify the root causes of performance issues.

Next, you will look at the key metrics that should be used for any performance investigation. Along the way, you will also look at what the combination of the metric indicates.

Metrics

You will be primarily focusing on the following key metrics; these metrics play a key role when investigating a performance problem issue. They provide an immediate glance of what's happening inside the MongoDB system and which of the system resources (i.e. CPU, RAM, or disk) are the bottlenecks.

- Page Fault

- Opcounters

- Lock percent

- Queues

- CPU time (IOWait and Users)

To view the below mentioned chart, you can click the Deployment link under Deployment Section. Select the MongoDB instance that has been configured to be monitored by Cloud Manager. Next, select required graphs/charts from the Manage Charts section.

Page fault shows the average number of page faults per second happening in the system. Figure 9-6 shows the page faults graph.

Page Faults

Figure 9-6. *Page faults*

OpCounters shows average number of operations per second being performed on the system. See Figure 9-7.

Opcounters

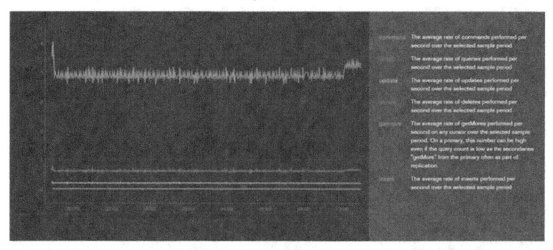

Figure 9-7. *OpCounters*

In the Page Fault to Opcounters ratio, the page faults depend on the operations being performed on the system and what's currently in memory. Hence a ratio of page faults per second to that of opcounters per second can provide a fair picture of the disk I/O requirement. See Figure 9-8.

Figure 9-8. *Page fault to Opcounters ratio*

If the ratio is

- < 1, this classifies as low disk I/O.

- Near 1, this classifies as regular disk I/O.

- > 1, this classifies as high disk I/O.

The Queues graph displays the operations count waiting for a lock to be released at any given time. See Figure 9-9.

Queues

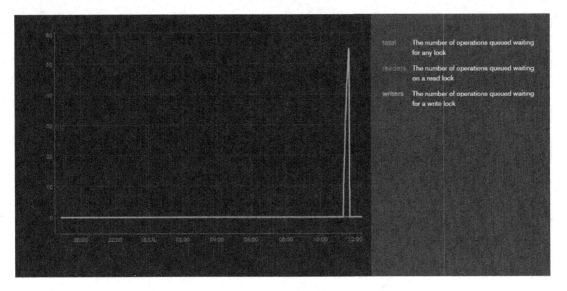

Figure 9-9. *Queues*

The CPU Time (IOWaits and User) graph shows how the CPU cores are spending their cycles. See Figure 9-10.

CPU Time

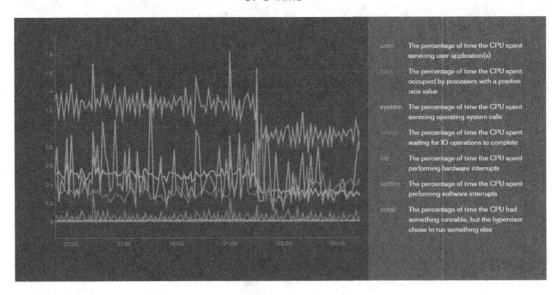

Figure 9-10. *CPU Time*

IOWait indicates the time the CPU spends waiting for the other resources, such as disks or the network. See Figure 9-11.

Chart

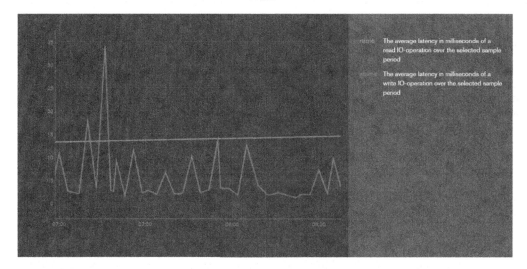

Figure 9-11. *IOWait*

User time indicates the time spent performing computations such as documents updating, updating and rebalancing indexes, selecting or ordering query results, or running aggregation framework commands, Map/Reduce, or server-side JavaScripts. See Figure 9-12.

Chart

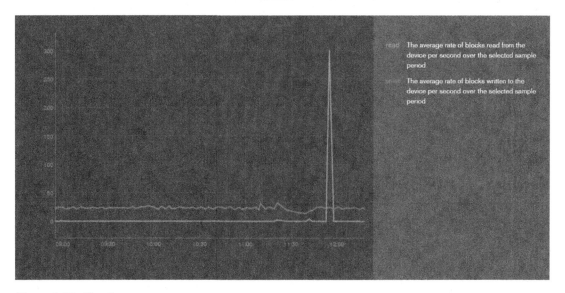

Figure 9-12. *User time*

To view the CPU Time graphs you need to install munin.

These key metrics and their combinations should be used to investigate any performance problems.

Summary

In this chapter you looked at how various utilities that are packaged as part of the MongoDB distribution can be used to manage and maintain the system.

You learned about the main operations that as an administrator you must be aware of for a detailed understanding of the utilities. Please read through the references. In the next chapter, you will examine MongoDB's use cases and you will also look at the cases where MongoDB is not a good choice.

CHAPTER 10

MongoDB Use Cases

"MongoDB: Is it useful for me or not?"

In this chapter, we will provide the much needed connection between the features of MongoDB and the business problems that it is suited to solve. We will be using two use cases for sharing the techniques and patterns used for addressing such problems.

Use Case 1 - Performance Monitoring

In this section, you will explore how to use MongoDB to store and retrieve performance data. You'll focus on the data model that you will be using for storing the data. Retrieving will consist of simply reading from the respective collection. You will also be looking at how you can apply sharding and replication for better performance and data safety.

We assume a monitoring tool that is collecting server-defined parameter data in CSV format. In general, the monitoring tools either store the data as text files in a designated folder on the server or they redirect their output to any reporting database server. In this use case, there's a scheduler that will be reading this shared folder path and importing the data within MongoDB database.

Schema Design

The first step in designing a solution is to decide on the schema. The schema depends on the format of the data that the monitoring tool is capturing.

A line from the log files may resemble Table 10-1.

Table 10-1. Log File

Node UUID	IP Address	Node Name	MIB	Time Stamp (ms)	Metric Ve
3beb1a8b-040d-4b46-932a-2d31bd353186	10.161.1.73	corp_xyz_sardar	IFU	1369221223384	0.2

© Shakuntala Gupta Edward, Navin Sabharwal 2015
S.G. Edward and N. Sabharwal, *Practical MongoDB*, DOI 10.1007/978-1-4842-0647-8_10

The following is the simplest way to store each line as text:

```
{
_id: ObjectId(...),
line: '10.161.1.73 - corp_xyz_sardar [15/July/2015:13:55:36 -0700] "Interface Util" ...
}
```

Although this captures the data, it makes no sense to the user, so if you want to find out events are from a particular server, you need to use regular expressions, which will lead to full scan of the collection, which is very inefficient.

Instead, you can extract the data from the log file and store it as meaningful fields in MongoDB documents.

Note that when designing the structure, it's very important to use the correct data type. This not only saves space but also has a significant impact on the performance.

For example, if you store the date and time field of the log as a string, it'll not only use more bytes but it'll also be difficult to fire date range queries. Instead of using strings, if you store the date as a UTC timestamp, it will take 8 bytes as opposed to 28 bytes for a string, so it'll be easier to execute date range queries. As you can see, using proper types for the data increases querying flexibility.

You will be using the following document for storing your monitoring data:

```
{
_id: ObjectID(...),
Host:,
Time:ISODate(''),
ParameterName:'aa',
Value:10.23
}
```

■ **Note** The actual log data might have extra fields; if you capture it all, it'll lead to a large document, which is an inefficient use of storage and memory. When designing the schema, you should omit the details that are not required. It's very important to identify which fields you must capture in order to meet your requirements.

In your scenario, the most important information that meets your reporting application requirements is the following:

1. Host

2. Timestamp

3. Parameter

4. Value

Operations

Having designed the document structure, next you will look at the various operations that you need to perform on the system.

Inserting Data

The method used for inserting data depends on your application write concerns.

1. If you are looking for fast insertion speed and can compromise on the data safety, then the following command can be used:

```
>db.perfpoc.insert({Host:"Host1", GeneratedOn: new ISODate("2015-07-15T12:02Z"),
ParameterName:"CPU",Value:13.13},w=0)
>
```

Although this command is the fastest option available, since it doesn't wait for any acknowledgment of whether the operation was successful or not, you risk losing data.

2. If you want just an acknowledgment that at least the data is getting saved, you can issue the following command:

```
>db.perfpoc.insert({Host:"Host1", GeneratedOn: new ISODate("2015-07-15T12:07Z"),
ParameterName:"CPU",Value:13.23},w=1)
>
```

Although this command acknowledges that the data is saved, it will not provide safety against any data loss because it is not journaled.

3. If your primary focus is to trade off increased insertion speed for data safety guarantees, you can issue the following command:

```
>db.perfpoc.insert({Host:"Host1", GeneratedOn: new ISODate("2015-07-15T12:09Z"),
ParameterName:"CPU",Value:30.01},j=true,w=2)
>
```

In this code, you are not only ensuring that the data is getting replicated, you are also enabling journaling. In addition to the replication acknowledgment, it also waits for a successful journal commit.

■ **Note**   Although this is the safest option, it has a severe impact on the insert performance, so it is the slowest operation.

Bulk Insert

Inserting events in bulk is always beneficial when using stringent write concerns, as in your case, because this enables MongoDB to distribute the incurred performance penalty across a group of insert.

If possible, bulk inserts should be used for inserting the monitoring data because the data will be huge and will be generated in seconds. Grouping them together as a group and inserting will have better impact, because in the same wait time, multiple events will be getting saved. So for this use case, you will be grouping multiple events using a bulk insert.

Querying Performance Data

You have seen how to insert the event data. The value of maintaining data comes when you are able to respond to specific queries by querying the data.

For example, you may want to view all the performance data associated with a specific field, say Host.

You will look at few query patterns for fetching the data and then you will look at how to optimize these operations.

Query1: *Fetching the Performance Data of a Particular Host*

```
> db.perfpoc.find({Host:"Host1"})
{ "_id" : ObjectId("553dc64009cb76075f6711f3"), "Host" : "Host1", "GeneratedOn":
ISODate("2015-07-18T12:02:00Z"), "ParameterName" : "CPU", "Value" : 13.13 }
{ "_id" : ObjectId("553dc6cb4fd5989a8aa91b2d"), "Host" : "Host1", "GeneratedOn":
ISODate("2015-07-18T12:07:00Z"), "ParameterName" : "CPU", "Value" : 13.23 }
{ "_id" : ObjectId("553dc7504fd5989a8aa91b2e"), "Host" : "Host1", "GeneratedOn":
ISODate("2015-07-18T12:09:00Z"), "ParameterName" : "CPU", "Value" : 30.01 }
>
```

This can be used if the requirement is to analyze the performance of a host.

Creating an index on Host will optimize the performance of the above queries:

```
>db.perfpoc.ensureIndex({Host:1})
>
```

Query2: *Fetching Data Within a Date Range from July 10, 2015 to July 20, 2015*

```
>db.perfpoc.find({GeneratedOn:{"$gte": ISODate("2015-07-10"), "$lte": ISODate("2015-07-20")}})
{ "_id" : ObjectId("5302fec509904770f56bd7ab"), "Host" : "Host1", "GeneratedOn"
.............
>
```

This is important if you want to consider and analyze the data collected for a specific date range. In this case, an index on "time" will have a positive impact on the performance.

```
>db.perfpoc.ensureIndex({GeneratedOn:1})
>
```

Query3: *Fetching Data Within a Date Range from July 10, 2015 to July 20, 2015 for a Specific Host*

```
>db.perfpoc.find({GeneratedOn:{"$gte": ISODate("2015-07-10"), "$lte": ISODate("2015-07-20")},
Host: "Host1"})
{ "_id" : ObjectId("5302fec509904770f56bd7ab"), "Host" : "Host1", "GeneratedOn"
................
>
```

This is useful if you want to look at the performance data of a host for a specific time period.

In such queries where multiple fields are involved, the indexes that are used have a significant impact on the performance. For example, for the above query, creating a compound index will be beneficial.

Also note that the field's order within the compound index has an impact. Let's understand the difference with an example. Let's create a compound index as follows:

```
>db.perfpoc.ensureIndex({"GeneratedOn":1,"Host":1})
>
```

Next, do an explain of this:

```
>db.perfpoc.find({GeneratedOn:{"$gte": ISODate("2015-07-10"), "$lte":
ISODate("2015-07-20")}, Host: "Host1"}).explain("allPlansExecution")
.................................................................
"allPlansExecution" : [
        {
                "nReturned" : 4,
                "executionTimeMillisEstimate" : 0,
                "totalKeysExamined" : 4,
                "totalDocsExamined" : 4
                "indexName" : "GeneratedOn_1_Ho
.................................................................
                                "isMultiKey" : false,
                                "direction" : "forward",
        }]
.................................................................
```

Drop the compound index, like so:

```
>db.perfpoc.dropIndexes()
{
        "nIndexesWas" : 2,
        "msg" : "non-_id indexes dropped for collection",
        "ok" : 1
}
```

Alternatively, create the compound index with the fields reversed:

```
>db.perfpoc.ensureIndex({"Host":1,"GeneratedOn":1})
>
```

Do an explain:

```
>db.perfpoc.find({GeneratedOn:{"$gte": ISODate("2015-07-10"), "$lte":
ISODate("2015-07-20")}, Host: "Host1"}).explain("allPlansExecution")
{
        .............................................
        "executionStats" : {
        "executionSuccess" : true,
        "nReturned" : 4,
        "executionTimeMillis" : 0,
        "totalKeysExamined" : 4,
        "totalDocsExamined" : 4,
.............................................
"allPlansExecution" : [ ]
.............................................
}
>
```

You can see the difference in the explain command's output.

Using explain(), you can figure out the impact of indexes and accordingly decide on the indexes based on your application usage.

It's also recommended to have a single compound indexes covering maximum queries rather than having multiple single key indexes.

Based on you application usage and the results of the explain statistics, you will use only one compound index on {'GeneratedOn':1, 'Host': 1} to cover all the above mentioned queries.

Query4: *Fetching Count of Performance Data by Host and Day*

Listing the data is good, but most often queries on performance data are performed to find out the count, average, sum, or other aggregate operation during analysis. Here you will see how to use the aggregate command to select, process, and aggregate the results to fulfil the need of the powerful ad-hoc queries.

In order to explain this further, let's write a query that will count the data per month:

```
>db.perfpoc.aggregate(
... [
... {$project: {month_joined: {$month: "$GeneratedOn"}}},
... {$group: {_id: {month_joined: "$month_joined"}, number: {$sum:1}}},
... {$sort: {"_id.month_joined":1}}
... ]
... )
{ "_id" : { "month_joined" : 7 }, "number" : 4 }
>
```

In order to optimize the performance, you need to ensure that the filter field has an index. You have already created an index that covers the same, so for this scenario you need not create any additional index.

Sharding

The performance monitoring data set is humongous, so sooner or later it will exceed the capacity of a single server. As a result, you should consider using a shard cluster.

In this section, you will look at which shard key suits your use case of performance data properly so that the load is distributed across the cluster and no one server is overloaded.

The shard key controls how data is distributed and the resulting system's capacity for queries and writes. Ideally, the shard key should have the following two characteristics:

- Insertions are balanced across the shard cluster.

- Most queries can be routed to a subset of shards to be satisfied.

Let's see which fields can be used for sharding.

1. **Time field**: In choosing this option, although the data will be distributed evenly among the shards, neither the inserts nor the reads will be balanced.

   As in the case of performance data, the time field is in an upward direction, so all the inserts will end up going to a single shard and the write throughput will end up being same as in a standalone instance.

   Most reads will also end up on the same shard, assuming you are interested in viewing the most recent data frequently.

2. **Hashes**: You can also consider using a random value to cater to the above situations; a hash of the _id field can be considered the shard key.

   Although this will cater to the write situation of the above (that is, the writes will be distributed), it will affect querying. In this case, the queries must be broadcasted to all the shards and will not be routable.

3. Use the key, which is evenly distributed, such as **Host**.

   This has following advantages: if the query selects the host field, the reads will be selective and local to a single shard, and the writes will be balanced.

   However, the biggest potential drawback is that all data collected for a single host must go to the same chunk since all the documents in it have the same shard key. This will not be a problem if the data is getting collected across all the hosts, but if the monitoring collects a disproportionate amount of data for one host, you can end up with a large chunk that will be completely unsplittable, causing an unbalanced load on one shard.

4. Combining the best of options 2 and 3, you can have a compound shard key, such as *{host:1, ssk: 1}* where *host* is the host field of the document and *ssk* is _id field's hash value.

   In this case, the data is distributed largely by the host field making queries, accessing the host field local to either one shard or group of shards. At the same time, using ssk ensures that data is distributed evenly across the cluster.

   In most of the cases, such keys not only ensure ideal distribution of writes across the cluster but also ensure that queries access only the number of shards that are specific to them.

Nevertheless, the best way is to analyze the application's actual querying and insertions, and then select an appropriate shard key.

Managing the Data

Since the performance data is humongous and it continues to grow, you can define a data retention policy which states that you will be maintaining the data for a specified period (say 6 months).

So how do you remove the old data? You can use the following patterns:

- **Use a capped collection:** Although capped collections can be used to store the performance data, it is not possible to shard capped collections.

- **Use a TTL collection:** This pattern creates a collection similar to capped collection, but it can be sharded.

   In this case, a time-to-live index is defined on the collection, which enables MongoDB to periodically remove() old documents from the collection. However, this does not possess the performance advantage of the capped collection; in addition, the remove() may lead to data fragmentation.

1. **Multiple collections to store the data:** The third pattern is to have a day-wise collection created, which contains documents that store that day's performance data. This way you will end up having multiple collections within a database. Although this will complicate the querying (in order to fetch two days' worth of data, you might need to read from two collections), dropping a collection is fast, and the space can be reused effectively without any data fragmentation. In your use case, you are using this pattern for managing the data.

Use Case 2 – Social Networking

In this section, you will explore how to use MongoDB to store and retrieve data of a social networking site.

This use case is basically a friendly social networking site that allows users to share their statuses and photos. The solution provided for this use case assumes the following:

1. A user can choose whether or not to follow another user.

2. A user can decide on the circle of users with whom he wants to share updates. The circle options are Friends, Friends of Friends, and Public.

3. The updates allowed are status updates and photos.

4. A user profile displays interests, gender, age, and relationship status.

Schema Design

The solution you are providing is aimed at minimizing the number of documents that must be loaded in order to display any given page. The application in question has two main pages: a first page that displays the user's wall (which is intended to display posts created by or directed to a particular user), and a social news page where all the notifications and activities of all the people who are following the user or whom the user is following are displayed.

In addition to these two pages, there is a user profile page that displays the user's profile-related details, with information on his friend group (those who are following him or whom he is following). In order to cater to this requirement, the schema for this use case consists of the following collections.

The first collection is user.profile, which stores the user's profile-related data:

```
{
_id: "User Defined unique identifier",
UserName: "user name"
ProfilDetaile:
            {Age:.., Place:.., Interests: ...etc},
FollowerDetails: {
            "User_ID":{name:..., circles: [circle1, circle2]}, ....
            },
 CirclesUserList: {
            "Circle1":
                    {"User_Id":{name: "username"}, ......
                    }, .......
            }        ,
      ListBlockedUserIDs: ["user1",...]
}
```

- In this case, you are manually specifying the _id field.

- Follower lists the users who are following this user.

- CirclesUserList consists of the circles this user is following.

- Blocked consist of users whom the user has blocked from viewing his/her updates.

The second collection is the user.posts collection, with the following schema:

```
{
_id: ObjectId(...),
by: {id: "user id", name: "user name"},
VisibleTocircles: [],
PostType: "post type",
ts: ISODate(),
Postdetail: {text: "",
Comments_Doc:
 [
{Commentedby: {id: "user_id", name: "user name"}, ts: ISODate(),
Commenttext: "comment text"}, .....
]
}
```

- This collection is basically for displaying all of the user's activities. by provides information on the user who posted the post. Circles controls the visibility of the post to other users. Type is used to identify the content of the post. ts is the datetime when post was created. detail contains the post text and it has comments embedded within it.

- A comment document consists of the following details: by provides details of the user id and name who commented on the post, ts is the time of comment, and text is the actual comment posted by the user.

The third collection is user.wall, which is used for rendering the user's wall page in a fraction of a second. This collection fetches data from the second collection and stores it in a summarized format for fast rendering of the wall page.

The collection has the following format:

```
{
_id: ObjectId(...),
User_id: "user id"
PostMonth: "201507",
PostDetails: [
{
_id: ObjectId(..), ts: ISODate(), by: {_id: .., Name:.. }, circles: [..], type: ....
, detail: {text: "..."}, comments_shown: 3
,comments: [
{by: {_id:.., Name:....}, ts: ISODate(), text:""}, ......]
},....]}
```

- As you can see, you are maintaining this document per user per month. The number of comments that will be visible the first time is limited (for this example, it's 3); if more comments need to be displayed for that particular post, the second collection needs to be queried.

- In other words, it's kind of a summarized view for quick loading of the user's wall page.

The forth collection is `social.posts`, which is used for quick rendering of the social news screen. This is the screen where all posts get displayed.

Like the third collection, the fourth collection is also a dependent collection. It includes much of the same information as the `user.wall` information, so this document has been abbreviated for clarity:

```
{
_id: ObjectId(...),
user_id: "user id",
postmonth: '2015_07',
postlists: [ ... ]
}
```

Operations

These schemas are optimized for read performance.

Viewing Posts

Since the `social.posts` and `user.wall` collections are optimized for rendering the news feed or wall posts in a fraction of a second, the query is fairly straightforward.

Both of the collections have similar schema, so the fetch operation can be supported by the same code. Below is the pseudo code for the same. The function takes as parameters the following:

- The collection that needs to be queried.

- The user whose data needs to be viewed.

- The month is an optional parameter; if specified, it should list all the posts of the date less than or equal to the month specified.

```
Function Fetch_Post_Details
(Parameters: CollectionName, View_User_ID, Month)
SET QueryDocument to {"User_id": View_User_ID}
IF Month IS NOT NULL
APPEND Month Filter ["Month":{"$lte":Month}] to QueryDocument
Set O_Cursor = (resultset of the collection after applying the QueryDocument filter)
Set Cur = (sort O_Cursor by "month" in reverse order)
while records are present in Cur
                Print record
End while
End Function
```

The above function retrieves all the posts on the given user's wall or news feed in reverse-chronological order.

When rendering posts, there are certain checks that you need to apply. The following are a few of them.

First, when the user is viewing his or her page, while rendering posts on the wall you need to check whether the same can be displayed on their own wall. A user wall contains the posts that he has posted or the posts of the users they are following. The following function takes two parameters: the user to whom the wall belongs and the post that is being rendered:

```
function Check_VisibleOnOwnWall
(Parameters: user, post)
While Loop_User IN user.Circles List
                If post by = Loop_User
return true
                else
return false
end while
end function
```

The above loop goes through the circles specified in the user.profile collection, and if the mentioned post is posted by a user on the list, it returns true.

In addition, you also need to take care of the users on the blocked list of the user:

```
function ReturnBlockedOrNot(user, post)
        if post by user id not in user blocked list
                return true
        else
                return false
endfunction
```

You also need to take care of the permission checks when the user is viewing another user's wall:

```
Function visibleposts(parameter user, post)
if post circles is public
                return true
If post circles is public to all followed users
        Return true
set listofcircles = followers circle whose user_id is the post's by id.

if listofcircles in post's circles
        return true
return false

end function
```

This function first checks whether the post's circle is public. If it's public, the post will be displayed to all users.

If the post's circle is not set to public, it will be displayed to the user if he/she is following the user. If neither is true, it goes to the circle of all the users who are following the logged-in user. If the list of circle is in posts circle list, this implies that the user is in a circle receiving the post, so the post will be visible. If neither condition is met, the post will not be visible to the user.

In order to have better performance, you need an index on user_id and month in both the social.posts and user.wall collections.

Creating Comments

To create a comment by a user on a given post containing the given text, you need to execute code similar to the following:

```
Function postcomment(
Parameters: commentedby, commentedonpostid, commenttext)
Set commentedon to current datetime
Set month to month of commentedon
Set comment document as {"by": {id: commentedby[id], "Name": commentedby["name"]},
"ts": commentedon, "text": commenttext}
Update user.posts collection. Push comment document.
Update user.walls collection. Push the comment document.
Increment the comments_shown in user.walls collection by 1.
Update social.posts collection.  Push the comment document.
Increment the comments_shown counter in social.posts collection by 1.
End function
```

Since you are displaying a maximum of three comments in both dependent collections (the user.wall and social.posts collections), you need to run the following update statement periodically:

```
Function MaintainComments
SET MaximumComments = 3
Loop through social.posts
        If posts.comments_shown > MaximumComments
                Pop the comment which was inserted first
                Decrement comments_shown by 1
        End if
Loop through user.wall
        If posts.comments_shown > MaximumComments
                Pop the comment which was inserted first
                Decrement comments_shown by 1
        End if

End loop
End Function
```

To quickly execute these updates, you need to create indexes on posts.id and posts.comments_shown.

Creating New Post

The basic sequence of operations in this code is as follows:

1. The post is first saved into the "system of record," the user.posts collection.

2. Next, the user.wall collection is updated with the post.

3. Finally, the social.posts collection of everyone who is circled in the post is updated with the post.

```
Function createnewpost
(parameter createdby, posttype, postdetail, circles)
Set ts = current timestamp.
Set month = month of ts
Set post_document = {"ts": ts, "by":{id:createdby[id], name: createdby[name]},
"circles":circles, "type":posttype, "details":postdetails}
Insert post_document into users.post collection
Append post_document into user.walls collection
Set userlist = all users who's circled in the post based on the posts circle and the posted user id
While users in userlist
Append post_document to users social.posts collection
End while
End function
```

Sharding

Scaling can be achieved by sharding the four collections mentioned above. Since user.profile, user.wall, and social.posts contain user-specific documents, user_id is the perfect shard key for these collections. _id is the best shard key for the users.post collection.

Summary

In this chapter, you used two use cases to look at how MongoDB can be used to solve certain problems. In the next chapter, we will list MongoDB's limitations and the use cases where it's not a good fit.

CHAPTER 11

■ ■ ■

MongoDB Limitations

"When starting with a new database, you should also be aware of its limitations to better use the database."

In this chapter, we will list MongoDB's limitations and the use cases where it's not a good fit.

MongoDB Space Is Too Large (Applicable for MMAPv1)

Let's start with the issue of disk space. MongoDB (with storage engine MMAPv1) space is too large; in other words, the data directory files are larger than the database's actual data.

This is because of preallocated data files. This is by design in order to prevent file system fragmentation.

The files in the data directory are named as <dbname>.0, <dbname>.1 and so on. The size of the first file as allocated by the mongod is 64MB; all subsequent file sizes increase by factor of 2, so the second file will be 128MB, the third file will be 256MB, and so on until it reaches 2GB, post which all files will be 2GB in size. Though the space is allocated to the data files while creation, there might be files that are 90% empty. This unused allocated space is mostly small for larger databases.

- This option can be disabled by using the -- noprealloc option. However, it's not recommended to use this on a production environment, and it's supposed to be used only for testing and with small data sets where drop databases are called frequently.

- **Oplog**: If mongod is a Replica set member, then there will be a file named oplog.rs in the data directory. This file is present in the local database and is a preallocated capped collection. On a 64-bit installation, the allocation for this file defaults to approximately 5% of disk space.

- **Journal**: The journal files are also contained in the data directory that stores the writes on the disk before the same can be applied to the databases by MongoDB.

- MongoDB pre-allocates **3GB** of data for journaling, which is over and above the actual database size(s), making it not fit for small installations. The workaround available for this is to use –smallflags in your command line flags or /etc/mongod. conf files until you are running in an environment where you have the required disk space. But this feature makes it not fit for small installations.

- **Empty Records**: When the documents or collections are deleted, the space is never returned back to the operating system; instead, MongoDB maintains a list of these empty records, which can be reused.

  To reclaim this deleted space, either the compact or repairDatabase option can be used but be aware that both options require additional disk space to run.

© Shakuntala Gupta Edward, Navin Sabharwal 2015
S.G. Edward and N. Sabharwal, *Practical MongoDB*, DOI 10.1007/978-1-4842-0647-8_11

> ▪ **Note** No such limitation exists with the WiredTiger storage engine. Instead, storage size reduces by 50% due to compression of data files. Also, once the collection is dropped, disk space is automatically reclaimed, which is unlike the MMAPv1 storage engine mentioned above.

Memory Issues (Applicable for Storage Engine MMAPv1)

In MongoDB, memory is managed by memory mapping the entire data set. It allows the OS to control the memory mapping and allocate the maximum amount of RAM. The result is that the performance is non-optimal and the memory usage cannot be effectively reasoned about.

1. Indexes are memory-heavy; in other words, indexes take up lot of RAM. Since these are B-tree indexes, defining many indexes can lead to faster consumption of system resources.

2. A consequence of this is that memory is allocated automatically when required. In a shared environment, it's trickier to run the database. In general, as with all database servers, it's best to run MongoDB on a dedicated server.

32-bit vs. 64-bit

MongoDB comes with two versions, 32-bit and 64-bit.

Since MongoDB uses memory mapped files, the 32-bit versions are limited to storing only about 2GB of data. If you need more data to be stored, you should use the 64-bit build.

Starting from version 3.0, commercial support for 32-bit versions is no longer provided by MongoDB. Also, the 32-bit version of MongoDB does not support the WiredTiger storage engine.

BSON Documents

This section covers the limitations of BSON documents.

- **Size limits**: As with other databases, there's a limit to what can be stored in the document. The current versions support documents up to 16MB in size. This maximum size ensures that a document cannot not use excessive RAM or excessive bandwidth while in transmission.

- **Nested depth limit**: In MongoDB, no more than 100 levels of nesting are supported for BSON documents.

- **Field names**: If you store 1,000 documents with the key "col1", the key is stored that many times in the data set. Although arbitrary documents are supported in MongoDB, in practice most of the field names are the same. Keeping short field names is considered a good practice for optimizing the usage of space.

Namespaces Limits

Be aware of the following limitations from the namespace perspective.

- **Length of a namespace**: The length of each namespace including collection and database name must be smaller than 123 bytes.

- **Namespace file size** (applicable for the MMAPv1 storage engine): A namespace file size cannot be greater than 2047MB. The default size is 16MB; however, this can be configured using the `nssize` option.

- **Number of namespaces**(applicable for the MMAPv1 storage engine): Number of namespace = (namespace file size/628). A namespace file of 16MB will support approximately 24,000 namespaces.

■ **Note**   No such limitations exist for the WiredTiger storage engine.

Indexes Limit

This section covers the limitations of indexing in MongoDB.

- **Index size**: Indexed items cannot be greater than 1024 bytes.

- **Number of indexes per collection**: At the most 64 indexes are allowed per collection.

- **Index name length**: By default the index name is made up of the field names and the index directions. The index name including the namespace (which is the database and the collection name) cannot be greater than 128 bytes.

  If the default index name is becoming too long, you can explicitly specify an index name to the `ensureIndex()` helper.

- **Unique indexes in sharded collections**: Only when the full shard key is contained as a prefix of the unique index is it supported across shards; otherwise, the unique index is not supported across shards. In this case, the uniqueness is enforced across the full key and not a single field.

- **Number of indexed fields in a compound index**: This can't be more than 31 fields.

Capped Collections Limit - Maximum Number of Documents in a Capped Collection

If the max parameter is used for specifying the maximum number of documents in a capped collection, it can't be more than 232 documents. However, if no such parameter is used, there's no limit on the number of documents.

Sharding Limitations

Sharding is the mechanism of splitting data across shards. The following sections talk about the limitations that you need to be aware of when dealing with sharding.

Shard Early to Avoid Any Issues

Using the shard key, the data is split into chunks, which are then automatically distributed amongst the shards. However, if sharding is implemented late, it can cause slowdowns of the servers because the splitting and migration of chunks takes time and resources.

A simple solution is to monitor your MongoDB instance capacity using tools such as MongoDB Cloud Manager (flush time, lock percentages, queue lengths, and faults are good measures) and shard before reaching 80% of the estimated capacity.

Shard Key Can't Be Updated

The shard key can't be updated once the document is inserted in the collection because MongoDB uses shard keys to determine to which shard the document should be routed. If you want to change the shard key of a document, the suggested solution is to remove the document and reinsert the document when he change has been made.

Shard Collection Limit

The collection should be sharded before it reaches 256GB.

Select the Correct Shard Key

It's very important to choose a correct shard key because once the key is chosen it's not easy to correct it.

■ **Note** What's considered a wrong shard key depends completely on the application. Say the application is a news feed; choosing a timestamp field as a shard key would be a wrong shard key because this will end up inserting, querying, and migrating data from one shard only, and not from the complete cluster. If you need to correct the shard key, the process that is commonly used is to dump and restore the collection.

Security Limitations

Security is an important matter when it comes to databases. Let's look at MongoDB limitations from security perspective.

No Authentication by Default

Although authentication is not enabled by default, it's fully supported and can be enabled easily.

Traffic to and from MongoDB Isn't Encrypted

By default the connections to and from MongoDB are not encrypted. When running on a public network, consider encrypting the communication; otherwise it can pose a threat to your data. Communications on a public network can be encrypted using the SSL-supported build of MongoDB, which is available in the 64-bit version only.

Write and Read Limitations

The following sections cover important limitations.

Case-Sensitive Queries

By default MongoDB is case sensitive.

For example, the following two commands will return different results: `db.books.find({name: 'PracticalMongoDB'})` and `db.books.find({name: 'practicalmongodb'})`. You should ensure that you know in which case the data is stored. Although regex searches like `db.books.find({name: /practicalmongodb/i})` can be used, they aren't ideal because they are relatively slow.

Type-Sensitive Fields

Since there's no enforced schema for documents in MongoDB, it can't know you are making a mistake. You must make sure that the correct type is used for the data.

No JOIN

Joins are not supported in MongoDB. If you need to retrieve data from more than one collection, you must do more than one query. However, you can redesign the schema to keep the related data together so that the information can be retrieved in a single query.

Transactions

MongoDB only supports single document atomicity. Since a write operation can modify multiple documents, this operation is not atomic. However, you can isolate write operations that affect multiple documents using the isolation operator.

Replica Set Limitations - Number of Replica Set Members

A replica set is used to ensure data redundancy in MongoDB. One member acts as a primary member and the rest act as secondary members. Due to the way voting works with MongoDB, you must use an odd number of members.

This is because a node needs majority of votes to become primary. If you use an even number of nodes, you will end up in a tie with no primary being chosen because no one member will have the majority of vote. In this scenario, the replica set will become read only.

You can use arbiters to break such ties. They can help support failover and save on cost. To learn more about replica set functioning, please refer to Chapter 7.

MongoDB Not Applicable Range

MongoDB is not suitable for the following:

- Highly transactional systems such as accounting or banking systems. Traditional RDBMS are still more suitable for such applications, which require a large number of atomic complex matters.

- Traditional business intelligence applications, where an issue-specific BI database would generate highly optimized queries. For such applications, the data warehouse may be a more appropriate choice.

- Applications requiring complex SQL queries.

- MongoDB does not support transactional operations, so a banking system certainly cannot use it.

Summary

In this chapter, you learned about MongoDB's limitations and the use cases where it's not a good fit.

In the next chapter we will cover the How To's of MongoDB.

CHAPTER 12

MongoDB Best Practices

"Getting started with MongoDB is easy, but once you start developing applications you will come across scenarios where you may need best practices to achieve particular use cases."

In the previous chapters, you became acquainted with MongoDB. The intent of this chapter is outline well-known issues using other user's experiences but also to provide various How To's that can help your journey with MongoDB be a smooth ride.

As you know, MongoDB works with documents, uses RAM for storing data to enhance performance, and uses replication and sharding to further provide data safety and scalability.

This chapter will cover tips that you should be aware of, from the deployment strategy to enhancing querying to data safety and consistency to monitoring.

Deployment

While deciding on the deployment strategy, keep the following tips in mind so that the hardware sizing is done appropriately. These tips will also help you decide whether to use sharding and replication.

- **Data set size**: The most important thing is to determine the current and anticipated data set size. This not only lets you choose resources for individual physical nodes, but it also helps when planning your sharding plans (if any).

- **Data importance**: The second most important thing is to determine data importance, to determine how important the data is and how tolerant you can be to any data loss or data lagging (especially in case of replication).

- **Memory sizing**: The next step is to identify memory needs and accordingly take care of the RAM.

  Like other data-oriented applications, MongoDB also works best when the entire data set can reside in memory, thereby avoiding any kind of disk I/O.

  Page faults indicate that you may exceed the available deployment's memory and should consider increasing it. Page fault is a metric that can be measured using monitoring tools like MongoDB Cloud Manager.

  If possible, you should always select a platform that has memory greater than your working set size.

  If the size exceeds the single node's memory, you should consider using sharding so that the amount of available memory can be increased. This maximizes the overall deployment's performance.

© Shakuntala Gupta Edward, Navin Sabharwal 2015
S.G. Edward and N. Sabharwal, *Practical MongoDB*, DOI 10.1007/978-1-4842-0647-8_12

- **Disk Type**: If speed is not a primary concern or if the data set is larger than what any in-memory strategy can support, it's very important to select a proper disk type. IOPS (input/output operations per second) is the key for selecting a disk type; the higher the IOPS, the better the MongoDB performance. If possible, local disks should be used because network storage can cause poor performance and high latency. It is also advised to use RAID 10 when creating disk arrays (wherever possible).

- **CPU**: If you anticipate using map reducing, then the clock speed and the available processors become important considerations. Clock speed can also have a major impact on the overall performance when you are running a mongod with the majority of data in memory. In circumstances where you want to maximize the operations per second, you must consider including a CPU with a high clock/bus speed in your deployment strategy.

- **Replication** is used if high availability is one of the requirements. In any MongoDB deployment it should be standard to set up a replica set with at least three nodes.

  A 2x1 deployment is the most common configuration for replication with three nodes, where there are two nodes in one data center and a backup node in a secondary data center, as depicted in Figure 12-1.

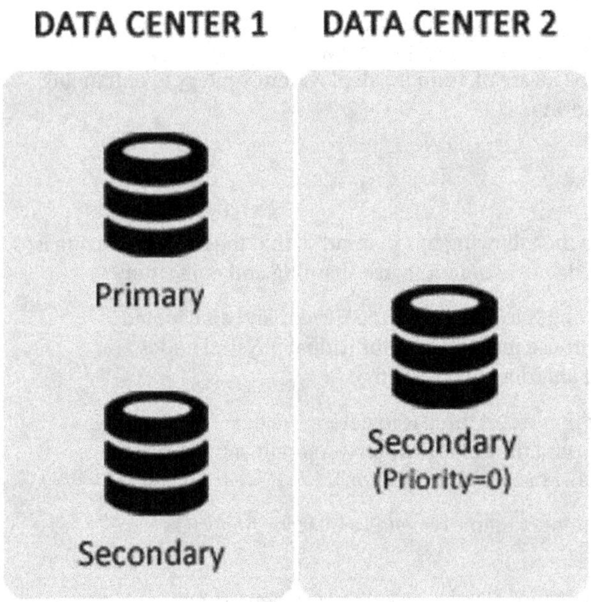

DATA CENTER 1   DATA CENTER 2

Figure 12-1. *MongoDB 2*1 deployment*

Hardware Suggestions from the MongoDB Site

The following are only intended to provide high-level guidance for a MongoDB deployment. The actual hardware configuration depends on your data, availability requirement, queries, performance criteria, and the selected hardware components' capabilities.

- **Memory**: Since memory is used extensively by MongoDB for a better performance, the more memory, the better the performance.

- **Storage**: MongoDB can use SSDs (solid state drives) or local attached storage. Since MongoDB's disk access patterns don't have sequential properties, SSDs usage can enable customers to experience substantial performance gains. Another benefit of using a SSD is if the working set no longer fits in memory, they provide a gentle degradation of performance.

   Most MongoDB deployments should use RAID-10.

   When using the WiredTiger storage engine, the use of a XFS file system is highly recommended due to performance issues.

   Also, do not use *huge pages* because MongoDB performs better with default virtual memory pages.

- **CPU**: Since MongoDB with a MMAPv1 storage engine rarely encounters workloads needing a large number of cores, it's preferable to use servers with a faster clock speed than the ones with multiple cores but slower clock speed. However, the WiredTiger storage engine is CPU bound, so using a server with multiple cores will offer a significant performance improvement.

Few Points to be Noted

To summarize this section, when choosing hardware for MongoDB, consider the following important points:

1. A faster CPU clock speed and more RAM are important for productivity.

2. Since MongoDB doesn't perform high amounts of computation, increasing the number of cores helps but does not provide a high level of marginal return when using the MMAPv1 storage engine.

3. Using SATA SSD and PCI (Peripheral Component Interconnect) provides good price/performance and good results.

4. It's more effective to spend on commodity SATA spinning drives.

5. MongoDB on NUMA Hardware: This point is only applicable for mongod running in Linux and not for instances that run on Windows or other Unix-like systems. NUMA (non-uniform memory access) and MongoDB don't work well together, so when running MongoDB on NUMA hardware, you need to disable NUMA for MongoDB and run with an interleave memory policy because NUMA causes a number of operational problems for MongoDB, including performance slowness for periods of time or high processor usage.

Coding

Once the hardware is acquired, consider the following tips when coding with the database:

- The first point is to think of the data model to be used for the given application requirement and to decide on embedding or referencing or a mix of both. For more on this, please look at Chapter tk. There's a trade-off between fast performance and guaranteed immediate consistency, so decide based on your application.

- Avoid application patterns that lead to unbounded growth of document size. In MongoDB, the maximum size for a BSON document is 16MB. Application patterns that make the documents grow in an unbounded way should be avoided.

  For instance, an application should not update documents a way that leads them to grow significantly. When the document size exceeds the allocated size, MongoDB will relocate the document. This process is not only time consuming, but is also resource intensive and can unnecessarily slow down other database operations. In addition, it can lead to inefficient use of storage.

  Note that the above mentioned limitation applies to the MMAPv1 storage engine. When using WiredTiger, the document is rewritten with every update.

For example, let's consider a blogging application. In this application, it's difficult to estimate how many responses a blog post will receive. The application is set to only display a subset of comments to the user, say the most recent comment or the first 10 comments. In this case, rather than creating an embedded model where the blog post and the user responses are maintained as a single document, you should create a referencing model where each response or group of responses are maintained as separate documents and then add a reference to the blog post in the documents. In this way, the unbound growth of the documents can be controlled, which will happen if you follow the first model of embedding the data.

- You can also design documents for the future. Although MongoDB provides the option of appending new fields within the documents as and when required, it has a drawback. When new fields are introduced, there might be a scenario where the document might not fit in the current space available, leading to MongoDB finding a new space for the document and moving it there, which might take time. So it is always efficient to create all the fields at the start if you are aware of the structure, irrespective of whether you have data available at that time or not. As highlighted above, the space will be allotted to the document and whenever value is there only needs to be updated. In doing so, MongoDB will not have to look for space; it merely updates the values entered, which is much faster.

- You can also create documents with the anticipated size wherever applicable. This point is also to ensure that enough space is allotted to the document and any further growth doesn't lead to hopping here and there for space.

This can be achieved by using a garbage field, which contains a string of the anticipated size while initially inserting the document and then immediately unsetting that field:

```
> mydbcol.insert({"_id" : ObjectID(..),......, "tempField" :
stringOfAnticipatedSize})
> mydbcol.update({"_id" : ...}, {"$unset" : {"tempField" : 1}})
```

- Subdocuments should always be used in a scenario when you know and will always know the names of the fields that you are accessing. Otherwise, use arrays.

- If you want to query for information that must be computed and is not explicitly present in the document, the best choice is to make the information explicit in the document. As MongoDB is designed to just store and retrieve the data, it does no computation. Any trivial computation is pushed to the client, leading to performance issues.

- Also, avoid $Where as much as possible because it's an extremely time- and resource-intensive operation.

- Use the correct data types while designing documents. For example, a number should be stored as a number data type only and not as a string data type. Using strings takes more space to store data and has an impact on the operations that can be performed on the data.

- Another thing to note is that strings in MongoDB are case sensitive. Hence a search for "practicalMongoDB" will not find "Practicalmongodb".

  Hence when doing a string search, you can do one of the following:

  - Store data in a normalized case format.

  - Use a regular expression with /I while searching.

  - Use $toUpper or $toLower in the aggregation framework.

- Using your own unique key as an _id will save a bit of space and will be useful if you are planning to index on the key. However, you need to keep the following things in mind when deciding to use your own key as _id:

  - You must ensure the uniqueness of the key.

  - Also, consider the insertion order for your key because the insertion order will identify how much RAM will be used to maintain this index.

- Retrieve fields as needed. When hundreds or thousands of requests are fulfilled per second, it's certainly advantageous to fetch only fields that are needed.

- Use GridFS only for storing data that is larger than what can fit in a single document or is too big to load at once on the client, such as videos. Anything that will be streamed to a client is a good candidate for GridFS.

- Use TTL to delete documents. If documents in a collection need to be deleted after a pre-defined time period, the TTL feature can be used to automatically delete the document after it reaches the predefined age.

Say you have a collection that maintains documents containing details of the user and the system interaction. The documents have a date field called **lastActivity**, which tracks the user and the system interaction. Let's say you have a requirement that says that you need to maintain the user session only for an hour. In this scenario, you can set the TTL to 3600 seconds for the field `lastActivity`. A background thread will run automatically and will check and delete documents that are idle for more than 3600 seconds.

- Use capped collections if you require high throughput based on insertion orders. In some scenarios, based on data size you need to maintain a rolling window of data in the system. For example, a capped collection can be used to store a high-volume system's log information to quickly retrieve the most recent log entries.

- Note that MongoDB's flexible schema can lead to inconsistent data if care is not taken. For example, the ability to duplicate data (embedded documents) if not updated properly can lead to data inconsistency, and so on. So it's very important to check for data consistency.

- Although MongoDB handles seamless failover, per good coding practice, the application should be well written to handle any exception and to gracefully handle such a situation.

Application Response Time Optimization

Once you start developing the application, one of the most important requirements is to have an acceptable response time. In other words, the application should respond instantly. You can use the following tips for optimization purposes:

- Avoid disk access and page faults as much as possible. Proactively figure out the data set size the application will be expected to deal with and add more memory in order to avoid page faults and disk read. Also, program your application in such a way that it mostly access data available in memory so page faults will happen infrequently.

- Create an index on the queried fields. If you create an index on the filter that you executing, the way the index is stored in memory will lead to less consumption of memory and hence will have a positive effect on the queries.

- Create covering indexes if the application involves queries that return a few fields as compared to the complete document structure.

- Having one compound index that can be used by maximum queries will also save on memory because instead of loading multiple indexes in memory, one index will suffice.

- Use trailing wildcards in regular expressions to reap the benefits from the associated index.

- Try to create indexes that reduce the possible documents to select from radically. An index on field "Gender" will not be as beneficial as an index on field "Phone Number."

- Indexing is not always good. You need to maintain an optimal balances of indexes used. Although you should create indexes for supporting your queries, you should also remember to delete indexes that are no longer used because every index has a cost associated for insert/update operations. If an index is not used but still it exists, it can have an adverse effect on the overall database capacity. This is especially important for insert-heavy workloads.

- Documents should be designed in a hierarchical fashion where related things are grouped together and are depicted as hierarchy wherever applicable. This will enable MongoDB to find the desired information without scanning the entire document.

- When applying an AND operator, you should always query from small resultset to a larger resultset because this will lead to querying a small number of documents. If you are aware of the most restrictive condition, that condition should go first.

- When querying with OR, you should move from a larger resultset to a smaller resultset because this will limit the search space for subsequent queries.

- The working set should fit in memory.

- Use the WiredTiger storage engine for write-heavy and I/O intensive applications due to its support of compression at the block as well as the index level.

Data Safety

You learned what you need to keep in mind when deciding on your deployment; you also learned a few important tips for good performance. Now let's look at some tips for data safety and consistency:

- Replication and journaling are two approaches that are provided for data safety. Generally it's recommended to run the production setup using replication rather than running it using a single server. And you should have at least one of the servers journaled. When it is not possible to have replication enabled and you are running on a single server, journaling provides data safety. Chapter tk explains how writes work when journaling is enabled.

- A repair should be the last resort for recovering data in the case of a server crash. Although the database might not be corrupted after running a repair, it will not contain all of the data.

- In a replicated environment, set W to the majority of safe writes. This is to ensure that the write is replicated to the majority of the members of the replica set. Although this will slow down the write operations, the write will be safe.

- Always specify wtimeout along with w when issuing the command in order to avoid the infinite waiting time.

- MongoDB should always be run in a trusted environment with rules to prevent access from all unknown systems, machines, or networks.

Administration

The following are some administration tips:

- Take instant-in-time backups of durable servers. To take a backup of a database with journaling enabled, you can take a file system snapshot or do a normal fsync+lock and then dump. Note that you can't just copy all of the files without fsync and locking because copying is not an instantaneous operation.

- Repair should be used to compact databases because it basically does a mongodump and then a mongorestore, making a clean copy of your data and, in the process, removing any empty "holes" in your data files.

- Database Profiler is provided by MongoDB. It logs fine-grained information on all the database operations. It can be enabled to either log information of all events or only events with durations exceeding a configurable threshold, which defaults to 100ms.

■ **Note**   The profiler data is stored in a capped collection. As compared to parsing the log files, it may be easier to query this collection.

- An explain plan can be used to see how a query is being resolved. This involves information such as which index is used, how many documents are returned, whether the index is covering the query, how many index entries were scanned, and the time the query took to return results in milliseconds. When a query is resolved in less than 1ms, the explain plan shows 0. When you make a call to the explain plan, it discards the old plan and initiates the process of testing available indexes to ensure that the best possible plan is used.

Replication Lag

Replication lag is the primary administrative concern behind monitoring replica sets. Replication lag for a given secondary is the difference in time when an operation is written in primary and the time when the same was replicated on the secondary. Often, the replication lag remedies itself and is transient. However, if it remains high and continues to rise, there might be a problem with the system. You might end up either shutting down the system until the problem is resolved, or it might require manual intervention for reconciling the mismatch, or you might even end up running the system with outdated data.

The following command can be used to determine the current replication lag of the replica set:

```
testset:PRIMARY>rs.printSlaveReplicationInfo()
```

Further, you can use the rs.printReplicationInfo() command to fill in the missing piece:

```
testset:PRIMARY>rs.printReplicationInfo()
```

MongoDB Cloud Manager can also be used to view recent and historical replication lag information. The repl lag graph is available from the Status tab of each SECONDARY node.

Here are some tips to help reduce this time:

- In scenarios with a heavy write load, you should have a secondary as powerful as the primary node so that it can keep up with the primary and the writes can be applied on the secondary at the same rate. Also, you should have enough network bandwidth so that the ops can be retrieved from the primary at the same rate at which they are getting created.

- Adjust the application write concern.

- If the secondary is used for index builds, this can be planned to be done when there are low write activities on the primary.

- If the secondary is used for taking backups, consider taking backups without blocking.

- Check for replication errors. Run `rs.status()` and check the `errmsg` field. Additionally, the secondary's log files can be checked for any existing error messages.

Sharding

When the data no longer fits on one node, sharding can be used to ensure that the data is distributed evenly across the cluster and the operations are not affected due to resource constraints.

- Select a good shard key.

- You must use three config servers in production deployments to provide redundancy.

- Shard collections before they reach 256GB.

Monitoring

MongoDB system should be proactively monitored to detect unusual behaviors so that necessary actions can be taken to resolve issues. Several tools are available for monitoring the MongoDB deployment.

A free hosted monitoring service named MongoDB Cloud Manager is provided by MongoDB developers. MongoDB Cloud Manager offers a dashboard view of the entire cluster metrics. Alternatively, you can use nagios, SNMP, or munin to build your own tool.

MongoDB also provides several tools such as mongostat and mongotop to gain insights into the performance. When using monitoring services, the following should be watched closely:

- **Op counters**: Includes inserts, delete, reads, updates and cursor usage.

- **Resident memory**: An eye should always be kept on the allocated memory. This counter value should always be lower than the physical memory. If you run out of memory, you will experience slowness in the performance due to page faults and index misses.

- **Working set size**: The active working set should fit into memory for a good performance, so a close eye needs to be kept on the working set. You can either optimize the queries so that the working set fits inside the memory or increase the memory when the working set is expected to increase.

- **Queues**: Prior to the release of MongoDB 3.0, a reader-writer lock was used for simultaneous reads and exclusive access was used for writes. In such scenario, you might end up with queues behind a single writer, which may contain read/write queries. Queue metrics need to be monitored along with the lock percentage. If the queues and the lock percentage are trending upwards, that implies that you have contention within the database. Changing the operation to batch mode or changing the data model can have a significant, positive impact on the concurrency. Starting from Version 3.0, collection level locking (in the MMAPv1 storage engine) and document level locking (in the WiredTiger storage engine) have been introduced. This leads to an improvement in concurrency wherein no write lock with exclusive access will be required at the database level. So starting from this version you just need to measure the Queue metric.

- Whenever there's a hiccup in the application, the CRUD behavior, indexing patterns, and indexes can help you better understand the application's flow.

- It's recommended to run the entire performance test against a full-size database, such as the production database copy, because performance characteristic are often highlighted when dealing with the actual data. This also lets you to avoid unpleasant surprises that might crop up when dealing with the actual performance database.

Summary

In this chapter we provided various How To's to help you on journey with MongoDB.

Index

■ N

Printed in the United States
By Bookmasters